THE
WEIGHT
OF THE
EVIDENCE

Titles by Michael Innes:

APPLEBY'S END

APPLEBY ON ARARAT

THE BLOODY WOOD

THE CASE OF THE JOURNEYING BOY

THE CRABTREE AFFAIR

DEATH ON A QUIET DAY

DEATH BY WATER

HARE SITTING UP

LAMENT FOR A MAKER

THE LONG FAREWELL

THE MAN FROM THE SEA

A NIGHT OF ERRORS

ONE MAN SHOW

PICTURE OF GUILT

THE SECRET VANGUARD

SILENCE OBSERVED

THE WEIGHT OF THE EVIDENCE

THE
WEIGHT
OF THE
EVIDENCE

Michael Innes

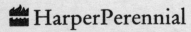 HarperPerennial

A Division of HarperCollins *Publishers*

THE
WEIGHT
OF THE
EVIDENCE

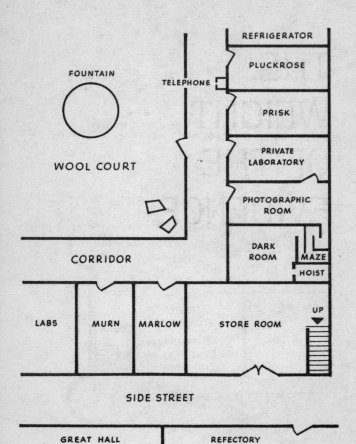

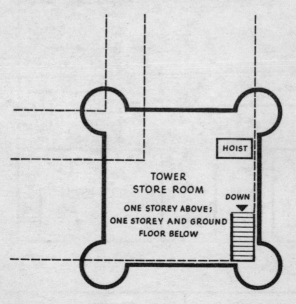

THE UNIVERSITY NESFIELD
WOOL COURT & SURROUNDING
BUILDINGS: WITH TOWER OVER

HOIST

TOWER
STORE ROOM

ONE STOREY ABOVE;
ONE STOREY AND GROUND
FLOOR BELOW

DOWN

1

It was soon apparent that Pluckrose had been murdered. A brief inspection of the corpse suggested that the only other possibility was what lawyers call an Act of God—and that of the kind which patently violates Natural Law. Of those concerned perhaps only Professor Prisk considered the fatality so felicitous as to make this explanation plausible. And yet between Prisk and Pluckrose there was, so far as was generally known, no deep-seated occasion of malice. Simply, these two had been required to share a telephone. Such are the antipathies of the cloister.

Not that the place was in fact cloistered in any substantial sense. The provincial universities of England, although often abundantly medieval in point of architectural inconvenience, have little of the organisation characteristic of traditional places of learning. The staff—a word which at Oxford or Cambridge might be used of persons employed in a hotel—is not accommodated in spacious common rooms and cosy suites. Sometimes it is provided with a cellar in which the extravagant may drink coffee-essence at eleven o'clock; sometimes there is also an attic with chairs, where meetings may be held; a mid-day meal is obtainable by those who will grab from a counter with one hand and from a cutlery basket with the other. The scholars live in remote suburbs, often surrounded by two, three, or even four children and a wife; they "come in" three times a week (giving it out to be four) or four times a week (giving it out to be five). To warm the sombre private rooms with which they are provided small gas stoves are supplied; but lurking caretakers pounce with an extinguishing hand upon these should a few minutes' absence justify the economy; nor has the sternly pencilled notice *Don't touch the stove*! ever been known to restrain such cold and flint-hearted janitors. In short, the amenities of communal life are scanty, and perhaps the professors and lecturers are expected to go much out and acquaint themselves with the world. Unfortunately neither Pluckrose nor Prisk nor many of their colleagues has lust or talent for this; for them the Scholar, as for Chaucer the Monk, is of little estimation without his right professional seclusion. But although they cannot bring with them from Oxford and Cambridge the immemorial organisation of a learned community they can and often do bring the somewhat attenuated charities which such societies produce. The matter of the telephone had rankled, as it might not have done in a larger air.

The death of Pluckrose, a beguilement from the first, was presently a sensation. Everybody was scared and shocked; everybody was literate; the result was a lavish expenditure of that sort of wit by which—psychologists assure us—the bewildered mind endeavours to maintain a perilous equilibrium. "*Gather the rose,*" murmured young Roger Pinnegar as he swept gowned down windy corridors; "*gather the rose of love.*" And "*Gather the rose of love while yet is time,*" he said aloud to Mr. Marlow under the great clock; "*Gather the rose of love while yet is time while loving thou mayst loved be with equal crime.*" "*Vivez,*" said Mr. Marlow readily; "*Vivez si m'en croyez, n'attendez à demain, cuillez dès aujourd'hui les roses de la vie.*" "*Mitte,*" said old Tavender, popping out of the Classics lecture room; "*Mitte sectari rosa quo locorum sera moretur.*" All three academic gentlemen giggled— Marlow and Pinnegar the more loudly in that their Latin was uncertain. "And I stick by that," said Tavender, waving his hand in what was presumably the direction of Quintus Horatius Flaccus. "Chuck it. Leave it alone. Forget about it. He's horridly dead. Well, let it go at that."

"Go, lovely rose," said Pinnegar automatically.

"Pluckrose is in his grave," said Marlow.

"Professor Pluckrose Pounded to Pot-pourri," said Pinnegar.

"Deceased Savant Smells Sweet," said Marlow. "Dead Biochemist Blossoms in Dust."

"Pounded?" asked Tavender, lowering his voice; "*really* pot-pourried?"

"Absolutely so." Pinnegar nodded almost soberly. "And by the Martians. There's the rub. By an inhabitant of earth—yes. Why not? Pluckrose was like that. But the Martians, so inappropriately named—"

"*Lucus,*" said Tavender, "*a non lucendo.*"

"—the Martians, stolid and phlegmatic by their dull canals: why should they take to pounding Pluckrose

3

with their planetary artillery? Ask Orson Welles."

"When you come to think of it," said Tavender, "Pluckrose was pretty close. What did one know of him? Not much."

Pinnegar nodded. "Most secret and inviolate Pluckrose. Did he keep a mistress? Was he quietly devoted to a mother of incredible age? Had he formed a curious private collection of—"

An electric bell of ingeniously piercing quality shrilled overhead. Doors banged. Students filled the corridors. Girls hurried past, bespectacled, notebooked, serious; girls loitered past, nudging, giggling, powdering; men skylarked, shouted, bit into sandwiches. Down the five ill-disposed wings of Nesfield University, vaulted, machine-carved, echoing and damp, surged conflicting columns of adolescent humanity, a rout of jostling automotive sponges hurried from pool to pool of a knowledge codified, timetabled and approved. Islanded in the midst, like three jackdaws among a charm of lesser fowls, Tavender, Marlow and Pinnegar maintained their own characteristic and esoteric jabber. Outside, in a little plot of ground known as the Wool Court, Pluckrose, pounded and pashed, lay with a tarpaulin between him and a smeared and smoky sky.

"A couple of years ago I had to do with a university murder," said Appleby. "But that was in the south. Oxford, was it—or Cambridge? I forget. So many of these things happen."

"Umph," said Inspector Hobhouse. The sound indicated that for him the humour of New Scotland Yard was without appeal.

4

"Anyway, the corpse was called Umpleby. A good North Country name."

Hobhouse rose massively to a repartee. "There's a fair number of us managing things down there."

"To be sure. Well, I sat with the local inspector just as I'm sitting with you now. And he explained the affair just as you've been doing. Not so lucidly perhaps, but competently enough."

"Umph," said Hobhouse. His voice held an appreciable change of tone.

"We sat and studied a plan just like this one." Appleby tapped a sheet of paper before him. "But there was one difference that I remember. Beer."

"Beer?"

"They sent us in beer." Appleby's eye traversed the empty table. "Two uncommonly handsome tankards."

"Is that so?" Hobhouse was impressed but cautious. "You wouldn't say that a thing like that was lowering to the dignity of the force?"

"Not the way it was done. With the compliments of the College—that sort of thing. Do you know, I remember that beer better than I remember the crime? It was a confused affair."

"Umph." Hobhouse too scanned the long bleak table, momentarily depressed. "When we go out to lunch," he said, "I think I can find you—"

"Capital. But first perhaps we'd better go over the ground again. I'm rather slow, as you've seen."

"Not a bit." Hobhouse was almost genial. "But if you ran over the facts as you've had them so far—"

"Pluckrose was a biochemist of some eminence. Nobody on the scientific side here is in quite the same street. There may be something in that." Appleby felt in his pocket. "Why not light your pipe?"

5

"I suppose they wouldn't object?" Hobhouse looked doubtfully round the room. "It's not what you'd call a very homey spot, is it?"

Appleby too looked about him—thoughtfully, as if here might be an unexpected key to the riddle which lay in front. The place was some species of board-room; presumably the professors of the university, as also the council of local notabilities by whom they were controlled, held their deliberations here. Large and square and high and gloomy, with walls of oily brown paint relieved by inconsequent outcrops of bare stone, it would have, if disfurnished, much the appearance of a sanitarily conceived receptacle for polar bears or hippopotami in a nineteenth-century zoological park. Gothic windows, anxious to present a symmetrical effect when viewed from without, had disposed themselves into a bewildering chaos when viewed, as now, from within; rafters, obedient to the necessities of some warren of rooms and corridors superimposed, edged themselves into positions suggestive of an obscure system of antipathies and affinities above; there was a fireplace so large that it held a massive bookcase stuffed with fading university calendars and superannuated reports. Above this last hung a sizeable canvas by Burne-Jones: an affair of enigmatic and epicene figures wandering amid a complicated system of trellises and vines. The rest of the wall space was covered up to a height of some twelve feet with a jumble of mutton-chopped or bewhiskered worthies in photogravure and daguerreotype and oil; similar worthies, more substantially commemorated in gleaming white marble, were dotted round the room on pedestals, while here and there a nymph or goddess, fashioned in the same forbidding medium, cowered and postured in futile pudicity and alarm. The whole evinced that curious unawareness of even the elements of aesthetic decorum to which the learned seem peculiarly prone. The room was itself a sort of murder; was a clumsy bashing of the simple rules of seemliness; was a brutal bludgeoning of the innocent and unoffending eye. Enormously criminal—thought Appleby extravagantly—must be the people who tolerated such a horror. Murder—yes. But murder considered as one of the fine arts? Surely not. But yet—Appleby frowned. But yet to kill a man seemingly out of interplanetary space—He struck a match, puffed, and turned to Hobhouse once more.

"A scientist of eminence. You know, they very seldom go in for the sort of thing that leads to a sticky end. Jealousies sometimes—but not very often. Personal irritabilities and squabbles often enough. But such things with them are commonly peripheral."

"Ah," said Hobhouse.

"I mean that they exist only on the fringes of the mind, on those borders of the whole psychical field where there isn't enough energy or attention or whatever it be to produce any very drastic consequences. It's with other types—artists, for instance—that you sometimes get odd shifts of energy to those fringes. Then you may find mere irritations and obscure antagonisms suddenly issuing in violence, vendetta, a settled and effective hate. But not on the whole with scientists. And another thing. Commonly they are either moral—sexually, I mean—or immoral in a methodical, businesslike and undangerous way."

Hobhouse looked up. "You don't," he said somewhat unexpectedly, "paint a very attractive portrait."

7

His eye went gloomily round the worthies on the walls. "And, by the way, is this what you call running over the facts?"

Appleby grinned, unoffended. "It's what I call running round them. Winding into the subject, you might say."

"I see." And Hobhouse's gaze transferred itself fleetingly to a hideous and Gothecised clock—uselessly, for the clock was of the kind which has exchanged time for eternity long ago. "A kind of lager is the best beer we brew down here."

"Very well. You tell me that Pluckrose, eminent scientist, was killed by a meteorite—a giant meteorite. It fell plop on him yesterday morning as he was sitting on a deck-chair in the little quadrangle called the Wool Court. There was no pretence that the fatality was actually an astral affair. A mass which had in fact fallen through the entire stratosphere—"

"Ah," said Hobhouse.

"—which had in fact fallen right through the air from outer space would, of course, be fairly hot, and would pretty well bury itself where it fell. Neither of these phenomena was observed. We must conclude, then, that someone took this massive and unlikely object and deliberately pitched it down on top of the victim. Why?"

"Why indeed, Mr. Appleby. Why indeed."

"I don't mean what was the motive for the total crime. I mean simply, what was the motive for proceeding in just this way? It cut out—or, speaking theoretically, all but cut out—the best security which a murderer can achieve: the appearance of natural death. Pitch a coping stone at a man—or a piece of lead roofing or a shower of tiles—and it may remain

8

possible so to fix things that the appearance of accident results. But this does not apply to a meteorite, because meteorites are not part of the customary furniture of roofs." Appleby paused. "You must forgive the obviousness of all this. We're considering the facts. And what, when one comes to think of it, constitutes a thing a fact? Its obviousness, I should say. Do you agree?"

Hobhouse, very properly ignoring this invitation to metaphysical discussion, shook his head. "You might be hoisting a meteorite to a museum or store-room or such like on an upper storey. And it might fall and kill somebody. And then you might be so scared—"

"Quite so. In theory the possibility of simple misadventure remains. But, in practice, wouldn't you say it could be ignored?"

"I don't know as to that." Infinite caution was plainly Hobhouse's line. "After all, there *is* a sort of store-room just in the appropriate place. You can't quite ignore that." And he laid the stem of his pipe on the plan before them.

"True enough. And in a tower which actually overshadows the spot where Pluckrose was sitting. But there is no provision for hauling up heavy objects from the Wool Court. What is provided is a sort of lift or hoist inside the building itself. One could hardly rig up a heavy affair of beams and pulleys on an outside wall without being spotted. Nor, when the lift was available, would it be sensible."

"Unless the meteorite was too heavy for the lift."

"To be sure. Suppose, then, that somebody about the university had a meteorite he wanted to store, and that he decided on this place in the tower. The lift is too small, or otherwise unsuitable. Wouldn't he then find some more convenient place altogether? Or, if he decided to persevere, is it believable that he would attempt the whole laborious business himself, rather than call in porters and so forth, who would make comparatively light of the job?"

"But suppose, Mr. Appleby, that some sort of secrecy was intended? A point about this out-of-the-way store-room in the tower is that it seems hardly ever visited. Suppose the meteorite was to be some sort of scientific surprise, so that the fellow who found it wanted to keep it quiet for a time—"

"Then, I agree, this particular store-room wouldn't be a bad place. But only if the thing could be got unobtrusively up in the lift. To rig up some sort of derrick at a window in broad daylight—"

"The Wool Court is fairly secluded." Hobhouse was obstinate. "And the fellow mightn't mind being seen just by some stray colleague. He'd reckon on simply tipping him the wink not to talk about his innocent little surprise."

"Very well. But it's all slightly improbable?"

"Yes."

"And we are then to suppose that this same fellow panics when the accident occurs, and keeps quiet for more than twenty-four hours thereafter?"

"Yes."

"That in itself being another improbability?"

"Yes."

"And to postulate the coincidence of two minor improbabilities is to establish a major improbability?"

Hobhouse took his pipe from his mouth and smiled. "Wasn't there one of the ancients, Mr. Appleby, that always used questions to put one down?"

"Socrates. And the method must often have been

extremely tiresome. But I say that, on the present showing, simple accident is no more than a faint theoretical possibility."

"In other words: murder. Someone got this meteorite up to the store-room at the top of the tower, waited until Pluckrose was in position below, and then tipped it out of the window."

Appleby nodded. "Say it looks like murder. And now comes something odd. Actually there are—I think you said four?"

"Four."

"There are four of these store-rooms one on top of another. And, although not much used, the clerk of works and the head porter check through them once a year. They last did this, as it happens, about three weeks ago. And there was no meteorite. Nothing odd in that. But what is a trifle queer is that there was quite a number of things which would have served equally well. For instance in the uppermost room but one there was a small steel safe and two deed boxes and a stone cannon-ball and a cast iron sink. And a dozen miniature reinforced concrete pillars used by people who study something called the Strength of Materials."

Hobhouse puffed tobacco smoke approvingly. "Very nice, Mr. Appleby. A good memory is the most important thing a detective officer can have, if you ask me."

"Umph," said Appleby.

"Well, it may be different in London, I don't doubt. But you've got to the queer part now, all right. There was no need to haul up this meteorite affair at all. Any of those things lying around would have served. The meteorite was a mere wanton freak, like. You agree,

11

sir?" Hobhouse's glance was swift and shrewd.

"Dear me, no. That's to be in altogether too much of a hurry—lager or no lager." Appleby frowned absently at a clout-clutching, sharp-nosed Aphrodite across the room. "Perhaps there was little premeditation and the fellow didn't go up and make an inspection first. He just bundled himself and the meteorite into the hoist, knowing nothing of the safe and the sink and what-not. Or, again, we may be going astray through thinking of quite the wrong type of person. *You* agree?"

Hobhouse shook a tolerant head. "Now, now, there's no call to go trying to catch each other out. I don't follow you, I freely admit."

"The meteorite didn't come straight from space. We know that because it was cold and because it shows faint traces of vegetable growth—a lichen or something of the sort. Now, the sort of person we tend to have in mind as the criminal—a scholar or scientist—would at once understand the conclusiveness of evidence of this sort. So, with a little reflection, would ordinary educated people like ourselves. But an uneducated man? Might he not believe that by possessing himself of, and using, this meteorite he was cunningly contriving an almost conclusive appearance of simple misadventure? Might he not, in fact, believe that he was constructing the most irrefrangible of alibis? For no man can be accused of loitering suspiciously in the neighbourhood of Mars or Saturn."

Hobhouse chuckled. "Nor of Venus, for that matter—in just that sense." He put down his pipe. "You've hit on a very important notion there," he added soberly.

"Possibly—or possibly there may be nothing in it.

And now consider the topographical lay-out of the affair." Appleby looked at the plan. "What's this thing in the middle of the Wool Court—an aspidistra?"

"A coconut palm," said Hobhouse solemnly.

"Rubbish."

"Actually it's a fountain. To me, it gives a distinctly watery effect. But I dare say leafy might be applied to it too." Hobhouse, now on very good terms with the officer from London, chuckled comfortably. "And these things in the angle of the wall are deck chairs."

"Indisputably. What we have, then, is a corner of the ground floor of the main building. It's like a fat L turned the wrong way round. On the inner side of this is a thin L which represents a corridor. And inside that, again, is the Wool Court and its fountain. The fountain plays?"

"Commonly it trickles away. But it's on the main and can make quite a display. And, oddly enough, it was full strength when the body was discovered, and drenching the whole place. Nobody knows who turned it on."

"I see." Appleby studied the plan again. "Now take the corridor. Nothing remarkable about that. Windows looking on the Court—"

"I wouldn't say looking. They begin about seven feet up and are full of what is probably called stained glass." Hobhouse too, it seemed, was not without his aesthetic reactions.

"Windows, in fact, that make this corner of the court pretty secluded. Anything also about the corridor? Double doors giving on the court." Appleby's finger moved up the paper. "What's this blob?"

"It's not a blob; it's a telephone. In a little locked box on the wall."

13

"How very odd."

"Economy. Pluckrose had to share it with the man next door. Caused trouble, it appears."

"But presumably not murder. Pluckrose had this room at the end?"

"Yes. And then comes Prisk, the professor of Romance languages. And then Pluckrose's private laboratory."

Appleby frowned. "Aren't these people oddly mixed up?"

"Uncommonly, I should say. But, you see, the university has grown pretty rapidly"—Hobhouse was not without civic pride in this announcement—"and at the same time people have refused to budge from their familiar quarters. It seems that in little matters like that there's nobody who can order professors and such-like about. So here's Pluckrose, and then Prisk, and then Pluckrose's lab and then the photographic room and then—"

"Wait a minute." Appleby had again put a finger on the plan. "Whatever is this affair in the corner?"

"Of the lab?" Hobhouse puffed at his pipe, much pleased. "You'd never guess. It's a maze."

"Ah, for the photography."

Hobhouse's face fell. "Yes. The dark-room is next door, and the only entrance to it is through this little pitch-black maze. It prevents the accidental ingress"—Hobhouse paused as if to admire this phrase—"of light."

"And the dark-room takes up part of the breadth of the building here and in the other part is the hoist. But the main doors of the hoist open on what is the next room again, a big one in the angle of the building.

14

In fact, the lowest of the store-rooms. And now turn the corner and we come to a man called Marlow."

"Yes. But don't turn the corner before you notice that the lowest store-room had only one pair of doors: on the far side and giving on a road—a public road, that is, but with nothing but university buildings opposite. Here's the refectory and here's the Great Hall."

"I see. Now Marlow: I think you said he was senior lecturer in English? Good. And next to him?"

"An aged and bearded person called Murn. Some sort of assistant to Pluckrose. And after that come more labs."

"At which we call a halt. But we remember that above the store-room is another store-room, and above that two further store-rooms again. And the two uppermost store-rooms are a bit bigger than those below. In fact there's a jutting-out or overhanging affair supported on corbels. And at each corner is a further overhang: a little windowed pepper-box affair of a turret. On this final architectural quiddity the whole crime turns."

"Just that." Hobhouse picked up a match and held it suspended above the table. "It meant that Pluckrose, sitting in his deck-chair some feet from the wall of the Wool Court, was directly beneath one of the pepper-box windows." He let the match fall. "So that once you'd got the meteorite up on the window sill the thing was a mathematical certainty."

Appleby sighed. "It's nice that there should be a bit of certainty somewhere. And now I think we'd better go and actually inspect. After that—luncheon."

"I hope that you gentlemen will lunch with me?"

They turned round. Hobhouse thrust his pipe in his pocket and scrambled to his feet. Standing in the doorway of the dismal, tank-like room was a tall man dressed in scarlet and gold.

2

The tall man doffed his robes and threw them over a chair. The only bright thing about him now was his eyes, which were of a startling blue and deep-sunken in massive but finely chiselled bone. An odd fact about Henry VIIIth's upstart nobility, thought Appleby, is that in under a mere four centuries they have come to approximate so closely the old Norman type. The Duke of Nesfield looked every inch a duke, and he contrived to suggest that this feat in itself was one man's sufficient achievement. But that might be a trick, a sort of hereditary pose of proved utility. There was a cold glitter in those eyes which spoke of other things.

"Conferring degrees." The duke moved across the room and without facetiousness clapped his academic cap on the bald head of a conveniently offering bust. "I always do it myself when I'm about. It's what a Chancellor is for. That and putting his hand in his pocket. If he has one left. Horrible room." He paused

17

and his eye was still the dominant thing; it was searching and utterly remote from the inconsequence of his speech. "One stands like a macaw." He paused again and suddenly smiled. "Like a macaw," he repeated delightedly, "—that's it! Mr. Appleby, Mr. Hobhouse, don't you agree?"

The image was undoubtedly exact. And as undoubtedly a triumph of efficient dukeishness was the care to place nobody, even for a couple of minutes, on a plane of mere anonymity. Automatically he would enquire the names of the obscure and tiresome policemen he was about to meet. And now it was necessary to speak up—an activity to which Hobhouse appeared momentarily unequal. So Appleby tried. "A little bright plumage, sir, must be all to the good. But in here one could scarcely feel at home unless one was—well, say a dodo and pretty effectively stuffed."

"Quite so," said the duke—gravely but smiling still. "It is like a municipal museum. If only we could rebuild in a pure taste! I agree with dear old Pam that nobody has improved on the Palladian style. But of course I live in it and may be prejudiced by that."

Palmerston, Nesfield Court—the man did perhaps in his own way put the duke business rather heavily across. Appleby, who distrusted the ruling classes as chronically concerned to hush things up, decided that enough small talk had passed. For a moment there was silence. And then the duke spoke again. "A macaw," he said. "And the Vice-Chancellor beside one like a great crow. Very apprehensive lest the undergraduates should smoke or throw things or otherwise misbehave. And yet only a few minutes before he was telling me that there had been—a murder."

Appleby looked quickly up. The duke's voice had

dropped on the last two words, had dropped with a betrayal startling in one so consummately of the world. He had been greatly shocked. And something more than that.

Again there was a brief silence. "A scholar. And in the university! Professor—" There was the tiniest hesitation. "Professor Pluckrose."

That surely was it. Professor Pluckrose was nothing to the Duke of Nesfield; was no more to him than was Appleby or Hobhouse. But that a crime of violence should occur among men wedded to the pursuit of knowledge, and should occur here in the University of Nesfield—The shock lay there. Or so it was reasonable to guess. But now a servant had come into the room carrying a coat and hat, and it was clear that Hobhouse's lager must give place to whatever beverage it is proper for dukes to offer the higher constabulary. They went out amid a staring of students and scurrying of porters; a press-photographer, receiving a complex gesture which combined an affable nod and a firm shake of the head, put his camera down, resigned; there was an enormous and quite unreticent lemon-coloured limousine; they sank down as if embedded in the strawberry leaves of nobility. The car purred. Behind them was the sprawling university, garish here and dingy there. In front, humped and lurched against a long, gentle hill, was the town: not very dirty—for wool is cleaner than cotton—but dirty enough to satisfy the most devoted painter of a soiled urban world. How long would it last? thought Appleby, forgetting all about Professor Pluckrose. The lines of back-to-back houses sprawling in a sort of brittle corruption over the obliterated hills and cluttered valleys—how long could they endure? Not long.

That was the certain answer. They were a temporary apparition, the rash of a disgusting but mercifully passing disease. They would go and their inhabitants would go and the university would grow enormous and there would be a universe of high-school children and well-soaped engineers. And the man who failed to acknowledge that this would be a bit better was a fool. Would the duke go too? Probably he would. And he would take with him much of the world's arrogance and independence and eccentricity—there would be something to deplore in that. But at the moment he had little appearance of evanescence. Perhaps he no longer owned the chaos which sprawled and spewed about them. But he looked very comfortably in control.

"The Club?" said the duke, as if somebody had asked a question. "I think not. The Club is a very good sort of place. Clubs are a very good sort of place in general, I should say. But we have never taken to them. I go to the hotel."

They went to the hotel—vast, a sort of Egyptian or Babylonish Gothic, a dream of aimless commercial opulence. There was a railway station buried in it; when war came it would be bombed—so it too was fated to pass. Meantime the duke had his own room and—Appleby presently suspected—his own cellar. They helped themselves to bread and cheese, to a dark, acrid Italian wine miraculously transported and preserved. No servant showed his nose. The duke made coffee and said what he had to say.

"You know, the old Nesfield is going. It won't survive this coming war. And I for one shan't mourn it. A nasty rabbit-warren of a place."

Hobhouse, rather inclined to sit on the edge of his

chair, opened wide eyes like a shocked child. Appleby looked thoughtfully at the heavy hotel cutlery: this all seemed remote from the Pluckrose affair, but it was close to what he had been thinking half an hour before.

"And we shall have a sort of dog-kennel civilisation instead. Every man, every family-unit in a nice drudgery-proof kennel with plenty of bright paint and a good high fence round. Do you ever look at the book-stalls? All those magazines about homes and gardens and refrigerators and furniture polish? It's not a dream world, like the cinema. It's a world on the verge of becoming real. And, to my way of thinking, not a bad thing. But desperately insulating and unsociable. The rabbit-warren is at least a shoulder-rubbing sort of place, and that breeds communal feeling, ideas, discontents—the things which make the individual life get somewhere. What I fear is a vast bourgeois stagnation, with the discontents all snugly in the refrigerator and the frictions which alone make possible any effective movement industriously furniture-polished away. That's why our university—this sort of university—is so important."

"I see," said Appleby.

"Well, not many people do. All these little Toms and Dicks and Harrys—and Susans and Josephines and Gladyses too—come from the workers and the lower middle class; from the people who, a couple of generations from now, will be absorbed in an amorphous and classless material prosperity. Not, mark you, a prosperity running here and there to wealth. Just a nice whack all round and perhaps half as much again for the bureaucracy policing it. Now, where is a little breath of mind going to come from amid all this? From Susan and Harry, if you asked me. Lord knows what they're taught: Anglo-Saxon, Fitting and Turning, Political Economy—it doesn't matter very much. The point is that for several years, and when almost grown-up, they rub along in coteries and crowds, and sit chattering on benches which never see furniture-polish from one year's end to another. Moreover they are in contact with scientists and scholars—a sort of people who often don't very clearly know whether they possess homes and gardens or not. In fact, these universities may temper the coming, attractive materialism rather as chapels and institutes and so forth a little tempered the disgusting materialism of the last century. So I always support any extending of our university, even if the extension is just another dodge."

"A dodge?" said Appleby.

"A dodge by industrial people to get necessary training and technical research done partly at somebody else's expense. I always support it just the same. It keeps the young people together for a bit in something which at least isn't a factory and hasn't got a boss. Gives them a chance to hatch things."

And the Duke of Nesfield chuckled with a certain malice. The truth was, thought Appleby, that he enjoyed still being a boss himself, and the local university was one of the instruments left to him. No doubt the Toms and Susans ought to be grateful—but it was doubtful if they would quite like that malicious chuckle and that masterful tone. And meantime there was the curious problem of what this was all about—for it was beyond even the aplomb of the duke to disguise the fact that his luncheon had been something out of the way. Was he in the habit of buttonholing all and sundry—the fathers and uncles of Susan and

Tom—for the purpose of airing views on the provincial universities of England? Almost certainly not. And Appleby stood up and spoke at a gloomy guess. "You think, sir, that it will be a great pity if a struggling institution becomes the centre of some vulgar scandal; that it will be extremely fortunate if the affair turns out to have been an obscure accident?"

The duke had risen too. He looked at once puzzled, shocked and faintly amused. "Good Lord, no! If somebody murdered the fellow of course that somebody must hang. Anyway, I wish you both luck in getting to the bottom of it. You'll find the car waiting. So good of you to have spared time to an idle man."

And the Duke of Nesfield opened the door and shook hands at once affably and with a matter-of-fact condescension.

"By the way," he said, "I suppose it is—ah—Pluckrose? Good-bye."

Outside the hotel there were now two cars and four servants; they were ushered into the first car and driven away. Hobhouse spoke with caution. "Took the wind out of your sails, rather." His voice held a faint malice which would have done credit to their late host.

"No doubt. But you'd hardly believe what those people sometimes think they can have stowed away in hugger-mugger." And then Appleby smiled, recognising in himself a somewhat ruffled assumption of metropolitan self-importance. "But, I say—I suppose it is Pluckrose?"

"Is Pluckrose? What the deuce do you mean?"

"What the deuce did the duke mean—that's the problem. The whole absurd party was just for the sake of dropping that question. And what should Professor

Pluckrose be to the Duke of Nesfield?"

"Professor—ah—Pluckrose," said Hobhouse.

"Quite so. Either Pluckrose is just a name to him or he is foxing. And why should he do that? Even supposing him to take an active and masterful interest in this university of which he happens to be the titular head, why ever should he have some game to play when a professor gets murdered? It's been a rum go."

"A curious interlude," said Hobhouse sententiously.

"Interlude? We hadn't rightly got begun. Say an irregular prologue. And the result of it is that we come back asking if it *is* Pluckrose."

"Of course it's Pluckrose."

"I'm glad to hear it. Remember I haven't yet seen the body. And a meteorite dropped from a tower sounds as if it might be pretty obliterating. Pluckrose's clothes on somebody else's carcass. Such things happen."

Hobhouse grunted. "Down to the supposed victim's false teeth lying on the grass nearby."

"Yes, yes." The car slid between lamp-posts and trams—gliding effortlessly up the hill like an immaterial thing. And Appleby looked sombrely out over the grey proliferation of slate and stone. "But the line is fine-drawn sometimes between those tawdry fictions and actual crime. . . . Undoubtedly Pluckrose?"

"Undoubtedly. Much of him—was crushed. Quite remarkably so. But there was nothing like an obliteration of the features. That's common knowledge, so his grace is barking up a wrong tree. I'm surprised he didn't find out from Sir David."

"From the Vice-Chancellor, that is? His grace will never see you or me again. But with those he has frequently to meet he probably practices a good deal of reserve. And here we are. And what we want now is actors."

They stood in a windy outer vestibule, curiously eyed. "Actors?" said Hobhouse.

"No drama without actors. And yet we haven't had any—except a sort of strayed ducal reveller. I wonder how he gets that wine—Montalcino, I should say— to carry?" Appleby's glance was straying round the large lobby—tiled, sweating faintly, and inhospitable—to which they had come. "But look; there are a couple of possible actors. Let's begin with them." Two gowned figures, one elderly and the other young, were advancing up a corridor. "Ring up the curtain, Hobhouse. The gallery is agog."

"But I don't know anything about them." Hobhouse looked at Appleby with an eye startled and plainly meditating the potency of Montalcino. "I think the regular thing would be to take you to see Sir David."

"Bother Sir David. Likely enough we shall have to interview the whole learned lot before we're finished." And Appleby took a couple of steps across the lobby. "Good afternoon," he said, and fished a slip of paper from his pocket.

The two gowned persons said good afternoon politely.

"I am Detective-Inspector Appleby of New Scotland Yard."

The two academic gentlemen, who a moment before had been conversing together with dignity and eyeing the empty corridor with an unnecessary but impressive severity, now looked at Appleby dumbly and with at least momentary dismay. It was upsetting, no doubt.

"And this is Inspector Hobhouse of the Borough police. As you may know, we are enquiring into the death of Professor Pluckrose." Appleby looked at the elder of the two men. "Mr. Murn, I think?"

"You are mistaken, sir." The elderly man looked both offended and relieved. "My name is Crunkhorn."

Appleby looked at his slip of paper and his face lit up with sudden interest. "Mr. Crunkhorn!" he said. "That's capital. And may I suppose, perhaps, that this is—?"

"Church," said the younger man, innocently and obligingly.

"Exactly. Now I wonder if you could both give us a few minutes? We are using a room just along this corridor."

Mr. Crunkhorn bowed and they moved into the tank-like apartment where Hobhouse had earlier given his account of the case. Appleby politely set chairs. "We are lucky to have come upon you so readily," he said.

The young man called Church again looked scared. But Mr. Crunkhorn now wore an expression of settled severity. "We are somewhat at a loss, Mr. Appleby. I hold the chair of mathematics and Mr. Church is my colleague in that department. We have no special knowledge of Pluckrose. In fact, we were very seldom associated with him."

"Just so." Appleby nodded agreeably. "Inspector Hobhouse and I have been seeing the Vice-Chancellor."

Hobhouse gave an inarticulate mutter and stared stonily at the golden-tasselled cap of the Duke of Nesfield where it still perched incongruously on its bust. Plainly, this sort of thing was far from having his approval.

"Sir David is greatly upset—much grieved. He regarded Professor Pluckrose as a close personal friend."

"Indeed," said Crunkhorn—a shade grimly.

"And he advised us to come straight to you for what he called an objective and dispassionate view."

"Ah," said Crunkhorn.

"Nobody, he thought, would be better able to provide such a thing. And he made one or two remarks on the value of a mathematical training which interested me very much. I fear I was a classical man myself."

"Indeed." Crunkhorn spoke more mildly. "Our professor of classics is Hissey."

"Really?" Appleby was interested. "I used to attend his lectures when he was a don at St. Anthony's."

"Dear me." Crunkhorn, though staring a little blankly at this odd policeman, relaxed appreciably in his chair. "A sound scholar, I have been told. But somewhat out of his element here. These universities, you know, require for the most part technical men. Applied scientists—that sort of thing."

Silly old snob, thought Appleby. "These" universities won't have a soul of their own until they put the duke's Dicks and Harrys into their teaching jobs. Aloud he said: "And now I wonder if you can help us? Professor Pluckrose appears to have been murdered, I am very sorry to say. Is there any general picture into which such a thing would conceivably fit?" He paused. "Of course we quite realise that you may not think there is anything profitable to record."

Hobhouse stirred slightly, as if reluctantly acknowl-

27

edging the mature technique concealed in this last remark. Nothing like suggesting to a witness that he may be without anything interesting to say.

And Professor Crunkhorn said something. It had at least the virtue of being totally unexpected. "Galileo," he said. "I associate the affair with Galileo."

"I beg your pardon?"

"Galileo."

Appleby looked very blank. "Do I understand you to refer to—to the sixteenth-century astronomer?"

Professor Crunkhorn turned to his junior colleague. "Church," he asked, "do you remember when he was born?"

"I'm afraid I don't."

"Or when he died?"

"I can't say I do."

"Ah." Crunkhorn shook his head with facetious sadness over this piece of academic nescience. "But stay! The dates have just come into my head." He smiled amiably at his discomfited assistant. "1564 to 1642. We shall therefore do well to refer to him as a *seventeenth*-century astronomer."

Hobhouse breathed heavily, clearly indicating his conviction that this travesty of correct police procedure could lead only to buffoonery. Appleby however looked admiringly at Crunkhorn, as if delighted to meet so forthright and cogent a mind. "I certainly agree that we should assign Galileo to the seventeenth century. And it is most interesting that he should be implicated in Professor Pluckrose's death. Perhaps you could expand the matter a little?"

"Church sees what is in my mind. He will explain better than I can." And Crunkhorn again beamed amiably at his colleague. It was plain that one of this young

28

man's functions was to be taken round and baited, like a sort of learned bear.

"Meteorites," said Church uncertainly and gloomily. "They say the old person was killed with a meteorite." He paused for a moment, as if there was something enticing in the thought of this short way with old persons. "I suppose that might link up with astronomy after some fashion." He scowled at Appleby—an able youth, acutely conscious of being manoeuvred into saying something thoroughly feeble.

"To be sure," said Crunkhorn. "Your analysis, my dear Church, carries us some way—some *little* way. But it is a particular experiment of Galileo's which I have in mind. You know something, Church, of the architectural curiosities of Pisa?"

"There's a leaning tower."

"Splendid! There is indeed a leaning tower, and from it Galileo conducted one of his most famous experiments. Unfortunately it was an experiment tinged with that frivolity to which he was prone. He had, as you know, become a professor of mathematics at an early age, and this appears to have unsettled him."

Mr. Church, who was himself presumably committed to the business of becoming a professor of mathematics sooner or later, scowled more darkly than ever. Appleby was beginning to be interested in him.

"This experiment of Galileo's to which I refer was directed towards the establishment of the Law of Falling Bodies, according to which all bodies fall at the same rate in a vacuum and at the end of a given time have a velocity proportional to the time in which they have been falling, and have traversed a distance proportional to the square of that time." Crunkhorn looked expectantly at Hobhouse, as if soliciting that officer's learned acquiescence. "Now Aristotle had maintained otherwise, and Galileo's colleagues swore by Aristotle."

"The longest tyranny that ever swayed," said Church. This was apparently a quotation, and the young man brightened momentarily at the consciousness of having behaved in a suitably donnish way.

"No doubt. And Galileo determined to demonstrate in a particularly dramatic manner the truth of his own view on the matter. As it happened, his colleagues were in the habit of walking past the base of the leaning tower in a daily academic procession. Galileo climbed the tower, taking with him what we may call a one-pound shot and a ten-pound shot. And these he dropped at what he considered the appropriate moment. Such of his colleagues as were not distracted by a narrow escape from death were forced to confess that the shots had landed virtually simultaneously. Or rather they confessed that so it appeared to them. As Aristotle could not be wrong it was evident that their eyes must have deceived them."

"What you tell us is extremely interesting." Appleby spoke quite without irony. "And the tower here is not unlike a leaning tower: that is to say, it has overhanging turrets which would make it quite a good place for such experiments. But I think that when you say you associate the affair of Professor Pluckrose's death with Galileo you must have something further in mind?"

"I have. In the university of late there has been a peculiar spirit of levity abroad."

Church suddenly grinned. "But with Galileo it

seems to have been rather a matter of gravity. And with Pluckrose too."

Crunkhorn frowned; this joke clearly failed to conform to the best academic canons. "A spirit of levity among the younger members of our teaching body. 'Ragging' is, I believe, the word. The sort of thing one associates with undergraduates in spurious novels of university life. We have been perturbed by it. And inclined to wonder who is the moving spirit." Mr. Crunkhorn looked with frank speculation at Mr. Church.

"Jokes?" asked Hobhouse. "You don't suggest that Pluckrose had an enormous meteorite thrown at him by way of a practical joke?"

"I for one," said Church, "fail to remember such a thing even in a spurious novel. But I agree that there have been practical jokes and that there is probably a moving spirit. Which gets us back to Galileo, doesn't it? *Eppur si muove*." And Church laughed immoderately. After all, a young man quite well able to look after himself.

Crunkhorn frowned. "I certainly don't suggest that Pluckrose was deliberately killed for fun. Such a suggestion would be rational only if there were ground for supposing the presence of a criminal lunatic about the university. But the thing may well have been a violent and dangerous jest gone wrong—just what Galileo's demonstration would have been had an accident occurred." Crunkhorn hesitated. "I really do not know if I ought to take this train of thought further. But perhaps it had better be mentioned that Pluckrose had a good deal of mathematics. He was a biochemist and interested in genetics, which requires a certain amount of mathematics nowadays. He had enough mathematics to ride various hobbies. And one of these was ballistics. He held rather cranky views on that."

Hobhouse was looking glumly at the ceiling. Appleby came tactfully to his aid. "Ballistics?" he said. "You mean—?"

"The science of projectiles. The Navy applies its laws whenever it fires a gun."

"Rules," said Church, "worked out by Newton and others when the bosses told them that the targets must jolly well be hit. Which is the sort of supply-and-demand affair they call science."

And professor Crunkhorn and his assistant eyed each other with a sudden serious animosity. At the moment, thought Appleby, one of the radical issues between the old and the young. Is science the disinterested pursuit of knowledge which the world may apply if it will? Or is it an activity always dependent upon economic and political demands? Odd how this messy mystery is bringing all that sort of stuff in.

"And a meteorite falling from a tower," asked Hobhouse practically; "would that be ballistics?"

"In a sense, yes." Crunkhorn frowned and spoke carefully. "Suppose Pluckrose to have what was, for some, an irritating way of airing this hobby of his. He is always talking about shells and bombs in a bland, theoretical way. He sees these abominations obstinately in terms of science and not at all in terms of morals or of the imagination. Until somebody says to himself: 'I'll show him what it *feels* like to have a projectile drop by one's nose.' I think, gentlemen, that the explanation of the fatality might lie there."

There was silence. One may be a bit pompous and yet by no means a fool. And Appleby looked at

Church. The young man had gone slightly pale. The silence prolonged itself.

"It would be a tragedy," pursued Crunkhorn presently. "And the law, I think, would call it manslaughter of the gravest sort. For myself, I should regard with great charity a folly so dreadfully visited. Nor do I say positively that this is even the most likely manner of Pluckrose's death. It is merely a possibility, and one which, if the mystery continues, would certainly be discovered and canvassed. So I mention it now. Perhaps Church will tell us what he thinks of it."

Appleby looked thoughtfully from one to the other of these men. Was Crunkhorn obliquely accusing his junior colleague? Or was he, despite an obvious everyday friction between the two, concerned to tide one whom he believed innocent over the first shock of a suspicion he judged inevitable? Church was scared. Was he scared merely as any young and inwardly uncertain man might be with such sinister and unfamiliar matter hovering round him? For a moment nobody said anything and one could hear the silence of the motionless clock.

"Think of it?" Church took a hand out of a pocket and looked at it—a steady hand. "I hardly know. It seems to depend on whether the meteorite was just lying about."

"Exactly." Appleby decided there was something to be said for helping Church along. "And we don't know that it was. Where it came from is still a mystery."

Church looked relieved. "Then why a meteorite? It's not an easy thing to come by. And not really very close in idea to bombs and shells. An old cannon ball would be just as easy to secure, and would have been much more—more appositeness in the situation Crunkhorn imagines."

Crunkhorn nodded, seemingly with approval. "I think, gentlemen, you will acknowledge that to be true. And yet there may have been such a joke as I described—and more of it than I have been able to describe."

"Ah," said Appleby.

"Suppose that Pluckrose had had it hinted to him that it would be nice if Providence dropped a nice heavy bomb on *him*. And suppose he had replied with some piece of rationalism: Providence does not, in fact, drop bombs; Providence has no bombs to drop— something like that. Would not a meteorite then become, in Church's word, apposite? A thing which comes whizzing like a projectile out of outer space might well be regarded as a sort of celestial ammunition."

"We become hypothetical," said Church. "Not only a hypothetical dispute about ballistics scientifically or morally conceived, but a hypothetical course to that dispute involving certain specific and rather far-fetched forms of words. An unfriendly person—say a barrister in court—might even insinuate that Crunkhorn is coming hurriedly forward with a laborious and slightly eccentric theory of his own devising—and one of which a principal consequence is to fix the attention upon likely frictions between Pluckrose and persons of markedly disparate age."

This was counter-attack with a vengeance. And the young man, like his senior, had the trick of turning his phrases in a bookish but effective way. There was no mistaking the implication of this studied piece of syntax. People who come forward with cock-and-bull tales of Galileo may be suspected of having something to hide. . . . And now Crunkhorn had stood up. Perhaps he felt that he had indeed been injudiciously ingenious; perhaps he was simply angry. "I am afraid," he said, "that another appointment must put an end to this interview. I do not say somewhat irregular interview, because I am willing to give any help I can, and I would not stand upon forms. Good afternoon."

And with a whisk of gown the professor of mathematics departed. What is called a dignified exit, thought Appleby. The sort of thing most people imagine afterwards rather than manage to achieve on the spot. And now perhaps it would be a good thing really to see that Vice-Chancellor. Or view the body. Or go poking about the topography of the thing: the Wool Court, the tower, the store-rooms, the hoist. But here still was the young man called Church—and he was now sitting back in his chair, mopping his forehead with a handkerchief. "Cripes!" said Mr. Church. "This is a lousy go. The old bastard!"

"Hobhouse," said Appleby gravely, "make a note. Mr. Church can talk like a human being when he wants to." He looked sharply at the young man. "And so, as it happens, can we. Pluckrose—did you quarrel with him?"

"No."

"Did he annoy you on the subject of bombs and shells?"

"Yes."

"Did you, if not exactly quarrel, at least dispute with him?"

"I bickered. A hole like this is largely bicker, bicker, bicker."

"I see. Did you ever—"

"I didn't pitch the meteorite at him; it never occurred to me that it would be a funny thing to do; I never play practical jokes." Church paused for breath. "I don't believe you have seen the Vice-Chancellor or that he directed you to Crunkhorn. You picked on us quite arbitrarily and out came all that rubbish about Galileo. It's your own mess and you can jolly well clear it up yourselves. I'm off." And Church scrambled to his feet, suddenly a very belligerent young man.

Appleby rose too. "Very well. But I'm sorry you should go off just when we've begun talking sense." His eye caught a flicker of uncertainty in the other man. "I expected you to tell us why Crunkhorn took that line."

Church gave a sort of impatient snort, but paused at the door. "He took *that* line because you blarneyed him into taking *some* line. Your smart yatter about mathematics and dispassionate views nobbled him and he thought up Galileo as something ingenious and learned and then he just went on elaborating. Everybody about the place will have some dam' fool theory to air if you take them that way."

Hobhouse made a discouraged sound and drummed on the table; clearly he judged this last statement only too true. But Appleby was unperturbed. "Even yourself, Mr. Church?"

"I'm not going to air anything."

"Except your own constitutionally bellicose spirit?"

"To hell with you." Church was now almost cheerful and his hand had dropped from the door knob.

"Of course it's just as you please as to that." Appleby was cheerful too. "But Crunkhorn was doing more than just elaborating a theory. He was getting back at you. And then you got a nasty one back at him. It was almost as if you were accusing each other of homicide. Quite a startling thing to happen when one has, as you say, picked on two men at random. Can you explain it?"

"Of course I can explain it." Church, as well as belligerency, had plainly a liberal dash of intellectual arrogance. "The old boy disapproves of me in various ways. He's convinced I have a hand in this idiotic joking. And it really did drift into his head that I might have flattened out poor Pluckrose in the way he hinted. He was appealing to me after his fashion to own up should it really be true. Or perhaps, even, he was putting me on my guard. You see, he's a fatherly old person in some ways. He feels he's making a mathematician of me."

"And is he?"

The inconsequent question stumbled Church for an instant. Then he laughed. "As it happens, *I'm* the mathematician about the place. Not that Crunkhorn has too bad a brain. Caught young and suitably trained, he'd have made quite a fair confidential clerk." Church paused, and the pause had the effect of acknowledging that, to strangers, this was not a pleasant witticism. "Anyway, I like him—quite."

"And your suggestion that he was talking away in order to conceal something on his own account?"

Church hesitated. "That," he said seriously, "was extremely foolish. So long."

The door banged behind him. Hobhouse drew a long breath. "I didn't think there could be anything odder than that duke-business. But this—"

Appleby smiled. "We're working among a queer lot. Not like respectable thugs and burglars. And now we'll view the body and read the medical report and measure things and find the crucial finger-print." He frowned. "And surely there's something else?"

"See the Vice-Chancellor."

"Just that."

3

Sir David Evans was a handsome old man with philosophic pretensions and a mass of white hair. Because of the philosophy he sat in front of the immense bookcase groaning under Locke, Hartley and Hume; and because of the hair these sages were cased in a dark shiny leather sparsely tooled in gold. The effect was charming—the more so in that Sir David's features invariably registered rugged benevolence. Every few years a portrait of Sir David robed in black and scarlet and with Locke and Hume behind him would appear in the exhibitions which our greatest painters arrange at Burlington House. Of these portraits one already hung in the Great Hall of the university, a second could be seen in a dominating position as soon as one entered Sir David's villa residence, and a third was stowed away ready for offer to the National Portrait Gallery when the time came. What happened to the others nobody knew. England is at best a semi-barbarous country, and the demand for portraits of retired professors of philosophy is astonishingly small. It was said that the portraits could be met with in every university college in India, a country through which Sir David as a young lecturer had endeavoured to diffuse the light of Clear and Distinct Ideas, Exact Senses, and the outlines of that celebrated Modified Empiricism which he was then beginning to think up for himself. But this of the Indian portraits may well have been a slander, for there is no doubt that about Sir David slanders of every sort were rife. Mr. Shergold, Nesfield's present professor of philosophy, maintained that the Vice-Chancellor was among that unfortunate minority of bad men who get themselves generally reprobated and disliked. This, perhaps, was a judgment of a somewhat *a priori* sort, the presumed axiom—one widely current in such universities as Nesfield—being that a Vice-Chancellor, *ipso facto*, cannot be a good man. Sir David, in fact, was conceivably a man much traduced. And some will hold that the effect which he produced with his bookcase and his hair and his expression of benevolent power ought to be accounted towards righteousness. For one might wander the length and breadth of Nesfield University without coming upon a single other such contrived effect. The professors never framed themselves against anything at all—unless it were haphazardly and unconsciously against shelves which were a tumble of battered books and jumbled papers, with here and there a dusty picture hanging slightly askew on a nail. If there is innocent pleasure and even something of edification in a little careful dressing-up then in one particular at least Sir David Evans deserved well of the institution over which he presided.

A slender shaft of sunlight, filtering through the well-combed mane of Sir David, spotlit the polished leather spine of *Observations on Man, his Frame, his Duty and his Expectations*. And gropingly Sir David was endeavouring to do a little of this observing on his own account; before him lay a letter to which he was now applying himself with scholarly concentration for the second time:

My Dear Sir David,

I am most distressed to hear of an occurrence which may cause annoyance to the dear Duke and considerable *anxiety* to yourself. The death of Mr. Pluckrose is (doubtless) a loss to science; and must be, moreover, an occasion of sober reflection to us all. For he has been snatched away unprepared and, knowing him as we did, is it not a point of some nicety to determine whether our mourning may be tempered by a pious hope? As my father (the late Sir Horace Dearlove, K.C.M.G.) used to remark with the peculiar forcefulness characterising all his utterances: *In the midst of life we are in death*.

As you know, Mr. Pluckrose has been a member of my household for nearly fifteen years and I may fairly claim an almost intimate knowledge of his habits and *connections*. I wonder if I can help in any way?

With kind regards,
Yours sincerely,
Virginia Caroline Dearlove.

P. S. My housekeeper—a most dependable person—tells me that there is outstanding the sum

41

of thirty-eight pounds eleven shillings and four-pence. Who are the solicitors?

V.C.D.

The sunbeam, creeping diagonally towards the ceiling, had reached *An Essay concerning Human Understanding*. A mathematician—say Mr. Crunkhorn or Mr. Church—might have found considerable beguilement in calculating where it would arrive in ten minutes' time. Would it be *An Essay concerning Toleration*? or *The Reasonableness of Christianity*? And surely it would not be so undiscriminating as to miss *A Treatise of Human Nature*? But Sir David, immobile at his desk, was without thought of his sainted and Caledonian namesake. Miss Dearlove absorbed his attention, and continued to do so until there came a knock at the door. Whereupon Sir David put the letter in a drawer, slightly shifted his chair so as to recapture the requisite aureole of sunlight, and called to come in.

Hobhouse introduced Appleby. Sir David, without budging, extruded so pungent a benevolence that the effect was rather that of coming unawares upon a skunk. Appleby said conventionally that this was an unfortunate business. Sir David, by silence, indicated that philosophers do not form these hasty conclusions; at the same time he continued to show that he held his visitors in the highest charitable regard. Appleby and Hobhouse decided that they might as well sit down. Whereupon Sir David stood up and walked to a window. Appleby and Hobhouse stood up and Hobhouse contrived to trip over his bowler hat. Sir David, not too philosophically remote to accord these blunderings a gentle compassion, tucked his hands beneath the tails of his beautiful black coat and presently spoke. "It iss mysterious," he said. "Whatever it iss, it iss that."

Appleby and Hobhouse found themselves nodding gratefully. The Vice-Chancellor had said the cogent thing. One was much more aware of this than of the fact that he spoke in the accents of Wild Wales. It must be the way he holds his head, Appleby thought. And the way he closes his mouth and jerks up his chin at the end of it. All needed, no doubt, if one is to put philosophy across on the hard-headed young. "You knew Professor Pluckrose well?" he asked.

It was obvious that another man would have raised his eyebrows. But the Vice-Chancellor crinkled the corners of his eyes into the kindliest smile—much as a dog-lover might do when subjected to the gambollings of an over-obstreperous puppy. To ask Sir David Evans a question must be something quite out of the way. "You will enquire into his death," he said benevolently and with authority. He took a hand from under his coat tails and raised a finger. "You haf a notebook?"

Hobhouse—but with less alacrity than might have been expected—indicated that he had a notebook.

"Things to remember about professors," said Sir David—and paused. It is a lecture, thought Appleby. It is—thought Hobhouse, innocent of the higher education—a dictation. But Appleby listened and Hobhouse wrote. Sir David still had that overpoweringly cogent air.

"They are ampitious." Sir David slightly inclined his head, as one might do when saying something compassionate about perennial strangeness and oddity of children. "All professors are ampitious—ampitious to become professors somewhere else." He paused and appeared to decide that, to reach the intellect of his hearers, this must be expanded and illustrated. "Professors at Leeds or Sheffield or Hull, look you, are ampitious to be professors at Nesfield; and professors at Nesfield are ampitious to be professors at Leeds or Sheffield or Hull."

"Ambition," said Appleby solemnly, "should be made of sterner stuff."

Sir David looked momentarily so disconcerted that it was plain his acquaintance had not the habit of offering him little jokes. Then he put out a kindly hand and patted Appleby on the shoulder, thereby indicating that even if he had said something foolish he should not altogether lose heart. "It iss the prave music of a distant drum," he said. "They are anxious to get away and so they work at things which are too hard for them, as it iss very easy for professors to do. They worry pecause their prains lack certain microscopic neural tracks which would make them a little cleverer than they are. How foolish it iss." And Sir David shook his head slowly and charitably, comfortably convinced that his own neural tracks were just as he would desire them. "So that iss the first thing about professors; they worry and have preakdowns."

Hobhouse licked his pencil, marked a heavy full stop and then unflinchingly pointed the lead at Sir David Evans's nose. "This Mr. Pluckrose," he said, "—did he have a breakdown?"

This time the Vice-Chancellor seemed to welcome interrogation. "Pluckrose certainly had a preakdown. Otherwise, look you, why should he have had a preakup?"

"A break-up?" said Appleby, involuntarily chiming in on the questioning.

"First Pluckrose had a preakdown. And then he proke up altogether and did it."

"Did it?" Hobhouse had put down his notebook and was looking thoroughly blank.

"Killed himself," said Sir David—and shut his mouth and jerked up his chin.

It was almost as if Appleby and his colleague ought to take up their hats and retire as men sated and resolved. But Appleby had at least one question to ask. "Then," he said, "it isn't mysterious after all?"

The effect of this was to cause Sir David Evans to move abruptly across the room as if in search of something. But the sunbeam was now high overhead and inaccessible, so he had to content himself with simply sitting down again at his desk. "You mistake me," he said patiently. "What iss mysterious iss that he should choose that way."

"Ah." Appleby nodded understandingly. "It does take some explaining, sir."

"And yet I think I haf an idea." Sir David looked with penetration at his visitors, as if sizing up their ability to do Advanced Work. "You haf heard of the Oedipus Complex?"

"Yes."

"And of the Electra Complex?"

"Yes."

"And of the Sisyphus Complex?"

This time Appleby shook his head. "I don't think I have."

"Good!" Sir David was delighted. "That is very good. Up to now there has not peen such a thing, look you. I haf just discovered it. Pluckrose suffered from the Sisyphus Complex."

Hobhouse groaned. This, on top of Galileo and the Law of Falling Bodies, was too much. Forgetful of the respect ever due to the upper classes, Hobhouse was suddenly aggressive. "And how could Pluckrose have suffered from something you've just invented? It doesn't make sense."

For a moment benevolence removed itself from the features of Sir David Evans and severity held sway instead. And then again he smiled, pardoning not only impertinence but bad logic as well. "I haf distinguished the condition and given it a name. Surely you haf heard of Sisyphus?"

Appleby decided that this exercise might as well be his. "Sisyphus was an avaricious king who was punished in the lower world, where he had to roll uphill a huge stone which kept on tumbling down again."

"Exactly! The stone, look you, was beyond Sisyphus' weight. It was something he worked away at, but which he had not the necessary power to cope with. So it iss with the professors who do work too hard for them and haf preakdowns. They pecome conscious of their impotence and develop the Sisyphus Complex." Sir David was evidently highly pleased. "And so it was with Pluckrose, to be sure."

Appleby stared at him. "But you can hardly mean—?"

The Vice-Chancellor raised a finger. "Things to remember about myths," he said.

Hobhouse put his notebook in his pocket. Sir David ignored this act of insubordination.

"Efery man has his myth, mark you. Long ago the myths provided opjective equivalents"—Sir David paused and considerately repeated this hard phrase—

"provided opjective equivalents of efery possible human situation. Sooner or later efery educated man discovers his own myth. Pluckrose discovered that his myth was that of Sisyphus. Never would he get the stone to the top of the hill. Always—crash!—it would fall pack again. Pluckrose was haunted by the myth and then there was a preakdown and he proke up. In his death he concretised the myth which now opsessed him. Up he went with his great stone, look you. And down it came and crushed him." Sir David Evans, delivering himself of this remarkably psychological analysis with great power and conviction, almost deliquesced in kindly feeling. He bore the late Pluckrose no grudge on account of the quaint absurdity of his proceedings.

"But," said Appleby, "Sisyphus wasn't crushed. He just had to go on trying."

"Nefer mind, nefer mind! It is near enough. Here always is the great stone hanging over him, threatening destruction, it iss in his dreams, consider you. Always the great weight, ready to come crashing down. And always—"

"Do you mean he *arranged* it?" Hobhouse was bewildered and shocked to the point of positive interruption. "Do you mean that he arranged for this meteorite to come tumbling down and then went and *sat* under it?"

"Always Sisyphus is in his dreams. The great stone is there in his dreams, and in his waking dreams. It pecomes a muscular fact, pressing on him. He walks with his shoulders pent. Any mass—a puilding, a pus—terrifies him. The thing haunts him. He is opsessed." Sir David had quite ceased to be the rugged but benevolent philosopher and had become a frank little Welshman of the bardic and excitable sort. He was, in fact, well launched upon a piece of bad poetry. "He is opsessed. And then, walking over the moors one day—he finds the meteorite. A thing, look you, sent from hefen! He hurries away. But he has met his myth and he returns, again and again, compelled. The thing has grown a fetish. He comes to know efery contour of it by heart. Now in his dreams there is a real stone: here a well-known jagged edge; there a smooth knob like a pig pludgeon. And at last he acts: he tries to move the stone! He pushes, heaves, levers. The stone stirs, moves, falls pack again into its place. Now he is caught. He has pecome Sisyphus indeed. Then, one dark night—"

"Then, one dark night, he goes mad." Appleby interrupted civilly. "The theory, I take it, requires that?"

"To be sure." The Vice-Chancellor nodded, slightly resentful of this short-cut to his climax. "It iss a thing to remember about professors. They go mad. And Pluckrose iss compelled to raise the stone—up, up as far as it will go. Into his car, into the hoist, up and up to the tower. He will palance it on the window-sill, where it can be seen from the court. And next day he will be able to point and say: '*Ha-Ha!*'"

At this juncture Sir David threw back his beautiful mane of hair and laughed so loudly that Hobhouse jumped. The interview was becoming dream-shaped and monstrous, like something in Kafka. And the last sunbeam had disappeared, so that Hume and Hartley and Locke were growing shadowy and insubstantial.

"'*Ha-ha!*' he will say; 'see how high Sisyphus has raised his stone after all. None ever raised it higher, look you!'" Sir David was now craning his neck up at his own ceiling, and involuntarily Appleby and Hobhouse found themselves doing the same. "It is perilously palanced; he will give it just one more push—" Sir David thrust his arms outwards and upward. "Just one more inch, when—*crash!*" And Sir David's arms fell dramatically to his sides.

They stared at him, astonished. "You mean"—Appleby had to strive for words—"that he had an accident while contriving some insane piece of exhibitionism; that he came tumbling down with the meteorite and was crushed; that he didn't commit suicide after all?"

Sir David Evans looked momentarily surprised, as if he had failed to notice the position at which he had arrived. But then he nodded emphatically. "Just so. It iss death by misadventure. And during a preakdown such as professors have." He paused and looked about the room, now filling with dusk. "Where are the reporters? They must be told what we have discovered, mark you. And who is the City coroner now? I must write to him. It will not do to have mistakes." He raised a finger—a finger which was now wholly minatory and threatening. "You will enquire. You will infestigate. But there will be no mistakes, look you, no mistakes!"

"Damocles," said Appleby as they walked down the corridor.

"Huh?" Hobhouse at the moment appeared to find inarticulate sounds of most service to him.

"If Sisyphus, why not Damocles? It's true he had nothing to do with stones or meteorites. But they suspended a sword over his head by a single horsehair and expected him to take his ease under it. I think somebody might bring Damocles into the story. The Damocles Complex."

Hobhouse looked cautiously behind him, rather as if he expected Sir David Evans to be following them quietly on all fours. "I say, what did you make of all that? I suppose his mind broods on that sort of stuff—Sisyphus Complexes and the like."

"I'm sure it doesn't. That's the odd thing. The sort of academic philosopher Evans is or was invariably thinks Freud and what-not a mass of nonsense. It was a sheer fantasy for the benefit of two ignorant policemen. He got quite worked up as he went along, I admit. But it began as a deliberate determination to put a false interpretation on the whole business. Why?"

"He doesn't want a scandal." Hobhouse shook his head sagely. "It's to be hushed up as an accident. Rather the sort of thing you thought the duke was after."

"But he wasn't."

"Well, Evans is."

"I wonder."

Hobhouse's reply was again merely an indeterminate noise. They plodded down the long corridor in a dingy twilight which thickened as they moved. A symbol, Appleby thought, of the Pluckrose affair so far. The case was growing more confused without growing more substantial. The elements of it were evasive. As the Vice-Chancellor had justly said, it was mysterious—and yet the mystery was bodiless still, scarcely quick in the mind. It required a little contemplation and less talk. But the university was like a House of Fame or Temple of Rumour in some medieval poem. A Parliament of Prattlers, with the be-

nevolently powerful Sir David Evans as Speaker. . . .
Appleby pulled up. " The body—will it have gone?"

"They're waiting for dark."

"Then I think we'll go back."

Students were hurrying past in mackintoshes and
mufflers; electric lights, sparse, shadeless and inimical, flickered on with an effect of impatient dismissal.
The place was shutting down; sweetness and light
were over for the day; the quest of knowledge was off
until nine o'clock next morning. Outside the porter's
office women with pails and brooms were gathering;
among them and through a faint aroma of dust and
soap the porter, unbuttoned but magisterial, was moving with a timesheet in his hand. Doors banged and
the stream of students grew: spotty faces, eager faces,
faces already dulled and defeated by the machine,
faces full of temper and intelligence. Susan and Harry,
Dick and Josephine going home to tea, to swatting
over text-books, to a night at the pictures in families
or together holding hands; Josephine, Dick, Harry
and Susan unaware of the awareness of the Duke
of Nesfield, of the curious behaviour of their Vice-
Chancellor, of Galileo's work on the Law of Falling
Bodies. Appleby and Hobhouse threaded their way
through, seeking the fallen body of Pluckrose *fue*. So
young and fair a congregation. What should they know
of death? Beyond this door is the chill April evening
air that fills the Wool Court. Open it.

The evening had suddenly clouded so that now it
was almost dark. The fountain trickled, invisible—a
melancholy sound, a tiny pointless dissipation, a futile
ebbing away. Zealous policecraft had rigged up an
affair of waterproof canvas over the body, and Pluckrose was a desert traveller defeated within crawling

51

distance of water, an arctic explorer perishing to a drip of icicles. Bringing imagination to the detection of crime. Appleby stumbled, stooped, softly exclaimed, walked on. Hobhouse followed, dubious. From the corridor behind them came a final scamper of feet, a name shouted twice, an answering faint hail. The tower soared and impended; it was impressive at dusk.

"I don't know that we can do—" Hobhouse stopped as Appleby flashed a torch. There was the striped duck and splintered wood of the deck-chair. There was the meteorite, with effort heaved aside. And here was the body. Pluckrose crushed. Like a little old shabby rebel angel, disparted from his brightness, when the faithful host had finished hurling heaven's hills in battle and gone home to bed.

These persistent mythological associations. . . . Appleby spoke soberly: "Could he and the meteorite really have come down together? It's an idea, after all."

"The man was murdered." Hobhouse's voice, harsh suddenly and not to be cheated, came out of the dark. "No one would deliberately make such a crazy end."

"But perhaps it is true that he was mad? We want a better means of eliminating Evans' theory." Appleby paused and looked down at the body. Pluckrose, a small grey man with untidy eyebrows, looked at once very dead and very surprised. A trick of the last futile messages that had hurried, collided, jammed, run out of fuel, evaporated in a chaos of crushed nerves and glands. One's own death is surely the most surprising thing in the world—but dead men commonly look vastly indifferent. Appleby snapped off the torch. "The Law of Falling Bodies," he said.

"To hell with the Law of Falling Bodies." For this sort of thing Hobhouse too must have a seasoned eye. But on Hobhouse too the frozen twist of those muscles had its effect.

"Not at all. What did Crunkhorn tell us about Galileo's experiment? That the one-pound shot and the ten-pound shot arrived at the foot of the leaning tower virtually at the same time. In a vacuum they would each have touched the ground actually at the same moment. But then they were bodies each with the same high specific gravity. If he had chucked over a ten-pound shot and, say, a one-pound open book the results would have been different. So what about a meteorite and a human body falling a considerable distance through air? Wouldn't the meteorite be bound to arrive first?"

"Not if the human body was clinging to it."

"I suppose that's so. It's only the resistance of the air which gives different velocities to different objects falling. But could he cling? Not, certainly, through a very long drop. If one jumped out of an aeroplane clutching a bomb one would part company with it soon and arrive on the ground some seconds later. Or so I should guess."

Hobhouse looked up at the dark empty sky. "It's not a thing very easily verified by the police. Nor Pluckrose and the meteorite either."

"But we can hunt up the university's physicists and see what they say. And we may still find evidence that he was certainly sitting here in the chair when the thing fell. Although the court is secluded—"

Like a trick on the stage, light flooded them. Shafts of light, bars of darkness lay on the grass, bridged the fountain, broke into confused chequering over the body with its sheltering tent. They turned round. Across the court half a dozen tall windows had sprung to a garish brightness and through their upper halves could be seen a system of shafts and wheels and belts which now with a faint throb began to turn. So something happened of an evening after all. The throbbing grew louder and across the lower windows, of a semi-opaque sea-green glass, indeterminate shadows moved.

"Engineering," said Hobhouse. "They work only in the afternoon and again at night. I suppose a good many of the students are in jobs. Anyway, that side would be deserted in the morning. And even if there were people about they couldn't see out of the windows at ground level."

"I suppose not." Appleby was staring absently at the turning wheels. "Isn't it odd that the university should be so insistent that there should never be a view from its windows? The eye is turned inward."

"Umph." Hobhouse was unimpressed by symbolism. "It's time they collected the body. P.M. at ten in the morning and funeral at two."

"Relations?"

"One distant cousin, so far. There's a will at the bank and a solicitor hard at work writing letters to anyone who could possibly be concerned. Nice easy wicket, the Law."

"Home?"

"He lodged with a Miss Dearlove. I haven't seen her yet. What a mess these deaths and homicides are. Far more running about than with burglary or forgery."

"Yes." Appleby looked at the body and agreed with this professional view. "Distinctly a mess."

"But embezzlement can be very bad. And I always say carnal knowledge is worst."

"I rather agree with you."

Hobhouse lowered his voice. "Did you ever have a case of a man keeping—"

"What I want to know"—Appleby's voice was suddenly incisive in the darkness—"what I want to know is this. Does anybody round about here keep pets?"

4

Outside the university trams charged down the hill. This lot took people to the first house at the Royal, the Kings, the Lyceum. The next lot would take cinema-goers: the Majestic, the Super, the Palace. Then there would be a lot taking people to the second house at the Royal, the Kings, the Lyceum. The trams charged past in a clang of bells, their swaying motion more marked now that they were stubby pencils of light; it was funny that nobody was ever sick on charging and bucketing trams that pencilled and swayed away into the distance and became like bits broken off the Neons further on. Further on was lower down too so you could see from here the city spread in a sort of drab sparkle in the darkness and you could see a pool of darkness which was a park and you could see the station and hard bright lights in the shunting yards beyond the station.

It is odd—thought Appleby, saying good night to Hobhouse—that the mind when tired churns out such flawless modern prose. It is more than odd, he thought as he climbed the stairs of the private hotel; it is more than odd, it is suspicious. He poured chilly water at a Victorian ewer and basin and tried to go on beginning a Hemingway story where he had left off at the shunting yards. But the plunge of his hands in the cold water woke him and Hemingway became irrelevant and he thought of Aeschylus. Aeschylus might be relevant. He thought of what he had stumbled against in the dusk of the Wool Court. Sisyphus was poppycock. But there might be something in Aeschylus. There might be something in Aeschylus if these people's minds really worked in that sort of way—but he was inclined to doubt this.

When he went into the dining-room he found himself unexpectedly confronted at table with Professor Hissey. And Hissey recognised him. "Appleby?" he said in amiable surprise. "What brings you here? And what has happened to Williams and Merryweather and Grant? And do you ever hear from Harrison? I had a letter about a year ago. The natives, he says, are becoming interested—really interested—in Catullus. I can well believe it. Merryweather, I am sure, is a very capable lecturer. Harrison, that is to say." And Professor Hissey ate some soup.

It was rather difficult. Appleby decided to begin with Grant. "Grant—" he said.

"Williams, my dear fellow"—Hissey leant across the table confidentially—"do you remember Appleby? I have been told a most extraordinary thing. He became a policeman."

"Yes," said Appleby. "I became a policeman." It was really very difficult indeed.

"And do you like it?" Mr. Hissey betrayed no consciousness of there having been any hitch in the conversation. "I don't think I ever had a competent pupil become a policeman before. But some of the very incompetent ones have." He ate more soup. "In Africa, that is. They go about on motor bicycles. No doubt quite a different thing. We have no wine at table here. But if you care to join me in my room afterwards I can offer you a glass of port, my dear—Appleby." And Mr. Hissey first smiled at his former pupil in innocent triumph and then looked slowly round the dining-room, rather as if he found it faintly but pervasively unfamiliar. Appleby remembered that Hissey had always been a slightly absent-minded man.

"I should like a glass of port very much. I think I should say that I have come to Nesfield to enquire into the business of Professor Pluckrose."

Hissey looked perplexed. "Pluckrose?" he said. "I don't think Pluckrose *has* a business."

"I mean—"

"Some of them have businesses. Rather surprising in scholars, don't you think? Crunkhorn is said to own and manage a garage. It perplexes me, I confess. But you're too late with Pluckrose, anyway. I've just remembered. He's dead."

"That's just it, sir. Pluckrose has died in a mysterious way and I've been sent down to enquire into the circumstances."

"I see. You *said*, you know, into the *business*." Hissey was mildly reproachful. "One can't be too careful with tramps."

"Tramps?" Appleby looked rather blankly at his former preceptor.

"They may appear innocent and even deserving. But as likely as not they are concerned to rob you—

58

and prepared to offer violence if you resist." And Hissey shook his head, very worldly wise. "Of course I should never refuse a tramp a shilling or two if he asked for it. It is quite clear from the accounts that they give of themselves that they have a very hard time. It would be uncharitable to refuse. But when I walk in the country I always carry a big stick."

"I see." Appleby watched the fish go. "And you think that Pluckrose—"

"Pluckrose?" Hissey spoke as if some quite new term had been introduced into the discussion. "Killed by tramps, poor chap. I suppose the police will send up to investigate. Do you always see the *Hellenic Review?*"

At the Royal, the Kings, the Lyceum the first houses would be in full swing. Life, in fact, is extremely various. Perhaps the best technique for tackling its problems is a thoroughgoing inconsequence. "Not always," Appleby said. "Do many people at the university keep pets?"

"No," said Hissey. He appeared wholly unsurprised. "I don't think many people do." He considered. "The head porter keeps a tortoise."

"You disappoint me," said Appleby. "Keenly."

"I am extremely sorry." Hissey looked benevolently across the table at this extravagant animal-lover. "But I am really afraid that nobody else keeps—"

"You mistake me. I mean I am disappointed that the porter should keep a tortoise. I thought it might have something to do with Pluckrose—and Aeschylus."

Professor Hissey laid down his knife and fork. "My dear Merryweather—Appleby, I mean—there are no eagles round about Nesfield. Nor was Pluckrose bald."

Appleby chuckled to himself. Lead the old boy to his own ground and his mind became instantly cogent. "I didn't mean quite that. I don't suppose that Pluckrose was killed as Aeschylus was by having an eagle drop a tortoise on his bald head in mistake for a stone. I was thinking of something rather symbolical."

"Dear me," said Hissey.

"There was an oracle—wasn't there?—which said that Aeschylus would die by a blow from heaven. Now Pluckrose—despite your very interesting theory about tramps—appears to have died something like that. A meteorite fell on him. You could call that a blow from heaven, more or less. And in the court where they found his body I stumbled over a tortoise. It occurred to me that if the manner of his killing had some symbolical significance the person responsible might have dropped the tortoise out of the Aeschylus story, so to speak, just by way of underlining the blow-from-heaven idea."

"Dear me," said Hissey again. His features assumed a courteous consideringness. "*Dear* me."

In fact, thought Appleby, he is not impressed. Their minds *don't* work in that sort of way. Nor would mine have, perhaps, if it hadn't been for Sir David Evans and Sisyphus. The death of Pluckrose isn't wrapped up in Greek and Latin and Freudian complexes and the Law of Falling Bodies. It is wrapped up in one or more of the usual things: a woman, blackmail, drink, drugs and the rest. A policeman's lot is not a happy one. Appleby looked across at Hissey. Hissey had grown abstracted; his eyes appeared to be on the open page of an invisible *Hellenic Review*. Nevertheless when he spoke it was to ask mildly: "Have you any clues?"

"I don't know that I have. Not now that the tortoise is gone."

"The tortoise has *gone*?" Hissey was interested.

"I mean not now that we have eliminated the possibility of the presence of the tortoise's having had a special significance in regard—"

"I understand you," said Hissey placidly. Suddenly he looked dismayed. "Bless my soul! I had quite forgotten the Symposium."

"The Symposium?"

"Of course it is quite the wrong word." Hissey laughed merrily. "It is quite the wrong word, I am sorry to say. Colloquium would undoubtedly be better. Nothing but coffee is provided." Hissey again dissolved in innocent mirth. "But perhaps there is something a shade pedantic about Colloquium. The word is scarcely in common English use."

"I suppose not." Appleby had just finished a chunk of blanc-mange and was feeling as one often does feel after dinner in small provincial hotels. "In fact distinctly not. Colloquium is a most pedantic word."

"No doubt you are right." Hissey was slightly wistful. The possibility of changing from Symposium to Colloquium was clearly a matter to which he gave a good deal of thought. Now he looked at his watch. "What worries me is our glass of port. You see, I have to take the chair and so it is necessary that I should go. But perhaps you would care to come across too? I am sure everybody would be delighted that I should bring an old pupil of my own."

"You are very kind." Appleby was cautious. "Will the Vice-Chancellor be there?"

"Evans? Dear me, no." Hissey looked quite shocked.

"Or Professor Crunkhorn or Church?"

"Neither of them, I judge."

"I should like to come, very much." There might be something, Appleby thought, in getting a representative section of the academic body of Nesfield within one *coup d'oeil*. Particularly if his own identity were not yet generally known.

"This is most delightful!" Hissey had risen nimbly from his chair. "I think you will enjoy it. There are likely to be one or two interesting things. Prisk has a further batch of notes on the placenames of Provence. Young Marlow is bringing a tentative bibliographical analysis of the 1582 quarto of *Mumblechance*. Tavender will review some recent contributions to epigraphy. . . ."

"It sounds very interesting indeed. And I hope you are giving something yourself?"

Hissey was moving towards the door. He stopped and lowered his voice. "Well, as a matter of fact I did happen the other day upon something a little odd in Paley's Theocritus—"

"In Paley's Theocritus!" Appleby was extremely impressed.

Hissey beamed. "I judge it to be not altogether without interest. In fact I am rather tempted to save it up."

They were out in a sort of uncomfortable compromise between a vestibule and a lounge. Residential ladies, little palms, commercial travellers, a dull fire made a background as they passed. Over the way and a bit up the hill they would by now have shoved Pluckrose in an ambulance, a mortuary car, a van.

Hissey, winding a scarf, still beamed. "Because I am hoping to put out a book."

"Really? I am sure people have been waiting for it a long time. What is it going to be called?"

Hissey shook his head; stopped to put on a rusty bowler hat; shook it again. "I find it difficult to make up my mind. But something quite simple will do. What do you think of just *Annotatuinculae Criticae?*"

"I think that would be excellent."

Hissey, mildly happy, led the way into the night.

Professor Prisk held the chair of Romance Languages. But why, Appleby speculated, do professors have chairs? Why not desks? Or even boxes or bags? What Prisk ought really to have was a bag. He was using a sort of invisible bag now. It held what our Saxon forebears would have called his word-hoard. Prisk dipped into his invisible bag, drew a word apparently at random, fingered it jealously for some minutes, returned it and brought out another word. He was wholly absorbed in the contents of his invisible bag, so that Appleby thought he was rather like an ingeniously conceived allegory of miserliness. But clearly to have out and gloat over one's word-hoard like this was a highly esteemed activity. Everybody listened to Prisk with respect—even the two young men behind Appleby who had been inclined to chatter to each other under their breath. The room was subterraneous and full of tobacco smoke and the place names of Provence went on and on and Appleby was sorry he had come.

Prisk was a little, stout, aggressive man who lived in a world of words. His room was next to Pluckrose's. There was something about a telephone. . . .

63

From the corridor outside a chink of china suggested that the place names of Provence might not go on for ever after all. The young men behind were whispering again. Appleby shifted on a rather hard chair. There was a telephone locked up in a box outside Prisk's and Pluckrose's rooms. They had to share the telephone because the university was hard up. Just the sort of malicious economy you could trust Sir David Evans to think of.

Somebody had interrupted with a question. Prisk earnestly explained himself, his hand held suspended over the invisible bag. Several people emitted helpful noises, working on one of Prisk's words like children. There was animated discussion. Then Prisk was off again, word after word. The whole place was a world of words—which was what made it so difficult for a policeman to get up any steam in. An unsatisfactory day. That odd affair of the Duke of Nesfield—Appleby frowned, very much as if he had detected a possible flaw in the philological reasonings of the laborious Prisk. The telephone! Perhaps *that* was why the duke—

Appleby took paper and pencil from his pocket. Several people were making notes. *I am a policeman* he wrote *How does Prisk know a telephone call is for him*. When Appleby had written this he handed it to one of the young men behind him, continuing to give every appearance of serious attention to Prisk the while. At his back there was a mild sensation. And then the paper came back. *Thrilled* it read *One ring for Pluckrose two for Prisk*.

So there might be something in that. Appleby stuffed the paper in his pocket, aware that the place names of Provence had come to an end. They had come to an end disconcertingly because wholly without peroration or climax. It was just like the turning off of a tap. Only turn again the other way and there would be plenty more to come. But now there would be coffee and then somebody else would start. Pluckrose by this time was in the city mortuary, lying on a slab of marble like a fish in a shop. . . . An open cigarette case curved round Appleby's right shoulder and hovered before his chest. It belonged to one of the whispering young men. And at the same moment both young men made a flanking movement and appeared before him. "Cigarette?" said one. "Coffee?" said the other, and darted away. In a moment Appleby found himself edged into an empty alcove, with the two young men staring at him with frank curiosity. It was like having confessed at a children's party that one had an uncle who had been in prison or in the secret service or quite near the South Pole.

"My name is Marlow," said the first young man. "This is the first time we've ever met the power behind the village copper. Do you wear a sort of badge behind the lapel of your coat?"

"Marlow has no manners." The second young man spoke in accents of mild apology. "We ask no questions. And we are secret as the grave. But we give our modest advice. *Cherchez la femme.*"

"The mind of Pinnegar," said Marlow, "runs on sex and expresses itself in vulgar *clichés*. Trace the meteorite."

"Question his landlady. A sinister gentlewoman called Dearlove."

"Subject Prisk to a grilling examination."

"Arrest the Vice-Chancellor."

"Have you met old Murn? Have him shadowed."

"Discover who hung the skeleton in the maze."

"Drag the river for Lasscock."

"Enquire into the curious affair of Mrs. Tavender's tea-party."

"What's happened to Timmy Church's girl?"

There was a pause. But they looked as if they might begin again. "Thank you," said Appleby hastily. "Thank you very much indeed. The meteorite shall be traced and the woman hunted for. Prisk, the Vice-Chancellor and Miss Dearlove shall be interrogated, Murn shadowed if it should be necessary, the matter of the skeleton elucidated and Lasscock—whoever he may be—traced. Mrs. Tavender's tea-party shall be investigated, and so will the fate of Timmy Church's girl." He put down his cup. "I wonder if I might have more coffee? It would be nice to keep some sort of clear head."

Marlow, a tall man with a shock of auburn hair, went for coffee. Pinnegar stood still and looked impressed and perhaps scared. From the body of the room came a murmur of conversation mingled with mooings, gruntings and hissings as the assembled scholars continued to challenge each other on nice philological points. The effect, Appleby thought, was to make one look for those bird- and beast-likenesses which human features can always suggest. There were the usual parrots and porkers and fish. These, after all, are the common types. But here and there was something more *recherché*. Prisk, for instance, had a nose flattened after a fashion curiously suggesting the platypus. The grunting and hissing was reinforced by whistling and a sort of muted bellowing as some new class of phonetic phenomena gained the attention of the company. The mingling of noises human and brute, and the zoological analogies thus evoked, gave the whole affair the quality of some vast and suspended metamorphosis, some Circean magic in which there had been a hitch half-way through. . . . But these were unprofitable reflections. Could one say otherwise of the chatter of these two apparently light-hearted young men? Must he take them sufficiently seriously, for instance, really to enquire into the curious affair of Mrs. Tavender's tea-party?

"About the telephone"—Marlow had returned with coffee and a plate of biscuits—"do you think it was really meant to be *Prisk?*"

"By Jove, yes," said Pinnegar. "Appointment with Death. Something like that."

They weren't fools. Naturally not. Everybody here was presumably something above average intelligence—it was that perhaps which gave its irritating obliqueness to the whole affair. They like to approach things sideways. If crabs made noises then there might be added to the hissing and grunting—Appleby checked himself. Among the constitutionally oblique a little directness might be the most effective thing. "Oh, quite," he said. "Somebody might propose to make a comfortable little appointment with Prisk down by those deck-chairs. And because of this telephone-business the message might somehow deliver itself to Pluckrose instead. One doesn't see just how. But it's a possibility, isn't it? Like Timmy Church's girl."

The young men were intrigued. They were also decently uncomfortable. "Perhaps," said Pinnegar, "we ought not to have mentioned—" He was interrupted by the emergence from the pervasive zoological background of a single dominant noise. At first

67

merely like another pertinacious experiment in phonetics, it presently disclosed itself as a giggle. An elderly man was approaching them, giggling and rubbing his hands. Pinnegar hailed him with renewed cheerfulness. "Tavender," he called, "here is Monsieur Dupont of the *Sûreté*." He gestured towards Appleby. "He has your *dossier* in his pocket. He is particularly interested in your skill as an epigrapher."

Tavender—whose wife, presumably, had held the curious tea-party—bowed, giggled and looked at the ceiling, rather as if he expected it to yield some suitable form of words. As this didn't happen he simply bowed and giggled again—this, apparently, with much more of good humour than embarrassment.

"Epigraphy!" said Marlow. "That's the thing. Tavender or Hissey shall read the evidences of the meteorite. They can decipher inscriptions that are thousands of years old. Let him try his hand at something which is as fresh as paint."

"As blood," said Pinnegar. "For what is inscribed on the meteorite? Presumably particles of Pluckrose. Parts, pieces, portions, pashes. Or should one say petals? Death's fading rose."

"Rose leaves," said Marlow, "when the rose is dead—"

Tavender giggled, even more good-humouredly than before. He was, Appleby provisionally decided, a displeasing old person. And Marlow and Pinnegar were displeasing young men. At least they would read as that if one wrote their talk down and read it out in court. Perhaps they were sensitive little souls and mildly hysterical. That isn't nice in young men, but then again it isn't criminal. Perhaps they had imaginations and very little guts and they didn't like the

Pluckrose business at all. . . . Appleby, who did in fact have a constantly growing *dossier* in his pocket, had another look at Tavender. Tavender quite liked the Pluckrose business. He would like anything which showed large potentialities for the creating of discomfort, malice and all uncharitableness. For Tavender these things made the world go round. Poor old Hissey, thought Appleby. Coming to Nesfield and finding himself provided with so displeasing an assistant. But of course this might be quite wrong. In such matters even talented young detective officers can make mistakes.

"Monsieur Dupont," said Pinnegar, "has discovered that it was Prisk whom it was understood to murder. But the call on the telephone missent itself and Pluckrose seated himself in error and the meteorite precipitated itself upon him with the violence enormous. Now, one addresses himself to trace the projectile. Monsieur Dupont will radio-diffuse an appeal tomorrow."

Tavender, because all this was plainly meant to be droll, stopped giggling and contrived to look serious and sad. "It is a possibility," he said. "The murderer asks the switch-board for Prisk and the operator proceeds to give two rings. But Pluckrose happens to be by the machine—perhaps just about to make a call— and he picks it up on the first ring and says 'Hullo.' There is nothing much to a Hullo and the murderer thinks he has got Prisk. 'Come into the court and have a chat,' he says; 'there's a nice bit of sun.' 'Right,' says Pluckrose and rings off. Pluckrose goes out and the murderer goes up. Pluckrose finds nobody, so he sits down and waits. The murderer peers down from the tower; his man seems to be there; he drops what he has ready to drop. The theory is possible, and it has its appeal."

"Its appeal?" said Appleby. Suddenly he felt almost affectionately disposed towards Tavender. The man spoke clearly, consecutively and to the point. Which—in this particular society—was like a good deed in a naughty world. "Its appeal?" said Appleby. "My name is Appleby, by the way. And I'm a policeman, all right."

Tavender bowed and rubbed his hands. "It means," he said, "that Prisk is still on the list. If at first you don't succeed, shy, shy again."

Marlow laughed. Pinnegar looked sulky; he was not going to be amused by others if others were not to be amused by him. Appleby glanced across the room at Nesfield's professor of Romance Languages. Could Prisk really be in danger? Would they, perhaps, tie him up in his own invisible bag and chuck him into the fountain? Would a few Provencal place names bubble to the surface, and that be the end? Appleby frowned. The mental habits induced by this learned environment were extremely frivolous. "But you wouldn't maintain," he said gravely to Tavender, "that all this is at all probable?"

"Of course it isn't probable. If murder was a probable contingency among us it would be merely alarming. All this is wildly improbable. Who would ever have thought we should all have the chance of whispering criminal suggestions about each other?" Mr. Tavender rubbed his hands in a kind of sober delight. "But it has happened. A real murder. And we are concerned not with the probabilities but with what is feasible. One knows straight away that this of the telephone is improbable. But its feasibility depends on a number of factors which you would have to investigate. For instance, the possibility of the mistaken call."

"Ah," said Appleby.

"One ring for one man; two for another. Frequently there must have been muddles—and indeed it is known that the shared telephone caused friction between them. One would suppose that always as one of them picked up the receiver the possibility of mistake would be faintly in his head. And this militates against the notion I have put forward. But one must notice that other interesting possibilities open out."

"Quite so," said Appleby, and wondered what the other interesting possibilities were. He was rather inclined to believe that if Tavender said they existed then they did exist. The man had an unattractive manner. But he also had a clear head. Appleby glanced at Marlow and Pinnegar. They were both looking faintly discontented, as if the matter of Pluckrose had gone unexpectedly dull.

"For instance," said Tavender, "there is the matter of the skeleton in the maze. One sees possible correlations with that."

"Um," said Appleby. The skeleton in the maze had been part of that cluster of suggestions which had included too Mrs. Tavender's tea-party. And it sounded as if it might link up with the practical joking that had offended Professor Crunkhorn. But apart from this Appleby knew nothing of it. So he said "um" as quizzically as possible and offered Tavender a sceptical smile.

But Tavender, by vocation a badgerer of bewildered

youth, was not to be drawn. "Don't you think?" he said.

"I try to think." Appleby smiled cheerfully. "And what you say is extremely interesting."

"Really?" Tavender rubbed his hands and raised his eyebrows in surprise. "I fear I cannot agree with you. I have the strongest suspicion that my remarks have been quite without relevance to the essence of the affair. But, of course, you are in the better position to judge."

And Mr. Tavender giggled and Pinnegar and Marlow again grew cheerful. "Tavender," said Marlow, "believes that the skeleton in the maze is not the skeleton in the cupboard after all."

"He makes," said Pinnegar, "no bones about it."

Tavender stopped giggling and again looked at Pinnegar sadly. And again Pinnegar sulked. It was depressing, Appleby thought. A murder in Houndsditch or Soho was altogether a more cheerful affair. . . . But now there was a shuffling of feet and scraping of chairs in the body of the room. These learned people were going to return to their quiet fun.

The young men, however, were reluctant to resume their seats. Marlow had produced a sheaf of papers which presumably contained his tentative views on the 1582 quarto of *Mumblechance*, and with this he now tapped Tavender urgently on the shoulder. "The meteorite," he said. "The evidences of the stone. Resolve this heavy riddle."

"Well, it is widely believed that the meteorite must have had some symbolical significance." And Tavender looked hopefully at Appleby, as if expecting that he might confirm this reasonable supposition.

"If it had been me," said Pinnegar, " I would have used the sink."

"The sink?" asked Marlow.

"It is said that up in the tower there was, among other things, a cast-iron sink. That would have been symbolism enough. A sink of iniquity. To what was the late professor to be likened? The grease at the bottom of the sink." And Pinnegar laughed harshly— this time not caring whether others laughed or not. "And I can think of one not dissimilar object which would have been better still."

There was, thought Appleby, nothing in it. Pinnegar's remarks were directed by no special animosity towards the unfortunate Pluckrose. He was a young man who cultivated this Thersytes-like attitude for private emotional reasons of his own, and these had almost certainly nothing whatever to do with the case. Or so it seemed. Again there was always the tiresome fact that one might be wrong. A clever man might cloak a precise and purposive animosity behind just such a harsh pose. . . . And Appleby, thus professionally sniffing at a red herring, looked absently from Pinnegar to Tavender.

Tavender was moving away. But now he stopped. "*Does* a meteorite carry about a symbolism with it?" he asked. "Really, I think not. A few minds of a special sort"—he waved a hand round the room—"may pump such a thing in. But what then does a meteorite universally carry? Not symbolism but—?" He was looking ironically at Appleby, much as he might look at a good student whom he had found a question difficult enough to floor. "Not," he repeated, "symbolism. But—?"

"Associations," said Appleby.

"Well, well!" Tavender giggled and bowed and again moved away. "Well, well, well," he was saying. And his voice faded, as it had come, into the zoological background of the assembled philologists.

The dull fire had grown duller and sleep, soft embalmer of the still midnight, had claimed the commercial gentlemen and the resident ladies. Appleby thanked Hissey for his entertainment and climbed to his room. The proper thing now was to sum up the impressions of the day and put two and two together in such a way as quite to astonish Hobhouse in the morning. Or even one and one. . . . Appleby turned out the light and drew back the curtains and got into bed.

He would begin with the Duke of Nesfield. Appleby stared at a ceiling across which travelled the lights of trams hauling homewards citizens from the second house of the Royal, the King's, the Lyceum. He began with the duke.

By the way, I suppose it is—ah—Pluckrose? Well, what should make a man ask that? *He thought somebody else was so certainly for it that he was reluctant to believe that it wasn't really somebody else who had got it. And with a thing that could give such a bashing as a meteorite there might be room for deception or mistake.* Here was one reason why the Duke of Nesfield might feel prompted to ask that question. Perhaps the meteorite had been for Prisk and the telephone had put things wrong. But why should a duke drift in with such a supposition? No adding one to one here.

Somewhere down the street the lines must curve. The faintly jogging beams swept in an arc over the

74

ceiling and down a wall. Parabolas. Ballistics. . . . Yes, there was all that of Crunkhorn's next. But, as Church had maintained, a mass dropped from a window was no neat commentary on the way projectiles work; only a meteorite looping in from outer space could be that. A falling star. But a thing dropped is just a thing dropped. . . . Appleby was nearly asleep. The slanting beams, the slowly rising and then falling drone of the trams was hypnot—which must account for a sudden and surely illusory sense of almost-illumination. He stared at the ceiling, trying to analyse an ebbing certainty that he had *seen*. Which was not possible. All that area of the case—talk of Galileo and the like—was just academic top dressing and nowhere near the roots of the thing. Drugs can make you feel you *know* but it is illusory. And sleepiness is the same.

Appleby sat up and clasped his knees under the bedclothes. No need to be sleepy. Move on.

It was a pity about the tortoise; the animal had petered out with incongruous rapidity. But at least it would not appear again. There was comfort in even this fantastic elimination. Galileo, Aeschylus, Sisyphus—turn them out. Turn out Crunkhorn and Church altogether, perhaps; their talk had been odd but did not clamour for explanation. With Sir David Evans it was different. He had been moved to offer a major effort in bamboozlement. Perhaps it was just the philosopher's instinct. But almost certainly not. *Almost certainly Sir David Evans was part of the case.*

Nothing like a little mental italics, Appleby reflected, to bolster one's tenuous convictions. Try again. *There was something factitious about the attitude of old Hissey.*

That was a stiff one. Appleby lay down again and

stared at it—a little pool of dubious light in a corner of the ceiling. He shut his eyes and it was still there— a dull purple patch on the retina. It shrank as he stared at it, but refused wholly to dwindle away. And it represented something disingenuous in Hissey. Which was extraordinary. But—there it was. That about tramps: *One can't be too careful with tramps*. It had been a little too good to be true. . . .

Appleby was asleep. He slept for eight hours and when he woke up it was broad daylight. The ceiling was one flood of light. He stared at it, round-eyed. It stared back. He spoke to it. "Well, well!" he said. "Well, well, well." He fell to making notes.

5

It was Ladies' Day. Your first day, Appleby
had been taught, give to an outline of the whole affair.
And your second day give to a thorough rummage
among the women. As likely as not your third day will
see you on the morning train back to London. . . . It
was a little theoretical and there were special cases
where it didn't apply at all. But on the whole it was
a sound procedure and none the worse for having been
recommended by young Mr. Pinnegar the night before. *Cherchez la femme.*

Hissey had not appeared by the time Appleby finished breakfast. Perhaps he had picked up Paley's
Theocritus while shaving, and with that conversing
had forgot all time. But one must remember that there
were women in Hissey's world as in any other. They
were inobvious—a vestigial tradition of celibacy ad-
heres to academic society—but not the less potent
because of that. . . . Appleby rose and strolled out to
the hall. The hotel had a little porch with wicker

chairs, and on one of these an inviting patch of morning sunshine had just settled. Appleby made for it and sat down. An Englishman, as Dr. Johnson said, has more frequent need to solicit than to exclude the sun. Perhaps it is so with his women too—to get back to them. At least that is the continental view. An Englishman has to dissipate much energy in pursuing women and getting them going. Whereas in happier lands, if a man is to get anything done, a policy of judicious exclusions has to be the rule. These were irrelevant reflections. And there, rising above the slate roofs of the line of villas opposite, was that ugly but extremely relevant tower. The windows in those pepper-pot turrets were surprisingly large; the meteorite would tumble through one easily enough.

A tram stopped at the corner and disgorged a first clump of students: young men and women hatless and hatted, with attaché cases, hockey sticks, bundles of books in straps. More came off a tram coming the other way and the road was suddenly filled with students. They advanced in every possible combination. A man and a girl, two girls, three girls, three girls and a man, two men, a man alone, a girl and three men. Appleby, remembering that it was Ladies' Day, conscientiously studied the girls. One could see that they ranged from the extremely inhibited to the mildly nymphomaniac. It takes all sorts to make a world—certainly to keep a world going. . . . And now from a later tram there had descended a venerable old man with a white beard and a purple muffler. Behind him came another group of girls. He slackened his pace and they were past him, disregarding. It pleased him to walk along behind; it pleased him to review at leisure a rapidly moving bunch of silk and lisle clad legs. A most mild and scholarly old person; probably one of the professors. Why did he walk through the streets in a purple muffler? Born in the purple. Perhaps the muffler percolated through from a repressed emperor-fantasy; perhaps one day he would go mad (things to remember about professors: they haf preak-downs) and shave and announce that he was Napoleon. Appleby shook his head and fished out a notebook. *A girl.* That was rather more to the point. *What happened to Timmy Church's girl?* No, she didn't really sound all that relevant. It would be disgusting to go nosing off after Timmy Church's girl simply on the strength of a random remark of young Pinnegar's. *A landlady.* Much better. *A sinister gentlewoman called Dearlove.* Appleby fetched his hat.

It was a mild April day. The sun was up and had turned from red to gold as if it meant to stay; it splashed the long glass-roofed sheds of the railway station, ran along the canal, caught in a noose of light the grimy spire of Nesfield Cathedral, delicately explored the opulent curves of the municipal gasometers. Down the hill a mist was lifting; the city unveiled itself; it was possible to feel that the whole man-made mess was gratefully breathing in the Spring. Appleby climbed on the top of a bus. He paid twopence and was trundled across a sort of compromise between a common and a public park. There were dark grey tennis courts and a tentative golf course. There were conveniences for ladies and for gentlemen built of glazed yellow brick. There was a cast-iron band-stand. Dotted about were cast-iron seats made to look as if they had been put together out of roughly trimmed timber. And the whole was islanded amid long lurching rows of stepped-up houses, for here the crowded suburbs were built on a switchback principle across the system of narrow valleys running down to the town. Appleby had a pennyworth of reflection on this compost of the anal and the bizarre; took out a further pennyworth in occasional glimpses of distant dales; and then climbed down as the bus reached its terminus. Around him now was the dismal confusion of a cheap housing estate in the early stages of its development. He walked through this for ten minutes and was in open country. Crime, Sherlock Holmes had believed, was much more horrific in rural areas than in the town. But these cows, faintly steamy still beyond a hedge, were a picture of arcadian innocence. Were there cows in Arcady, or only goats and sheep? Appleby turned through massive but dilapidated gates and walked up an elm avenue. Miss Dearlove owned what ambition might style a manor house.

And Miss Dearlove owned cats. Numbers of these were following Appleby silently. Every now and then as he advanced up the avenue there would be a slither just behind him and the feline force would grow. It was as if some outflanking movement were being directed with much tactical skill from the mansion ahead. A blackbird fluted briefly. Appleby rounded a bend and now there were cats in front—a line of them advancing in open order down the drive. Again the blackbird fluted. And the cats in front, parting in a swift right and left incline, faded into the undergrowth. But there at last was the house straight ahead: large, grey and square. If the cats were proposing to close in and attack they were leaving it till very late. It was possible to see where patches of paint had peeled from the front door. Everything was in considerable disrepair. A quiet, peaceful spot nevertheless, and one doubtless grateful to a jaded professor after the hurly-burly of Nesfield.

But now from in front there came a murmur of mingling sounds. Narcoleptic doves maintained a futile drowsy cooing amid the chirmings and twitterings of a multitude of lesser fowl like desperate nursemaids crooning over a vast and lively dormitory of imbecile children. There was a plash of water as from a little cascade. Beyond the house a bull began to bellow. And suddenly, as if all this were an overture merely, there rang out from somewhere ahead first one and then another spine-chilling scream. Appleby stopped in his tracks. The scream rang out a third time, rose to a yell, died away to an indescribable gurgle. Appleby grinned. Even well-trained guerilla cats have their noisy moments. He advanced again and now there was the sound of a heavy-oil engine, uncertainly pulsing in an outbuilding to the right.

The house was late Georgian and dug into the ground—a costly arrangement seemingly devised for the sole purpose of keeping servants in a symbolical subjection. Appleby climbed a flight of steps and was looking down into a basement with windows heavily barred; from this troglodytic depth rose a clatter of cutlery recklessly handled in bulk. He tugged at a bell-pull and the result, startling in itself, was enhanced by the instant baying of a hound in some remote and echoing corner of the building; these effects almost drowned a less commanding but curiously displeasing snuffling and slobbering audible just on the other side of the door. The door opened upon an elderly maidservant; the maidservant sniffed; there was an answering slobber and snuffle from two shambling black spaniels at her feet. Appleby was led into a shadowy hall, lit from high above through a skylight of purple glass. A grandfather clock of the kind equipped with what are called Westminster chimes began to tackle the announcement that it was a quarter to eleven. The spaniels, horridly wheezing and whiffling, crawled about annoying cats. A vacuum cleaner roared in a nearby corridor; it was as noisy, Appleby rather desperately thought, as the kind that used to arrive once a year in a van and accomplish the spring cleaning in a single agonising day. . . . The maidservant took a deep breath and announced at the top of her voice that Miss Dearlove would be down soon. Appleby sat down and put his head between his hands. He could still hear the doves and the bull and the engine. And he was not sure that now he couldn't hear somebody killing a pig. But perhaps this was merely a hallucinatory carry-over from the philological proceedings of the evening before.

Poor old Pluckrose. That shabby and fallen archangel had certainly known what the pains of Pandemonium are. . . . Appleby looked up and became aware with some alarm that a large chunk of skylight had detached itself and was floating down at him in a leisured but purposeful way. Ballistics, he thought—and realised that it was merely a large and purple-clad lady descending a gloomy staircase. Miss Dearlove advanced, carrying his card. "Commander Appleby?" she said—and her voice was at once deep and tuned to a professionally cheerful chirp. "A relation of the dear Admiral, no doubt? I think it may be possible to receive you. I *hope* it may." And in the gloom Miss Dearlove graciously smiled.

"Inspector Appleby," said Appleby.

Miss Dearlove looked at the card again. "Though now I come to think of it—" She looked at Appleby in severe appraisal. "I fear that just at present—"

"My business concerns the late Professor Pluckrose."

"Ah." Miss Dearlove dived at her skirts and produced a contrivance which Appleby suspected might be called a reticule. "My housekeeper informs me—" She brought out a notebook and opened it. "Thirty-eight pounds, eleven shillings and fourpence."

"I beg your pardon?"

"Thirty-eight pounds, eleven shillings." Miss Dearlove paused. "And fourpence," she added briskly.

"You mean that Professor Pluckrose owed you—?"

"The professor owed the *establishment* that sum. These are matters in which he was a little *absent* at times."

"I see."

The clock had begun again and now there was a cuckoo-clock operating too. In a corner the spaniels had fallen into a senile quarrel and this disorderly behaviour was spreading to a number of cats. The doves, the vacuum-cleaner, the bull, the engine and the cascade were tireless; the hound was intermittent but effective; the clatter of the cutlery it was possible to feel was a little dying down.

"Poor Sir Archibald," said Miss Dearlove, "was a little the same. He was, of course, a very old man— a contemporary of my father's, the late Sir Horace Dearlove."

"Ah," said Appleby respectfully.

"K.C.M.G."

"I beg your pardon?"

"My father, the late Sir Horace Dearlove, K.C.M.G. But it was not so with the dear General. In these little matters, as in others of greater moment, he was the most punctilious of men." Miss Dearlove's eye returned to her notebook. "Thirty-eight pounds, eleven shillings and fourpence."

"Quite so. It is a charge which the executors will no doubt settle. I must explain that I am from the police. I understand that Mr. Pluckrose had been, ah—"

"Received," said Miss Dearlove.

"—had been received in your household for a number of years?"

"For some fourteen or fifteen. He was a person of retiring habits and relished the quiet of the country. We are a very quiet household, though I fear there is a *little* disturbance this morning."

"Disturbance?"

"I beg your pardon?" Miss Dearlove moved her left ear nearer Appleby.

"Disturbance?" Appleby raised his voice to a sort of modified bellow.

"The piano-tuner."

"I beg your pardon?"

"The piano-tuner." Miss Dearlove, also raising her voice, spoke so loudly that her face momentarily took on the same shade as her gown. "But presently I think he will leave us in quiet. You can hear him playing through a set piece now."

Appleby strained his ears, but in vain. The only fresh sound to be distinguished was a periodic and reverberating crash—extremely puzzling until one realized that somewhere near at hand a water-mill had been put into motion. "You were naturally acquainted," asked Appleby—as loudly as if he were addressing an aged metropolitan magistrate in court—"with the habits of the dead man?"

"That is so."

"And perhaps you can suggest—"

"Though, naturally, there were aspects of his personality which were unrevealed to me."

"I see," said Appleby.

"Mr. Pluckrose was a bachelor."

"Quite so."

"An *elderly* bachelor." Into this point Miss Dearlove, smiling brightly, contrived to inject an almost boundlessly sinister implication. "There were matters into which I did *not* enquire."

The water wheel was now operating smoothly and made less noise. But the whole house gently vibrated, and on the mantel-piece an elaborate contrivance of Venetian glass had begun to tinkle. "An *elderly* bachelor," agreed Appleby heartily. To what a god-awful age Miss Dearlove and her father the late Sir Horace belonged. Minds like drains. How infinitely wholesome and honest was that bellowing bull. "Naturally," Appleby pursued, "there would be—reticences."

"Precisely so." Miss Dearlove lowered her flowing purple skirt an inch further over her ankle. "How upset the university will be. How *very* upset must be dear Sir David Evans."

"Ah," said Appleby. In keeping a genteel boarding establishment Miss Dearlove was shamefully wasting her talents. As a rather low-class counsel on the criminal side a fortune awaited her power of abounding suggestiveness. One of the spaniels was rubbing itself against Appleby's trouser-leg. He gave it a covert but ungentle kick. The general melee, as he had calculated, obscured the creature's indignant yelp. "Sir David Evans and the dead man were close friends?"

"It might be said"—Miss Dearlove paused in search of a suitable expression—"that there was a mutually sensitive nerve."

"I see." Appleby raised his voice again against a sudden renewed screaming of cats. "Perhaps it would be possible for you to enlarge a little on that?"

"I believe them to have been not without interests in common." Miss Dearlove folded her hands in her lap as she continued to speak in this gnomic vein. "But this is a subject which we will not pursue."

"You would not care to say more than that these two men had common interests?"

"*Very* common," said Miss Dearlove.

And for some time the conversation continued under discouraging acoustic difficulties. From the murk of the Dearlove psyche little of illumination emerged. Pluckrose, as Appleby had rather gathered before, had been a busybody, with a diversity of interests outside his own particular scientific field. He was fond, he had said, of *looking over the fence*—and by this he had apparently meant getting up enough of some colleague's subject to make a nuisance of himself in an argumentative and critical way. This could not, Appleby reflected, be at all an uncommon academic foible, and should scarcely lead to murder. Still, in even so innocent a place as a university a busybody might conceivably hit upon some piece of knowledge not good for the health. Take forgery, thought Appleby. There are few things odder than the fascination which a career of learned and wholly unremunerative forgery can exercise upon persons of erudite and seemingly blameless life. Eminent Shakespearean scholars have been known to discover pedantically important documents in out-of-the-way libraries, to publish them with copious notes, to engage in severe debates on their significance with unsuspecting fellow-workers— and finally to be exposed as laborious coiners of counterfeit knowledge. Their motives are childish and scarcely criminal; they like to be laughing in their sleeve at persons who fancy their own acuteness. But the learned world does not relish such jokes and exposure is likely to be distinctly blighting. Now suppose that this rather nosy-parker Pluckrose had discovered that, say, Prisk—

But Miss Dearlove's peaceful retreat was a most unsuitable environment in which to endeavour to follow up a train of speculation. Appleby applied himself to asking a few final questions. "And now may I enquire if you have lately received any other members of the university staff?"

Miss Dearlove stiffened in her chair. "There was Mr. Marlow," she said. "He left."

This, plainly, was turpitude not merely hinted at but plainly spoken. Pluckrose and Sir Archibald and the dear General might have been elderly bachelors making too free, say, with wenches in a neighbouring village. That was one thing. But young Mr. Marlow had left. That was quite another. "Dear me," said Appleby. "Did he, indeed."

"Some months ago. I am inclined to suppose that he was unsettled by Nesfield Court."

Appleby sat up much as if one of Miss Dearlove's cats had stuck a set of claws in his leg. "The Duke of Nesfield's place?" he said.

"The dear duke's seat. I have no doubt that life

87

there is surrounded by every refinement of luxury. That is perfectly appropriate and proper in a noble household. But it was most unreasonable of Mr. Marlow on his return to quarrel with the modest comfort befitting private gentlefolk. I can think of only one explanation." And Miss Dearlove paused awfully. "The origins of Mr. Marlow must be low."

"That is very probably it," Appleby said easily.

"Only a plebeian young man would be likely to have his head turned by such a commonplace experience as temporary residence in a nobleman's family. And the actual excuse he gave for leaving us was almost insultingly baseless. He complained of noise." Miss Dearlove looked severely at Appleby. "—*of noise*," she repeated loudly.

"Good heavens!" Appleby looked properly amazed. "Can you tell me, by the way, what took him to the duke's?"

"Certainly. It was in no sense a matter of being received into a society of the county. As you may know, and as my dear father used to remark, we are if anything a shade too exclusive here. I remember the dowager duchess remarking when I was a girl—"

Appleby ruthlessly cut short these splendours. "It was in the nature of a professional engagement?"

"Precisely so. Mr. Marlow was engaged as a vacation tutor to the duke's youngest grandson, dear Gerald. Actually I believe as one of several tutors, though I am not clear as to that. Gerald is a most charming boy." Miss Dearlove paused. "But extremely stupid," she added unexpectedly.

"You say there may have been several tutors. Do you think that any of the professors of the university—

the senior men—would be likely to accept a job like that?"

"It would not be quite dignified." Miss Dearlove was judicial. "But then dignity is largely a matter of the way things are managed. It is a fact that I realised when adopting my own present means of subsistence many years ago. Certainly it would be less trouble to the dear duke to have younger men only. He would not have to go out of his way to be civil to them."

"But civility is never out of the duke's way." Appleby paused. "I was reflecting on that only yesterday, when I happened to have luncheon with him."

Even in the purple gloom of Miss Dearlove's hall it was possible to see that this was staggering information. It demanded, at this belated point, an entire social reorientation of the interview in progress. Miss Dearlove peered at the grandfather clock. "Dear Mr. Appleby," she said, "I hope that *to-day* you will be able to take luncheon *here*."

"I should be delighted. But unfortunately I must return to Nesfield at once." Appleby got up. "And Marlow is the only other university man you have had?"

"During the past ten years, yes. Except, of course, Mr. Lasscock. The senior lecturer in history. A quiet and charming man."

Drag the river for Lasscock. It had been one of the recommendations of those deplorable young men at Hissey's Symposium. "Mr. Lasscock is at home now?" Appleby asked.

"Yes. He has a slight chill and is spending the morning in the orchard. It must be half-term."

"Half-term?"

"Poor Mr. Lasscock commonly has a slight chill

about halfway through the academic term. His half-term holiday is quite a little joke with us. Though Mr. Marlow, I fear, used to be rather rude about it."

"I see." Appleby prepared to take his leave. "But, you know, the term isn't anything like half over. It has only been going for about three weeks."

"Dear me! That is quite true." Miss Dearlove looked perplexed.

"Perhaps it's—well—a real chill this time."

"I hardly think so." Miss Dearlove was quite decided. "You see, Mr. Lasscock is a peculiarly healthy man. He *never* has chills."

Appleby frowned. "Then there must be some other explanation. And I think I should like to introduce myself to him. Would you mind if I went out that way?"

Miss Dearlove rose, threaded her way expertly through a congeries of cats and majestically tugged at an ancient bell-rope. Then she turned round. "Dear Mr. Appleby, good-bye. And should you at any time care to be received—"

The water-wheel thumped and the engine pounded. The vacuum-cleaner had not failed and, just at this moment, the bull bellowed and the hound bayed. The rest of Miss Dearlove's words were lost in the clamour. But Appleby had a suspicion that it was the establishment's tariff which was being explained to him. Dignity is largely a matter of the way things are managed, after all.

The pseudo-convalescence or truancy of Mr. Lasscock had as its setting a restful and wholly charming scene. Always supposing, that was to say, that Mr. Lasscock was deaf—for the auditory characteristics of Miss

Dearlove's orchard were as shattering as its visual aspects were pleasant. High and mellow brick walls, comfortably fretted over with apricot and peach, radiated grateful warmth even on this day of early spring. Within these were irregular lines of apple-trees, gnarled and twisted and breathing the tranquillity of age. And within this again lay a prodigal kitchen garden: strawberry plants and raspberry canes, gooseberry bushes and asparagus beds, potatoes and cabbages and cauliflowers, carrots and onions and radishes and dwarf and climbing peas. All this Mr. Lasscock sat and contemplated—and with very much the expression, Appleby thought, which the Deity must have worn on the Seventh Day. Mr. Lasscock was an elderly, rosy person with untidy ginger hair, a brocaded dressing-gown and a large yellow muffler. And he sat and contemplated the fruits of the earth with a mild and benevolent attention. Clearly he liked to watch them grow. Conceivably he was providing a little sympathetic magic by way of helping things on. Yes, quite conceivably he was feeling himself into the radishes and the cauliflowers and then luxuriously opening his leaves to the sun. . . . Appleby drew nearer and saw that actually Mr. Lasscock's eyes were lightly closed—not grossly in plain sleep but with the flower-like quality of an infant replete upon the mother's breast. And the thump of the mill-wheel and the throb of the engine, the battle of wills between the myriad small birds and the doves, the mournful passion of the bellowing bull, the sudden, shrill and horrifying sexuality of circumambient cats: these things were all as lullaby to Mr. Lasscock. He sat close by the high brick wall, wrapped in warmth radiated as from some vast maternal flank. Around him the branches of an overhanging horse-chestnut, just breaking into big and flaky bud, threw a light dapple of shade. A rug was over his knees and under his slippered feet was an ancient hassock; by his side stood a table upon which were ranged a spirit kettle, lemons, sugar and a bottle of rum. Mr. Lasscock opened his eyes slowly as Appleby approached and immediately made as if to close them again. Then, perhaps reflecting on the unnecessary muscular effort this involved, he let them stay open in a placidly interested stare. "Nice mornin'," said Mr. Lasscock.

"Very pleasant indeed." Unlike the unfortunate Marlow, Lasscock's origins were plainly not low; his accent was at once aristocratic and about a century out of date, an interesting field of study for his philologically-minded colleagues. "Beautifully mild for the time of year. But don't you think it a great pity that there's such a lot of noise?"

"Noise?" Mr. Lasscock faintly frowned, as if stretching his sensory awareness to the full. "Well, I suppose there is. I rather think I can hear a bull. But bulls will be bulls, after all." He chuckled with a sort of rich and sleepy tolerance. "What I've never liked about this place is the mice. Hijjus noise they make in the wainscots—quite hijjus."

"If there are a lot of mice perhaps that's why Miss Dearlove keeps so many cats."

Mr. Lasscock shook his head slightly, as one who would politely indicate a disinclination to intellectual discussion. "Come to stop here?" he asked. "Have a peg. Kettle here because I've got a bit of a chill." Mr. Lasscock tightened the yellow muffler about his neck and passed a large silk handkerchief in a ritual way across his nostrils. "But hot rum-and-water capital at any time. Insijjus, in a way."

"No, thank you. And I haven't come to stop. Appleby is my name and I am a police officer come to enquire into the death of Mr. Pluckrose."

Mr. Lasscock opened his eyes a little wider. "Lunnon?" he asked.

"I beg your pardon?"

"Lunnon man?"

"Oh—yes. New Scotland Yard."

"Come down by train? What djew think of the breakfast they give you now?"

"The breakfast? It seems all right."

Mr. Lasscock nodded gravely. "Better than the luncheon. The luncheon is very bad, if you ask me. Death of whom?"

"Pluckrose."

"There used to be a buffet-car where you could get quite a decent grill. Much better arrangement, I always think." And Mr. Lasscock again lightly closed his eyes. He was as one who, having fully and faithfully coped with the narrow world of here and now, gratefully retires to the inner contemplation of more spacious scenes. For what, Appleby wondered, had this placid historian exchanged the clamour of Miss Dearlove's orchard? For the comparative peace of the field of Waterloo? Or was he running a calculating inward eye down the ranks of the barons at Runnymede? Was he taking a peep at the great Marlborough closeted with his duchess? Had an impalpable St. Stephen's Hall sprung up around him and was he watching the expression of Miss Frances Burney as she listened to that terrible indictment being piled up by Edmund Burke? Or—as the tenor of Mr. Lasscock's talk so far might hint—was he merely engaged upon some retrospective review of that morning's breakfast—that or an anticipatory consideration of his coming luncheon? Appleby sat down on a rustic bench and let these idle speculations float through his mind. For there was something infectious and hypnoidal in Mr. Lasscock's massive repose, much as there must have been in the inexpugnable somnolence of Mr. Wardle's Fat Boy. . . . "Disturbin'," said Mr. Lasscock, his eyes still closed.

The word had coincided with a sudden excruciating jabber of starlings in a corner of the orchard, and Appleby looked that way. When he looked back it was to find Mr. Lasscock's eyes open—open but narrowed in a disconcertingly keen and appraising glance. But this was gone in an instant and Mr. Lasscock was gazing blandly out across the orchard. "Disturbin'," he repeated. "Poppin' off in that ojus, messy way. Sound point about Pluckrose when alive was that you didn't need to think of him. Requires quite an effort to stick to that good habit now. Would lie on the mind, if one weren't careful, a horrid end like that. Wool Court, too. Place I often sit in myself." Mr. Lasscock's eyes were fixed idly upon a wren which had appeared on one of the nearer apple trees. The wren, being a Dearlove wren, was making as much noise as it possibly could; its whole body could be seen shaking and pulsing with the effort. And, oddly enough, Mr. Lasscock's body too suggested considerable tension; to Appleby's acute sense in such matters it was as if these vague and unfeeling remarks to which he was listening somehow required in the uttering as much nervous energy as the bird was putting into its shrill and innocent uproar. . . . "Tiresome," said Mr. Lasscock. "Irritatin'."

"Irritating? But all mysteries are that." Appleby spoke with brisk friendliness. "They give you a feeling that here is a place you simply must scratch. Don't you feel like that about this Pluckrose business—that you simply must get at the true facts? Rather as one might feel about an historical problem or something of that sort."

Over Mr. Lasscock's placid features a new expression momentarily spread. It might have been the expression of an obstinately lethargic child seduced into contemplating a bribe. But quickly it died away again and he slowly shook his head. "Can't say I feel like that about it. May hold in your line o' business, no doubt. But I don't intend to give Pluckrose a chance of lyin' on the mind. Queer thing, the mind. Read these Viennese fellows and you'll see one can't be too careful with it. Early spring. Soon be seeing the first migratory birds."

"No doubt." Perhaps, Appleby thought, this elderly and comfortable person, with his rug and hassock and rum and half-term holiday, was really only judiciously concerned to insulate himself against the thousand natural shocks that flesh is heir to. A wise man, after all, will find much less of satisfaction in analysing a deed of violence than in contemplating the life of birds or the procession of the seasons. And if one believes oneself to have the sort of mind one can't be too careful with—Still, lurking in Lasscock there was surely something more or other than this. Perhaps the unknown factor could be forced to declare itself. Appleby brought out a notebook—hastily, because Lasscock's eyes seemed to be on the point of closing once more—and poised a pencil ominously in air. "And now," he said, "be so good as to tell me when you were at the university last."

"Certainly." Lasscock was perfectly amiable. "Anythin' to oblige." He raised his right hand and began to twitch the fingers one by one. Then he frowned, as if this method of computation was either too laborious or confusing. "This nasty Pluckrose thing: what day did it happen?"

"The day before yesterday, Mr. Lasscock. Monday morning, in fact."

"Then I wasn't there. Not on Monday—and not since. Tiresome chill." Lasscock gave a twist to his muffler, made a pass with his handkerchief and pointed to the table. "That's the reason of the rum. Most sovereign stuff, I think you'd find. But perhaps you haven't got a chill?"

"Thank you"—Appleby spoke a shade austerely—"but I am perfectly well. We don't have half-terms in the police-force."

Lasscock showed no sign of being stricken by this barb. He leant forward and applied himself to lighting the spirit-kettle. "Well," he said, "glad to know you're all right. Treacherous time o'year. But charmin'. Notice the boles of the elm trees?"

"I must try to impress upon you that my business is to notice every circumstance which may be connected with the death of Professor Pluckrose. And you must have heard that it is almost certainly a matter of murder. So if you don't mind we will defer comparing nature notes till another time. And now—"

"Then I mustn't detain you." Lasscock tipped sugar into a glass and reached for the rum; he poured out a small tot of it, added water and settled himself comfortably back in his chair. A silver spoon clinked drowsily as he stirred. And slowly his eyes closed once more.

Appleby, momentarily baffled, stared at him in a kind of fascination. The endeavour to interrogate Lasscock was little more satisfactory than would be an attempt to cross-question a child in the womb. And indeed it was just such an environment that this elderly foetus carried about with him. Perhaps his tolerance of the hubbub of Miss Dearlove's orchard lay in that: it was like the great pounding of a near-by heart. . . .

But now Lasscock was speaking. Or rather, his voice was to be heard—for he was so lost in some drowsy other-world that one got the impression of a mere automatism in his speech. "Young man," said the voice of Lasscock, "Pluckrose is dead. Somebody dropped a horrid great rock on him from the tower. And I don't know anything more about it." One eye opened, as if to take stock of the effect of this categorical announcement. It closed again. "Good day to you," said Mr. Lasscock.

Appleby walked down the avenue. He observed the elm boles. He glanced behind him and saw that again there was an escort of cats. The sounds of the mill wheel and the engine, the bull and the doves and the hound and the cutlery and the vacuum-cleaner, still vibrated on his ear. He was out on the main road before he could hear what he wanted to hear: the ghost of his own voice reigning undisturbed in his own head and patiently setting about an analysis of the meagre gifts of the morning. *Miss Dearlove: sun-*

dry social pretence, several hints, no lies. Lasscock:
nothing in the nature of a big put-up job, but rather
a genuine revelation of a decidedly unathletic person-
ality, plus one lie—possibly not a very important one.
Appleby shook his head as he trudged. It was scarcely
encouraging. Still, the plot did a little begin to
thicken. Certain aspects of the case were falling into
at least an enigmatic relationship. For instance, the
Duke of Nesfield had come—oddly—to Appleby and
Hobhouse, and some time ago young Marlow had
gone—not particularly oddly—to Nesfield Court. *By*
the way, I suppose it is—ah—Pluckrose? Make it a
hypothesis that this queer question of the duke's proceeded from a train of circumstances to which Marlow's having gone to tutor the stupid Gerald stood in
some causal relationship—Appleby frowned at this
pedantic phraseology. Put it more simply. *Because*
Marlow had stopped at Nesfield Court the duke had
been surprised that it was *Pluckrose* who was killed.
That was it. And Appleby stared at it until he reached
his bus.

6

Hobhouse was not in his office; he had, a sergeant announced with some pride, gone out to trace the meteorite. No, it wasn't a matter of information having come in. The inspector had just thought of where such a thing would come from, and he had enquired, and it seemed likely he was right—as the inspector often was. And he had left a message. It appeared probable that the meteorite would be traced a very considerable eminence. Beyond this obscure joke the sergeant had—or feigned to have—nothing to report. Appleby arranged to call later and went out to get himself a meal.

The station buffet was the nearest place and he strolled in there. One sat at a long horseshoe-like counter; there were cauldrons of tripe and reservoirs of sausages; there was a brave clatter of pewter pots; there were barmaids to whom several gentlemen were usually offering jocose conversation at the same time. After Miss Dearlove's retired manor it was all remarkably peaceful. Appleby, having contributed his conventional quota of badinage, applied himself to his victuals and to meditation.

Somewhere in this vast building he had lunched the day before with a nobleman concerned to see that there should be no mistake about Pluckrose. The police must be sure of what really had been achieved by the murderer. Or—alternatively—they must be sure of what the murderer had really *intended*. Now, the duke had two kinds of contact with the University of Nesfield: he was its Chancellor and concerned himself a good deal with its affairs in a general way; he was a grandfather and had engaged one or more members of its staff as a holiday tutor. That it was this second and more personal contact with which the Pluckrose affair was somehow tied up, was, Appleby realised, only a guess. The duke himself had refrained from any mention of the circumstance—but little could be read into that. Probably there had been, at most, only one more tutor; for to turn a whole team of such people upon Gerald would be absurd. Gerald was apparently a schoolboy, and the attempt was presumably to screw him up to whatever shadowy standard of learning an Oxford or Cambridge college required of young men of his sort. Marlow was a lecturer in English, which meant that he could probably stuff Gerald with a little Latin and French or German as well. What else would be required? Presumably some mathematics—and that might mean that the second tutor had been Timmy Church. But this was mere speculation.

And perhaps all speculation beginning with the curious irruption of the Duke of Nesfield was of secondary importance; perhaps it was only the magnetism of the strawberry leaves which suggested that here was really a profitable point of attack. Hobhouse was out after the meteorite—and surely the meteorite was the thing. Where had it come from? Was there anything in Sir David Evans's extraordinary theory—or had Pluckrose known nothing of the meteorite until—? Appleby put down his knife and fork. Until what? Appleby stared unseeingly at the row of persons opposite him. He remembered the displeasing Tavender . . . something Tavender had said about the meteorite . . . a tentative conclusion to which he had himself come in the night. But at least the meteorite must be weighed and manoeuvred; the windows of that store-room must be measured; the hoist must be examined; Galileo-like experiments, perhaps, made. All this was the direct line on the case, and it ought to precede any further exploration of all those personal relationships which might or might not be involved. Mrs. Tavender's tea-party, for instance—what, as a field of enquiry, could be vaguer and more nebulous than that? Something thrown out by an irresponsible young man, like the dragging of the river for Lasscock. And yet there had been something in that; it had been based on the observation, not perhaps irrelevant, that Lasscock had been apparently absent from the university on Monday and Tuesday—the days of the crime and of Appleby's first investigations respectively. So perhaps there might be something in the tea-party too, and in some of the other suggestions Marlow and Pinnegar had made. For instance, there was that curious maze between the dark-room and Pluckrose's private laboratory. Somebody had once hung a skeleton there. But was that why Marlow— no, Pinnegar, it had been—had directed Appleby's attention to it? Appleby fished from his pocket the plan Hobhouse had sketched for him the previous day. Yes, undoubtedly there was something to look into there. Pluckrose's laboratory, the maze, the dark-room, the hoist, the lowermost of the store-rooms— these, with Prisk on one side, Marlow on another and the spot where the body had been found on a third: the whole thing was as compact and had as many possibilities as a well set-up scene in an abstract the-atre. Decidedly, thought Appleby finishing his tripe, he must go for all that.

Only this was Ladies' Day. And although the female element in the case appeared meagre it was by no means exhausted. Miss Dearlove did not look like being a very active element, but she had made one or two remarks which, as far as searching out the woman was concerned, might be described as a sort of passing the buck. For instance, when she had said of Pluckrose and Sir David Evans—

At this point Appleby, looking absently about him as he speculated, let his eye stray to a far corner of the buffet at which there were half a dozen small tables. The buffet too was a preponderantly masculine affair; if you were a woman, or accompanied by a woman, it appeared that you were prescriptively con-fined to this retired corner. And on one of the tables Appleby's glance halted. Those broad shoulders and that untidy hair were surely familiar; they belonged in fact to the belligerent young mathematician, Timmy Church. And opposite him was a girl of about his own age—what one might call a wholesome girl, Appleby thought; a girl of reasonable features, equable dis-position and sufficient intelligence. For a young scholar of somewhat unruly temperament it looked like a very sound match. Only at the moment things were clearly going far from smoothly; the girl was leaning forward and speaking with what looked like precise and controlled indignation; Church was leaning back with his hands in his pockets and his chin sunk on his chest—and probably scowling ferociously. And suddenly this melancholy scene came to a crisis. The girl paused for breath and then said something briefly and with particular decision; the young man jumped to his feet, banged down what looked like a half-a-crown on the table, and marched out without looking behind him.

Appleby sighed. Duty, duty must be done. He picked up his cup of coffee, moved across the room and sat down in the young man's vacant chair. "Are you," he asked, "Timmy Church's girl?"

The young woman, who had been continuing her meal quietly, laid down her knife and fork. "I don't know you," she said. "Please go away."

Appleby got to his feet again. "I'm sorry. But I assure you I'm something perfectly respectable. In fact a policeman."

She looked at him with startled eyes. "One of the policemen about the murder?"

"Yes. Indeed the principal policeman about the murder."

"Then you may sit down again. My name is Joan Cavenett."

Appleby introduced himself. Miss Cavenett, he thought, if not a cool card was yet having a good shot at appearing one. A business girl of the superior, private-secretary-to-someone-important sort. Or that was a good guess. At any rate, a young person much impressed with the necessity of coping with the world.

First, then, a little fishing after the young woman's background. "I'm sorry to see there's been a rumpus." Appleby looked at her gravely. "Have you known Mr. Church for long?"

"We were at Cambridge together."

"I see. Then don't you think you ought to have got your quarrelling over by this time?"

"You've no business to come barging over and talk about it." Joan Cavenett spoke with decision; nevertheless, Appleby noted, her tone was now not really hostile.

"I have, really. It's unpleasant, of course, but my business is to barge into pretty nearly everything. This quarrel hasn't anything to do with the Pluckrose affair? But of course it hasn't; it's older than that."

"Did Timmy tell you so?" Now she was looking at him with a smouldering eye.

"Of course not. He didn't say anything about you. It was just a piece of vulgar gossip. Somebody wondered what had become of you—I suppose because the two of you haven't been seen about together."

"How perfectly odious. Ordinary people ought to be able to mind their own business, even if policemen can't." She glanced at him suspiciously. "You don't *look* like a policeman."

"I'm a new and rather hazardously experimental sort. I have approximately the same smell as Mr. Church and yourself."

"It doesn't seem to me that that improves matters at all. If I'm to be badgered I'd rather be badgered by a man in thick boots and a helmet. I'd feel I knew better where I was." She paused. "Look here," she said, "I wouldn't go on quarrelling with him if I could help it. Not now that this has happened. I know he

104

was always arguing with this awful Pluckrose. And I know you think—"

Appleby interrupted her with a chuckle. "Mr. Church is an aggressive young man, isn't he? And you'll probably find later on that a temperament of that sort goes with a mild and perfectly normal leaning towards persecution fantasies. He's been telling you we're hunting him as a murderer?"

Miss Cavenett looked at him uncertainly. "More or less."

"Well, it's all bosh. An elderly professor called Crunkhorn—"

"He's his boss. Not a bad old chap really. But hasn't much mathematics."

Appleby chuckled again. "You're not really wholly estranged, you know, or you wouldn't go on repeating your young man's favourite dogmas. Well, this Crunkhorn—whom he rather irritates at times—seems to have had an idea that he might have perpetrated some joke which fatally miscarried and resulted in Pluckrose's death. But there's nothing in it at all. Timmy Church is no more suspected than the Duke of Nesfield is. Put it right out of your head."

She looked at him quickly, at once suspicious and enormously relieved. "Then—"

"Then you can, as far as that is concerned, go on quarrelling with him as long as you like. Except that it's rather silly and unnecessary, likely enough."

"It's nothing of the sort."

"Very well, then; it isn't." Appleby sipped his coffee and waited. A competent young woman, but at a very considerable strain. Ten to one, out it would all come.

"It's not just a silly tiff. We're not kids. He wants me to—" She hesitated. Appleby sipped again, outwardly unperturbed. Some intimate and probably utterly irrelevant disclosure. A policeman's lot—

"He wants me to—to commit bigamy," said Joan Cavenett.

"Well, well," said Apply. "That isn't too bad. It might be worse. So cheer up."

"Worse than bigamy? I don't believe a policeman can think there's anything worse than bigamy. A stupid, horrid thing you read about in corners of the paper."

Appleby shook his head. "It's very trying, no doubt. But at least it's something perfectly definite and clear cut. And trouble between lovers is really serious only when they don't at all know what it's about." He paused on this piece of homely wisdom and looked at Miss Cavenett with a slightly malicious eye. "By the way," he said, "—what's wrong with your present husband?"

The young woman opened her mouth as if to say something very decided indeed. Then she changed her mind and laughed softly. "Must you really play the benevolent uncle?" she asked. "And lighten the young people's troubles with quiet merriment? You understand perfectly well that it's Timmy who's married already."

"I've turned uncle because as policeman it's plainly not at all on my beat." Appleby smiled reassuringly. "But you might tell me about it, all the same."

"There's nothing to tell. I mean I know nothing about it. Once when we were talking about getting married Timmy just said in an off-hand way that it would be bigamy. And then he shut up and wouldn't say any more."

"Which was very unreasonable of him. But then

probably you made a bit of an ass of yourself too. Flared up and talked at him like something out of a book."

"Perfectly true." Joan Cavenett had finished her meal and now sat back with elaborate composure. "But he's kept it up, which seems stupid. He says it's no business of mine—which is absurd. And that it doesn't matter—which is absurd too. And when I said well, couldn't he get divorced, he said it was too difficult and that I had better forget about it."

"And so you better had."

"And be a—a bigamist?" She stared at him, amazed.

"If you want him I really wouldn't let any little irregularity stand in your way. The thing will clear itself up, likely enough." He was looking at her maliciously still. "He hasn't mentioned which you'll be?"

"*Which I'll be?*"

"Third or fourth or fifth? I mean, you don't know *how many* wives he's got already?"

She stood up. "This is horrible. And I thought you were going to be rather nice."

"I suppose he goes abroad fairly often?" Appleby spoke softly, looking up at her still from the table.

"Yes." She sat down again, suddenly limp and bewildered. "You seem to know a lot."

"What we do in my profession is guess. And I think I've guessed right. Your Timmy goes abroad just to get married. And I think it will be all right." Appleby was perfectly grave now. "It will be quite all right, Miss Cavenett."

"All right!" Suddenly she blazed out at him. "When he's conducting himself like a howling cad? If it was just that he'd had a mistress—"

107

"You're talking like that book again. And he's not conducting himself like a cad. On the contrary. He's conducting himself like an English gentleman."

"Isn't that out of the book too?"

"Maybe it is. But it's true."

She was silent for a moment and Appleby saw that she was trembling. "Will you explain?" she asked quietly.

"I think I'd better not—even though I have guessed. See him again yourself. Tell him you don't mind if he's Bluebeard."

"But I do."

"My dear, we men are all kids. You have to say things to us. But tell him too that somebody's told you he's quite the English gentleman. You'll enjoy seeing how startled and foolish he looks. And then say the same person thinks the secrecy business can be overdone. Caution is no doubt necessary, but is romantically attractive too. Tell him to contact his boss about it."

"His boss? Crunkhorn?"

Appleby had stood up. He laughed aloud. "Crunkhorn? I hardly think so. But of course one never knows."

Outside, the sky was delicately grey behind dark buildings. Newsboys were shouting and Appleby bought a paper. Sir Neville Henderson, he read, was reported to have had an interview with Hitler. Appleby shoved the paper in his pocket and crossed the street, frowning at the shape of things to come. From a railed-off plot of ground a pedestalled Queen Victoria looked down at him sourly—an old lady enormously bored with the business of clutching a truncheon and a thing like a plum pudding. What,

Appleby wondered, would she make of it all? What, for instance, would she make of the proceedings of Mr. Timothy Church? Mr. Gladstone would disapprove, but then the Earl of Beaconsfield—so much more discerning a man—would be enthusiastic. Would have his own reasons for being so, Appleby grimly thought. The opinion of the Prince Consort could alone provide comfortable certainty in the matter, and he most assuredly had died without leaving any memorandum on so unlikely a state of affairs.

Appleby was arrested by a fanfare of trumpets and the glimpse of a scarlet-clad figure climbing the steps of Nesfield town hall. The Assizes were on. Well, next time the judge would perhaps be dealing with the affair of Professor Pluckrose. And now it was time to get back to that. For surely the matter of Timmy Church and his Miss Cavenett, though interesting and odd in itself, could have no connection with the real business on hand. Or could it? Suppose that in this mysterious activity upon which he had stumbled Pluckrose had been the boss. And suppose it to be organised on a considerable scale. Might there not be danger—danger of a decidedly melodramatic but yet quite possible sort? But with this supposition nothing in Pluckrose's known character seemed to fit. No, it was unlikely that Timmy Church's peculiar form of bigamy was at the bottom of it all. And it was equally unlikely that Mrs. Tavender's tea-party had anything to do with it either. Nevertheless Mrs. Tavender was next on Appleby's list. For it was Ladies' Day still. He boarded a tram.

The Tavenders' was a quiet district. On the long tree-lined road on which their house was to be sought only one figure was visible, that of a man in a bowler

109

hat who was walking some hundred yards ahead of
Appleby. Presently this figure halted, walked on a few
paces, halted again. And now he was looking up at
the sky—rather, Appleby thought, as if hoping to receive guidance or information from that quarter. It
was, in fact, Professor Hissey. Perhaps he was working
out a nice point for *Annotatiunculae Criticae*. Appleby
drew level with him. "Good afternoon, sir," he said.

Hissey lowered his gaze from the heavens and
looked at Appleby with momentary suspicion. Conceivably he took him for one of those dangerous
tramps to ward off whom it is desirable to carry a big
stick. But presently his brow cleared and he took off
his hat—so that Appleby, who had been forgetful of
the nicety of academic manners, had hastily to make
the same gesture. "My dear Shrubsole," said Hissey,
"how do you do?"

"Very well, thank you." Williams and Merryweather and Grant, Appleby was reflecting, had been
one thing. But Shrubsole was really a bit steep. "A
nice afternoon for a walk."

"It is, indeed." Hissey appeared mildly puzzled.
"But, do you know, I hardly think I came out with
that object in view?" Once more he looked up at the
sky. "I am inclined to think that I am doing something
else."

"So am I. I'm going to call on Mrs. Tavender."

"How extraordinary! So am I." Hissey laughed delightedly. "But just for the moment it had somehow
slipped my mind. This, of course, is Mrs. Tavender's
afternoon. So come along, my dear fellow. Or come
away, as a Scot would so quaintly put it."

"And so would Shakespeare. Come away, come
away, death."

"Dear me, yes. How very interesting. Could Shakespeare, I wonder, have been a Scot? He has been shown, quite conclusively, to be a Welshman. And a German. And recently, I believe, an Italian too. You know, a most amusing essay might be written on the quite peculiar sense of evidence that the professional English scholars have developed." And Hissey, very pleased with this mild and learned pleasantry, took Appleby by the arm and walked him forward. "By the way, how very stupid of me to call you Shrubsole, my dear—"

"Appleby."

"Dear, dear—I am really very weak on human nomenclature. But much stronger, believe me, on human motive. I always know what a fellow is about, even if I can't put a name to him. How goes the hue and cry after poor Pluckrose's assailant today?" And Hissey smiled, innocently proud of his awareness of the world. "But here we are. A pleasant house, is it not? Mrs. Tavender has means, I have been told. A most superior woman, and with artistic interests."

Mrs. Tavender was large, vague and vehement, and her party had approximately the same qualities, so that it was easy for Appleby to slip in once more on the strength of a word of introduction from Hissey. How one learns to snoop around, he thought—and proceeded to lose himself skilfully in the crush. One walks about with a politely restrained shouldering movement, as if one were bent on reaching a friend at the other end of the room. And so nobody pays any attention and one collects a sort of cross-section of such conversation as is going forward.

Two largish rooms and a hall were required for Mrs.

Tavender's afternoon: they served as a somewhat uneasy meeting place for the learned and artistic societies of Nesfield. The walls were hung with pictures in tiers and rows, as in a gallery. There were surrealist compositions in which the cleverest bits proved to be scraps of colour photogravure cunningly fitted in; there were pictures made of tram tickets; there were nudes looking rather like heaps of salmon straight from the tin. And on pedestals about the floor there were Carvings and Objects—the latter being often assemblages of pebbles which discerning artists had picked up on their last visit to the sea. There were also Constructions: these were made of broom handles, wooden spoons, brightly coloured rubber balls suspended on string, and coils of a sort of chromium-plated barbed wire. And amid this aesthetic profusion the guests performed something between an obstacle race and a saraband. Mrs. Tavender urged them on. She wore an enormous necklace which she clutched before her bosom and swung to and fro as if to impart a more urgent tempo to the gathering. In a corner Mr. Tavender, giggling, disagreeable and acute, watched the whole performance with evident pleasure.

Appleby secured a cup of tea and a sandwich which had gone slightly curly at the edges. The artists ate more than the academics; for some of them the occasion was clearly quite an important fill-up. There were young men in flowing ties and velvet jackets; there were other young men who had been to Paris more recently and were extremely quietly and precisely dressed. The artists looked at the other guests and didn't say much. The other guests looked at the exhibits and seemed to feel in honour bound to talk copiously and in an animated way. If one were engaged upon the manufacture of what is called light fiction, Appleby thought, all this would be just the thing. But to one concerned with the ponderous verity of an errant and lethal meteorite the significance of the proceedings was depressingly hard to discern. . . . It was at this moment that a woman came up to Appleby and shook hands. A small woman, and of a genteel appearance modified by a large black hat—in fact, Appleby said to himself, a sort of artistic-academic centaur. And she was shaking hands with him firmly and kindly, as if she had seen through the restrained-shouldering business and were taking him for a lonely soul. And now she spoke. "Pata pata, ko-ko-ko," she said. "Rondi rondi, ripalo."

It sounded more or less like that. And, issuing as it did from a source whence intelligible communication had been expected, it was momentarily disconcerting. Appleby tried something cautious. "How do you do," he said.

The centaur looked at him with surprise and perhaps a hint of reproach. "You don't mean to say," she cried, "that you are *not* one of those interesting new Russians?"

"I'm afraid I'm not—in fact, not a Russian at all." Appleby spoke as apologetically as was reasonable. "I wonder why you should suppose—?"

The centaur laughed quietly and with much social assurance. "It must be because you don't put your hands in your pockets. Have you never noticed it of Russians? No well-bred Russian would dream of standing about a drawing room with his hands in his pockets. So interesting a people, don't you think?"

Appleby agreed that the Russians were of interest.

The centaur looked at him appraisingly for a moment, plainly selecting some further topic. "Have you," she asked brightly, "had anything much on hand lately?"

"Well, yes—a fair amount. A murder in Bermondsey."

"How very interesting!"

"And a woman trying to poison her grandmother in Bow."

"Indeed! Do you know, I would so like to see them sometime?"

Appleby was again somewhat dismayed. "Oh, yes," he said vaguely. "Quite."

"I take the greatest interest in the new anecdotal school. Genre painting is something we have long missed. I am a great admirer of Firth. And Tissot too. And my father was a close friend of Holman Hunt. We have really been most unfair to that generation for a long time. I should particularly like to see your poisoning."

Somewhat laboriously, Appleby took his bearings amid this prattle. "I'm afraid there's a mistake," he said. "It was a real murder and a real poisoning. You see, I'm a policeman, not a painter. My name's Appleby."

The centaur, it was impressive to observe, didn't bat an eyelid. "That," she said cheerfully, "is more interesting still. And it is poor Mr. Pluckrose, no doubt. In fact, you are the high official people are talking about. And a friend of our dear duke's."

Never before had Appleby been referred to as a high official. It was almost as difficult as being taken for a new Russian. "The Duke of Nesfield?" he said. "I met him yesterday for the first time."

The centaur smiled—mysteriously. "I knew from

114

the beginning that there was a great inwardness to this affair of Mr. Pluckrose. I am not at all surprised that the Foreign Office should be concerned."

"The Foreign Office!" Appleby was startled.

"But we shall say no more about that. A policeman you shall be." The centaur's voice was now both conspiratorial and arch. "I must tell you that my name is Isabel Godkin. I am Warden of our women's hostel, St. Cecilia's. Two hundred girls, Mr. Appleby. Two hundred quite *simple* girls. And I have to lick them into shape!" Miss Godkin gave a practised little laugh indicating comical dismay. "A little music, a little deportment, *something* of the outlook of gentlewomen. I assure you it is most fascinating work. A sort of finishing school that has to start from the beginning." This was evidently a well-worn gag, and Miss Godkin paused on it. "It is arduous but important—*quite* as important as their purely academic work. I do hope you will come and visit us one day."

"I should like to very much." Appleby looked at this awful woman gravely. "And I can see that it must be very exacting indeed. You must sometimes have the discouraging feeling that the whole process is an orgy of snobbery."

This time Miss Godkin's eyes did open wide. "I don't think that I have ever—"

"I suppose it's rather like the savings bank."

"The savings bank!"

"One gets people to put in a little money, and quite soon they feel they have a vested interest in the way that property is at present disposed. Similarly you teach your girls, say, to talk about dinner instead of tea, and soon they feel a sort of invisible tie-up with whatever is the Nesfield equivalent of Mayfair. Cardinal Newman observed somewhat similar efforts in Birmingham. He called them, if I remember aright, uncouth imitations of polished ungodliness." And Appleby smiled in the friendliest way at Miss Godkin. Stupid to be pricked into this assault and battery. Perhaps the Warden of St. Cecilia's would insist on his being expelled from Mrs. Tavender's afternoon forthwith. . . .

But Miss Godkin was smiling with the greatest friendliness too. "*How* like the dear duke!" she said. "A *most* stimulating conversationalist, is he not? And I am myself extremely interested in radical ideas. A number of my father's friends belonged to the Fabian Society at one time. Men with beards and very distinguished records in economics and so on. I do hope that you will visit us. It would be so *good* for my girls to know that in the Foreign Office there are really *progressive* minds. Some of them are a little inclined to socialism, I fear."

There is no coping, Appleby reflected, with an assured and thoroughly illogical woman. All that remained was to escape from Miss Godkin as quickly as possible. And then a thought struck him. Why should she have supposed that there was an "inwardness" to the Pluckrose affair? And why should she have taken it into her head that he himself came, of all places, from the Foreign Office? Before Appleby's mind as he pondered these question there rose the image of Joan Cavenett telling her odd story of the bigamous Church. Might it be possible—? Appleby turned to Miss Godkin again. "I suppose," he said, "that at St. Cecilia's they are for the most part local girls?"

"They are mostly country girls from the area that the university serves. If a girl has not a home in Nesfield she must live in the hostel. Lodgings for girls are no longer allowed. An excellent measure, I am sure you will agree."

"One is always glad to hear of things being no longer allowed." Appleby looked very seriously at Miss Godkin. "But do you have others as well? Foreign girls, for instance?"

"Ah!" Again Miss Godkin was conspiratorial. At the same time she was appreciably uncertain, so that Appleby had the impression that there was something by which she was herself a good deal puzzled. "We have had quite a number of late. From Germany, for the most part. And of very good family, some of them. For some time, now, Sir David—" Miss Godkin hesitated. "But I think you are likely to know more about it than I do."

This was mysterious and rather awkward. Appleby decided to persevere. "You say that Sir David Evans has had something to do with—"

He was interrupted by a cheerful voice behind him, and a hand was laid on his shoulder. "Well, well," said the voice. "Just the place where one would expect to find the Vice Squad at work."

It was young Pinnegar. Like Miss Godkin he appeared to have deferred to the aesthetic nature of the occasion by a modification of his attire, for he wore a decidedly outré jacket of orange-coloured corduroy. "Come to think of it," he said, "I fancy you're here on a tip of my own."

Appleby nodded. "Just that."

"Well, well." Pinnegar raised a bitten macaroon and pointed it at Miss Godkin. "This is Mr. Appleby—a cop. And I'm a nark. I passed him the word about

117

Mrs. Tavender's Disorderly House."

Miss Godkin, by looking coldly at the macaroon, indicated that this was a disagreeable jest.

"Odd phrase, when you come to think of it. Why disorderly? I've been told such places have a sort of drab propriety and decorum of their own. But of course what Appleby is really on the trail of is the busting of the bust. Pluckrose, having attempted to bust the bust, was himself busted. Appleby, that's it, isn't it?"

"Very possibly." Miss Godkin, Appleby noticed, though she looked disapproving was not bewildered. So there must be some sense in Pinnegar's gibberish. "Where is the bust?" he asked. "Can I see it?"

Pinnegar nodded. "The bust, bottle-bashed, is in the hall. This way." And he began to push through the crush. Appleby followed and so did Miss Godkin. And presently they were confronting a marble effigy of Sir David Evans. The thing was executed in a markedly modernistic manner but the material was the glaring white stone that had its chief popularity in the Victorian era. So Sir David's complexion, in nature ruddy or even florid, was represented as of a deathly pallor. But what was odd was that Sir David's hair, so snowy in the actual man, was here tinctured quite a bright green.

"I think it's fading," said Miss Godkin. "It was really a most eccentric thing to do."

"I wonder," asked Pinnegar, "if it could be anything to do with Jumblies? Was their hair green? I forgot. Perhaps the sense of the affair was this: Evans is no better than a Jumbly. He puts to sea in a sieve. His intellectual gear and tackle are grotesquely inadequate to the pretentious philosophical voyages he attempts. It's a new interpretation, anyway."

"But Mr. Hissey?" said Miss Godkin. "The thing really appeared to happen in the course of an argument between Pluckrose and Hissey. I was standing quite close and can vouch for that myself. We would have to suppose that Mr. Hissey was protesting against Pluckrose's plan to turn poor Sir David into a Jumbly. And I don't know that he would do that. I really believe that Pluckrose could have painted the real Sir David in stripes all over and Mr. Hissey wouldn't have minded a bit."

"They say," said Pinnegar, "that Lasscock was in it too. The argument, I mean. He was distinctly heard to call upon Pluckrose to desist. Quite an unwonted display of energy on Lasscock's part."

Miss Godkin nodded. "It is perfectly true. I myself saw Mr. Lasscock try to take the bottle from Pluckrose's hand."

"The bottle?" Appleby, half enlightened, looked from Miss Godkin to Pinnegar. "Am I to understand that Pluckrose, during one of these parties, emptied a bottle of green paint over Sir David Evans's bust?"

Pinnegar shook his head indulgently. "Officer, officer," he said, "how you jump to conclusions! Miss Godkin will agree that you have contrived a shockingly inaccurate reconstruction of the crime. Not *emptied* the bottle. *Broke* it. Think how much more dramatic that was. And not green paint. A colourless fluid in a clear glass container. Several people will swear to that. He brought it down with a bang, and instantly the bust went green on top. What you might call a display of parlour chemistry. But the effect is now fading somewhat, as Miss Godkin says. The thing happened a fortnight ago."

119

"I see." Appleby stared at the bust in considerable gloom. If there could be anything odder than the bigamous proceedings of Timothy Church it was surely this demonstration by the dead man. But that these two affairs were related either to each other or to the central drama of the meteorite it was hard to see. Appleby turned again to Pinnegar. "But was no explanation sought? After all, it was a most out-of-the-way thing to happen in a lady's drawing room. What had Pluckrose to say for himself?"

"Nothing at all, as far as I know. He just left. It was felt to be very awkward, of course. But Pluckrose was known to be rather eccentric."

"Did he have break-downs?" Appleby was remembering Sir David Evans's theory. "I mean, did he periodically break out into markedly neurotic behaviour?"

"I can't say I've ever seen him eating grass or climbing up the curtains. Miss Godkin, have you?"

"I have not. Nor did he strike me as a particularly unstable man. But undoubtedly he was an interfering one. When he came to tea it was invariably to tell me how St. Cecilia's ought to be run. I must admit that I resented it. After all, I have been some little time on the job. And I think I have learnt to concentrate on the elements. Many people have remarked that my girls *do* know how to do in and out of a room. And when to look at you and for how long. And *not* to be eternally buying cheap stockings. And to use—"

"Quite so." Once in an afternoon, Appleby felt, was enough for all that. "You would naturally resent Pluckrose's interference. But may I ask if it was all based on knowledge? I mean—"

"I quite understand what you mean." Miss Godkin

nodded briskly. "And the knowledge was there. What was particularly annoying about Mr. Pluckrose was the fact that he had always got the subject up. He would hold out the example of a new women's college in Oslo—something like that."

"It was his way of badgering people all round." Pinnegar had turned up again after a sortie in search of further macaroons. "He got up your stuff on the quiet and then tried to trap you with it. Disgusting habit. But you couldn't call it unacademic. Just pretty, mannerless and under-bred."

"I suppose Sir David heard about the affair of the bust?"

Pinnegar chuckled. "My dear man, he was here at the time. And as he went up to take his leave of Mrs. Tavender there was the thing staring at him. And I must say the old devil was superb. He looked at it and didn't move a muscle of his face. Just said good-bye in his benevolent and loathly way and toddled down to his car. Only next day he had Tavender to luncheon and heard just what had happened."

"And would you say he would be likely to harbour resentment against Pluckrose on account of the insult?"

Pinnegar grinned. "And heave a rock at him? It makes a nice theory for you to work on, I'm sure. But I don't think much of it. Miss Godkin, do you?"

"I do not. Sir David's attitude to the professors is peculiar. He may be said to take a kindly interest in seeing them make fools of themselves. Any imbecility on their part serves to reinforce some theory of his own. I couldn't tell you quite what the theory is, but I have long been convinced that it is there."

"And it doesn't apply to lecturers." Pinnegar was

happily finishing his last macaroon. "Just to professors." He looked round the room. "And I should think it calculated to irritate the mildest of them—even Hissey."

Appleby looked round too. It was the mild and absent Hissey who had been observed in some sort of argument with Pluckrose just before the embarrassing affair of the bust. Perhaps something could be extracted from him. But Appleby scanned the still thronging crowd of Mrs. Tavender's guests in vain. Hissey must have gone. For any enlightenment that he could offer it would be necessary to wait until they met that evening in the hotel. And now dusk was falling; it was time to hunt up Hobhouse again and learn if he had really traced the meteorite.

Mrs. Tavender was standing by the door. Appleby went up and shook hands with her. Mrs. Tavender said "So pleased" in a voice at once absent and emotional. They were the only words Appleby was ever to hear her speak; decidedly she was not one of the ladies in the case. Involuntarily moving to the urgent rhythm of Mrs. Tavender's beads, he passed through an outer lobby. Mrs. Tavender's husband was standing on the steps; clearly within Mrs. Tavender's orbit one would think of him as that. And yet Tavender was somebody in himself. With a shamble and a giggle and a great rubbing of hands he was coming forward now: in some obscure way a formidable man. Perhaps he had hidden qualities of will or intellect; perhaps he was just uncommonly acute. He stopped before Appleby with an uncertain grin. "On the trail?" he said—and clapped his hands with a disconcerting gesture, rather as if he were summoning invisible afreets or jinns.

"Off it—hopelessly astray." Appleby, mysteriously prompted to this mild exaggeration, shook a rueful head.

Tavender was delighted. His giggle became genuinely friendly; he raised and lowered himself on his toes, like some uncouth crooner before a microphone. "Well, well," he said. "Think of that! But at least you've seen our bust?"

"I've seen the bust."

"A great shame, don't you think? A perfectly new bust, too."

"New?"

"New, my dear sir—and exquisitely artistic, if you'll believe my wife." Tavender chuckled—informed, malicious and joyful. "You'll come to it all—in time."

Appleby was silent. I ought—he was thinking—to be annoyed. But I believe I am grateful—which is odd. And perhaps it might be possible to requite Tavender in his own quizzical coin. "Mr. Tavender," he asked, "would you say there was much bigamy about the university just now?"

For a moment Tavender blankly stared. And then his good humour became positively riotous. "Oh, well done, sir!" he said. "Very pretty, indeed! I wouldn't say that it will take you anywhere—or not positively— but it's a remarkable feat, all the same." He paused, suddenly oddly immobile. "Are you a reading man?" he asked.

Appleby smiled. "So-so. When I get the time."

"Read *Zuleika Dobson*. Read *Zuleika Dobson* by the incomparable Max!"

7

Nothing more tiresome, thought Appleby emerging through the Tavenders' front gate, than cryptic advice. *Zuleika Dobson* was a masterpiece of fantasy justly endeared to university men. But why should the chronicle of a lovely lady's catastrophic impact upon Oxford be likely to illuminate this affair of bedaubed busts and pulverising meteorites? And why—

"Acritochromacy," said a voice almost in Appleby's ear. He turned round. There was nobody to be seen; nevertheless the voice spoke again. "Acroasis," it said; "acroama, acroatic, acroamatical." There was a pause. "Acronarcotic," said the voice, rising in a sort of triumph; "acronyctous, acrophony, acrochordon." There was another pause. "Acrobat," said the voice— rather dejectedly this time. The Tavenders' gate opened once more and Professor Prisk appeared. "Acrid," he said. "Acrid," he repeated in a tone of sudden and disconcerting repugnance. "An irregular and recent formation." He advanced down the footpath and Appleby saw that he was alone. More strictly perhaps, he and his word-hoard had left the party together.

Appleby waited. "Good evening," he said.

His philological musings thus interrupted, Prisk halted and peered suspiciously down his spade-like nose. Then he spoke with an incisiveness that was somehow surprising. "How do you do. I hope you enjoyed our meeting last night. Though it has been hinted to me that your real business—"

"Quite true, sir. I'm after Pluckrose's death all right."

Prisk fell into step. "And may I ask if you have been following a trail to our artistic friends?"

"I don't think I could say that." Appleby hesitated. "I have been hearing about the curious affair of Sir David Evans's bust."

"Ah." Suddenly Prisk stopped in his tracks. "Acrocomic," he said triumphantly. "You are familiar with the word?"

"Decidedly not, sir."

"No more you should be. It's never been found."

"I see. Well, in that case—"

"But Cockeram cites it in 1626. You know Cockeram?"

"I'm afraid I don't."

"*An Interpreter of Hard English Words.* Interesting book. And the word means 'possessed of long hair.' What you said about the Vice-Chancellor's bust put me in mind of it." Prisk as he poured out this learned twaddle was striding along—it occurred to Appleby—in an incongruously businesslike way. In marked contrast with the absent-minded Hissey, he seemed to know just where he was going. So perhaps he knew

just what he was saying as well. . . . "Yahoo," said Prisk
suddenly.

"I beg your pardon?"

"Where do you think Swift got that? Houyhnhnm
is obvious—a mere neigh. But why Yahoo?"

Appleby considered. "It's a good word."

"Of course it's a good word. And the point is that
I'm put in mind of it by Pluckrose. The man was a
Yahoo. Remember to put that in your report." And
Prisk quickened his pace.

Quite a ferocious person, Appleby reflected. And
put most of it into pounding and pummelling and
torturing words. Was it conceivable that this curious
form of sublimation might on occasion fail and leave
Prisk with sufficient free belligerence to liquidate a
distasteful colleague? It was a fantastic supposition.
But then the meteorite and the bust were fantastic as
well. Appleby glanced curiously at the figure hurrying
along beside him. "You were unable to regard Pluckrose in an amiable light?"

"Jargon," said Prisk.

"I beg your pardon?"

"Amiable light is jargon. Don't talk it. And as for
Pluckrose he was infrahuman."

"Isn't that jargon too?"

"It may be." Prisk laughed robustly. "But it's true."

"I see. Of course there was the telephone."

"So you've heard of that?" Prisk swung so suddenly
round a corner that the two men bumped shoulders.
"Would you willingly share a toothbrush with a Yahoo? Of course not. Then why should I share a telephone with Pluckrose? I felt strongly about it. You
might consider it as a motive for murder."

"Everything shall be considered." Appleby found

that he was almost out of breath. "And I may say that odd little troubles do lead to homicide from time to time."

"Subhomi-cide. Infrahomi-cide. But why—when one comes to reflect on the thing soberly—should anyone think to murder Pluckrose?"

"Why indeed?" Appleby's tone expressed untroubled agreement. "Or why should anyone think to murder you?"

"But, my dear sir, nobody has thought to murder me." Prisk was suddenly speaking as if to an unreasonable child. "Even child. Pluckrose was a much more likely victim than I am. He interfered with people. Whereas I might be described as the most harmless and retiring of men." And Prisk laughed his oddly fierce and sinister laugh—a sensualist's laugh, Appleby found himself remarking. "A man too without possessions—barring a modicum of philological knowledge of no market value."

"No doubt, sir. But it is interesting that you appear to have considered the matter. The possibility, I mean, of there having been a mistake. A message going astray on that telephone—something of that sort." Appleby paused but Prisk said nothing. "Several of your colleagues have been debating it. You may feel it to be rather an uncomfortable theory. But it has this point of comfort. If, in fact, the murder of Pluckrose represented the miscarrying of a plan to murder you, then it isn't likely to be you who murdered Pluckrose."

"Well, well!" Prisk laughed again. "This, no doubt, is what they call deduction. And I certainly agree that Pluckrose's death can scarcely have been the unforeseen result of my attempting to commit suicide."

"Quite so. If the murderer was really after you then certainly you were not the murderer." Appleby paused as if to admire the logical irrefutability of this. "But of course there is another side to the thing— and one not quite so comfortable. It has been well expressed by our late host."

"Tavender?" Prisk's voice had subtly sharpened.

"Yes—and he seems to me rather an acute person. What he said was this: *Shy, shy again.*"

"Ah!" said Prisk. "The adage."

"Quite so, sir. Or if you like, the apophthegm. If at first you don't succeed, try, try again. Supposing Pluckrose to have been the intended victim, one meteorite was enough. But if it was really aimed at you and went astray, then it is conceivable that another may follow. Or that some further attempt on your life may be made. That's the uncomfortable side to it."

"Um," said Prisk. They had reached a main street and he came to a halt by a tram-stop. "This is an absurd discussion. I cannot understand why you should have wished to conduct it." He looked sharply at Appleby. "Such irregular interviews must be quite foreign to correct police procedure. And now, as I have a dinner engagement, I fear you must excuse me." And Prisk strode into the middle of the road and jumped with some athletic skill on a moving tram.

It was an exit not unlike that of the indignant Crunkhorn on the previous day. Only Crunkhorn before taking himself off had unburdened himself of quite a lot, whereas Prisk had been pretty close. His extreme distaste for Pluckrose was a matter of common knowledge—and it was virtually the only sentiment he had permitted himself. Undoubtedly the interview had been irregular. Was it possible—Appleby asked himself as he too boarded a tram—that it might be not without its sequel in due time?

"Nesfield Court," said Hobhouse triumphantly. "The lethal object, Mr. Appleby, came from Nesfield Court itself. And that's where you and I are going now."

"By all means. Only I don't think we ought to come down on his grace for another meal quite so soon. What about getting something to eat—and investigating that lager—first?" Appleby glanced at his watch. "Then it will be an after-dinner call."

They went out and ate roast beef and Yorkshire pudding. Or rather—for Hobhouse was a purist in these matters—they ate Yorkshire pudding and gravy first and roast beef afterwards. And Hobhouse told about the tracing of the meteorite. He had begun with museums and learned institutions generally and everywhere drawn a blank. Directors and curators were unanimous: most had never possessed a meteorite worth speaking of, and those who did were in the enjoyment of their property still. Moreover the directors and curators were able to compile a list of private persons whose scientific tastes suggested that they might possibly own such a thing; and here too there was a blank. Whereupon it had occurred to Hobhouse that great houses often run to something like a museum of their own. Nesfield Court had been the first place to try and Hobhouse had cautiously contacted the duke's man of business in the city. And after a good deal of telephoning to and fro among the mysterious powers which shared among them the stewardship of the noble household there had arrived the message that a meteorite there had been and that the meteorite had disappeared. At this Hobhouse had firmly announced that police officers would present themselves that evening to make further enquiries at Nesfield Court. And at this the Chief Constable, who had not hitherto taken any marked interest in the Pluckrose affair, announced that the proprieties required his presence with the party. But Hobhouse, as the result of an exercise of tact of which he now favoured Appleby with the fullest particulars, had persuaded the Chief Constable that it would be enough if he sent his car. As a result of this curious fragment of social logic Appleby and his colleague presently found themselves purring very comfortably out of town. Nesfield Court was some twenty miles away. Once clear of traffic, they would make it in half an hour.

Hobhouse settled himself in his corner. "And have you," he asked, "had a good day?"

It was a benevolent question, and probably the little Hobhouses heard it quite often when they got home from school. Appleby lit his pipe and considered it. "Well," he said, "not bad. A bit miscellaneous, perhaps. I've been after a minor act of vandalism perpetrated against a work of art. Say five pounds or twelve days. Then I've collected virtually conclusive evidence against a man called Lasscock on a charge of shamming ill and dozing in the sun. Penalty? Perhaps a tactfully expressed hope for his better health on the part of Sir David Evans. But I should say that before that I was working on a little affair of bigamy. It has the makings of quite a dramatic case in itself. Round Up of the Bigamy Club."

"Of the what?"

"The Society for the Promotion of Bigamy. I'm not sure it oughtn't to be the Royal Society. There is some suspicion that our friend Sir David is involved, look you. Which makes it so extremely respectable that any chance of a conviction is probably slight. Interesting, all the same. Or don't you think?"

In the darkness of the limousine Hobhouse could be heard breathing heavily. "In the matter of Pluckrose—" he began with massive irony.

"To be sure. And tomorrow will be much better. We'll abandon these fringes and go to the heart of the thing. The whole tempo will speed up. We'll mess about the Wool Court and reconstruct the crime."

"I don't think we could do that." Hobhouse was suddenly apprehensive. "The Chief Constable—"

Appleby chuckled. "I don't mean we'll put suspected persons through a sort of theatrical performance. Just the physics of the thing. Do you think you could supply a corpse? It would have to be quite a new corpse. And unsquashed."

"Certainly not!" Hobhouse's voice was as decided as it was scandalised.

"Don't you think that perhaps Nesfield Infirmary—? After all, it would only be a sort of slightly new post-mortem."

"It would be nothing of the sort." Logic came to Hobhouse's aid. "A post-mortem is performed in order to discover the manner of death of the corpse in question. In what you're suggesting the corpse wouldn't be the corpse in question. It would be a— a previous corpse. Decency is decency, Mr. Appleby."

"Perhaps you're right." Appleby was silent for a moment. "By the way, I can tell you this. There's going to be a great deal of sex in the Pluckrose affair. For instance, Pluckrose's landlady practically stated

131

to me that Pluckrose was a person of immoral habits. And that no less a person than Sir David Evans was a rival of his in his lewd loves."

Hobhouse sat up with a jerk. "Now you're talking!" he said. "What I always say is this: get your hands on the sex of the matter and you'll soon find your feet. Now, I'll tell you a curious case—"

The car sped through the night. It was an instructive, if not an edifying, journey.

They had passed a road-house, garish with neon, loud with music; they had overtaken a little column of night-travelling lorries, headlong and stinking; they had turned through great gates dimly glimpsed—and then the moon rose as they crossed Nesfield Chase. Slyly the moon edged itself over the horizon as if its purpose were eavesdropping on the earnestly discoursing Hobhouse; then in a moment it hung clear in the sky, suddenly indifferent and remote. To the left it gleamed coldly on an expanse of water flanked by a balustrade which seemed to run endlessly into distance; to the right it created out of darkness a great irregular chequer-board of trees and clumps of trees and blotched and shafted shadows upon a carpeting of blanched and close-cropped grass. Now they were on a bridge and in the water deer were drinking; now they were running by the stream and before them, correctly framed amid plantations and contrived waters, were the ruins of Nesfield Abbey—a silhouette of broken and impending arches caught by the invisible hand of wealth and invisibly sustained in air; a treasured and embalmed decay. The car purred on, circled, stopped. There was a high stone wall and wrought-iron gates flanked by prancing monsters:

portal-guarding lion-whelps, thought Appleby thinking of Tennyson. The driver discreetly tooted and there was a stir at a lodge door. "The park," said Hobhouse. He spoke in a low voice, rather as if in church. "It was his grandfather enclosed the chase as well." The car was moving again—down an avenue now.

The elm avenue ran like an arrow before them, still and dappled. Fast as the car was going, it was like walking up some endless aisle to the encountering of unknown mysteries. It is nice, thought Appleby, to be plebeian; you take nothing for granted and get all the thrill. The avenue curved, straightened again, curved once more—manoeuvreing to just the angle wanted. And then there was clear moonlight and the car was in the open. It was like pulling round a point in a dinghy and finding a battleship at anchor straight ahead.

To left and right Nesfield Court sprawled into distance—or would have sprawled had it not been labouriously braced against aesthetic appraisal by the massive perpendiculars of Corinthian columns rising to a succession of pediments, or marshalled by platoons and companies into symmetrically disposed porticoes and colonnades. Beneath all this was an ordered multitude of flights of steps, advancing and retiring upon each other like a frozen ballet; and beneath this again was a system of terraces at once cold and lavish, mathematically embellished with classical statuary: hounds and boars, nymphs and satyrs, Laocoon and Hercules and Niobe all tears. Appleby looked at it all as the car slowed down. There was a lot of it and it had been there for quite a long time. Moreover it would last. Even when England had turned into the duke's dog-kennel paradise it would stand. Even when given over to the occupancy of tired workers or imbecile children it would continue to make its own assertions and not theirs. At the moment it made Pluckrose seem very small; before this vast facade of stone that shabby little figure shrivelled further, took on the dimensions of some ink-spinning spider crushed between the pages of an academic textbook. How curious, then, the power of the moral conscience. How curious that the judges of this class-ridden and materialistic modern England would license the pulling of Nesfield Court stone from stone if it were demonstrable that the riddle of this obscure scholar's death could only be solved that way!

The car had stopped before a bifurcation of the drive. Appleby saw the driver's questioning face, and smiled. "Hobhouse," he said, "how do you think we get in?"

"Get in?" Hobhouse was looking dubiously up at the moonlit vistas of pale stone. "Drive up to the front door, of course. Get on."

They drove on past long flights of empty and unwelcoming steps. It was rather as if they were sculling round the battle ship and looking for an accommodation ladder. Suddenly the bonnet of the car nosed up into the air; a flight of steps had parted before them and they were mounting a steep stone ramp. Darkness gathered round them and then once more they were on a level and had come to a stop. Great pillars soared all around with here and there a shaft of moonlight striking uncertainly through. It was like being lost in a forest of immemorial elms. They sat and peered rather helplessly into the thicker darkness. "Well," said Appleby, "I think there can be no doubt that this is the front door. What about ringing the bell? Or do you think one just gives a knock?"

Hobhouse showed no disposition to get out. "Perhaps—"

"I expect you're right. They probably open this one only for the Royal Family. We'd better search elsewhere."

The car moved forward; the bonnet sharply dipped; presently the unending steps and terraces and balustrades were gliding past them once more. They turned a corner. "Do you know," said Appleby, "I believe that was just the side of the house? There's far more of it this way on."

"If this were a taxi we'd have had a bob's worth round the place already." Hobhouse was becoming restive. "And as yet I haven't seen a single light. The place might be uninhabited."

"Probably nine-tenths of it are. I think I see an archway a bit along. Let's turn in."

The archway proved to have something like the dimensions of a tunnel; they drove through and now the building rose on all sides of them. Still there was no gleam of light; great walls, blank or with shuttered windows, rose intermittently before them; they crawled uncertainly through further tunnels and drove slowly round court after deserted court.

"It's like a dream," said Hobhouse flatly, and then: "lights!" he added dramatically—much as a castaway might announce a sail.

The buildings were lower and more irregular now, and straight ahead a cluster of lights had revealed itself. The car crawled to a standstill; a shaft of light shot across the darkness nearby as a door was opened and shut; another door, wide open, showed a vista of

135

empty, stone-flagged corridor.

"Offices," said Appleby. "Laundries and harness-rooms and lord knows what. Rather a come-down after such a regal approach. But human contact is something. Out we get. And don't forget to be properly respectful to the head groom."

Hobhouse shook his head. "Drive on," he said firmly.

"But don't you think—?"

"Mr. Appleby, we have the dignity of the constabulary to observe. It wouldn't do. It wouldn't do at all."

Appleby sighed and the car drove on. "Hobhouse," he asked suddenly, "whom are you going to ask for, anyway?"

"Ask for?" Hobhouse appeared not to have considered this point.

"Supposing that in the next half-hour we find what looks like the policemen's entrance, whom are you going to ask for—the duke?"

"It's really rather difficult to say. If it were the Lord Mayor of Nesfield, now, I'd certainly ask for the Lord Mayor."

"And if it were a baronet somewhere about the country?"

"I'd ask for the baronet."

"And if it were an earl?" The courts now were growing loftier again, and the lighted windows were larger and showed blinds of uniform cream. "Or, say, a marquis?"

Hobhouse shook his head, much disturbed. "They have all sorts of folk around them. What would you say to asking for his grace's secretary?"

"I think you ought to ask for the major-domo."

"It sounds kind of queer to me, Mr. Appleby."

Appleby chuckled. "It is. Of course you might try the steward."

"Would the steward be a gentleman?" Hobhouse had sunk his voice confidentially.

"Not in the sense you mean."

"Then it wouldn't do. Particularly with the Chief Constable's car." Hobhouse pondered. "What about not asking for anyone? What about just saying, 'I am Inspector Hobhouse of the Borough Police'? And then just expecting something to happen?"

"That will be capital." A paralysing place, Appleby was thinking—when the car jerked to a stop. They had come suddenly upon a sort of junior version of the portals at which they had made their first assault—another ramp running up under a small portico. Only here there were lights in the roof and panels of light from windows flanking a closed door.

They got out and explored. "There isn't a bell," said Hobhouse, suddenly dejected.

"A bell? Of course not. This little place scarcely counts as an entrance. It's just a convenient place to put out the cat. Try a knock."

Hobhouse knocked, and presently knocked again; there was no result. "It looks like another blank," he said.

"Nonsense. Look at the lights." It was Appleby who was impatient now. "Try the door. If it's open we'll simply walk in."

"Walk in!" Hobhouse was scandalised.

"We'll come upon a porter or footman in no time. In you go."

Doubtfully Hobhouse pushed open the door and they entered a vestibule which was all pale green enamel and Chinese Chippendale. In front were curtained glass doors with light streaming through. Hobhouse looked about him and seemed to gather resolution from the costliness and strangeness of the place. He advanced upon the glass doors, opened one wing and marched through without a pause. Then suddenly he gave a bound backwards, cannoned violently into Appleby and slammed the door to.

"Hobhouse, what on earth—"

"Somebody took a shot at me." Hobhouse's hand had dived into his overcoat pocket; his glance was warily on the door.

"Took a shot at you? Nonsense. There wasn't a sound."

"I felt it go past my ear. A graze."

"My dear man—" Appleby stopped and stared. From Hobhouse's left ear there was a trickle of blood.

And then the door opened again and the tall figure of the Duke of Nesfield was before them, politely curious. "I hope," he said, "that you are not hurt? Perhaps it was a stupid place to set the thing up. But then nobody ever comes in this way." He came forward and shook hands, a man very far from proposing to show surprise at the identity of his unexpected guests. "My friends and I took a fancy to darts some months ago, and to-night we are having a little reunion. You play?" He stood aside and they entered what proved to be a billiard room. "More coffee, Thomas." He glanced at Hobhouse. "And a bottle of iodine."

Appleby looked about him. Yes, there was the darts board, set up on a wall close by the door. And standing beside it, as one who studies the strategy of the later stages of the game, was young Marlow. And over by the billiard table, surveying the newcomers with frank distaste, was that acid and severe Romance philologer, Professor Prisk.

8

"Marlow," said the duke, "is streets ahead of us. He has the advantage of playing regularly in a Nesfield pub. A thing, unfortunately, I can't do; it would be an affectation. And a thing the professor can't do either; it would be an impropriety."

"Indecorous would be a better word." Prisk took careful aim. "And I think eccentric would be better still. Perhaps I may take it up. Pluckrose was our eccentric professor, as Mr. Appleby here has found out. And now another is needed in his room."

"Talking of Pluckrose's room—" began Marlow.

"Whisky?" The duke had strode over to a great silver tray on which stood an array of decanters and now spoke rather abruptly to the company at large. Prisk and Marlow, it seemed to Appleby, represented once again the duke's fondness for little parties with some ulterior object. And this, surely, could only have to do with the Pluckrose mystery. Nevertheless the duke was not at all disposed to let Pluckrose's name turn up at random. For the moment at least he had imposed upon Hobhouse and Appleby the part of casual visitors, and now he had shut up Marlow with businesslike directness. "Whisky?" he repeated. "Although darts ought really to do with beer."

"Say rather with ale," said Prisk vigorously. "Ale for an Englishman is a natural drink, so that it be neither ropy nor smoky, nor have no weft or tail. But beer is a natural drink for a Dutchman." He held up a dart in the air, much as if gesturing at a blackboard. "I cite no less an authority than Dr. Andrew Borde's *Regiment of Health*, a pioneer work in dietetics, published in 1557. Dr. Borde, who was in holy orders, died in prison shortly after being arrested by his bishop on a charge of keeping three punks or croshabells in his rooms at Winchester." Having delivered himself of this piece of musty bawdry Prisk turned back—rather vaguely, it suddenly seemed to Appleby—to the game. In fact Prisk was slightly drunk—or what Dr. Borde might have called disguised in liquor. And the liquor was the duke's. Perhaps the object of the present party could be glimpsed here. Perhaps the duke was employing the mellowing resources of the Nesfield Court cellars to worm his way a little further into the Pluckrose affair. But Marlow was unkindled by wine; indeed he had the appearance of being carefully sober. And he was looking at Prisk now with a certain calculating malice.

"Borde?" said Marlow; "I think Prisk would find sounder advice in Platt. Sir Hugh Platt's *Jewell House of Art and Nature*. He recommends salad oil. A good swig of salad oil will float upon the wine which you shall drink, and suppress the spirits from ascending to the brain."

"Oh, most barbarous!" Prisk flung a dart—so inaccurately that Appleby trembled for Hobhouse's other ear. The result appeared to discourage him; he turned away, lowered himself carefully into a chair and began solemnly to recite:

"Who ever casts to compass weighty prize,
"And thinks to throw out thundering words of threat:
"Let pour in lavish cups and thrifty bits of meat,
"For Bacchus fruit is friend to Phoebus wise.
"And when with Wine the brain begins to sweat,
"The numbers flow as fast as spring doth rise."

He paused and frowned, as if he had lost the thread of this paean. "Duke" he said heavily, "if only our dear Gerald were here the reunion would be complete."

"Very true, professor." The duke too had sat down and was taking the band from a cigar. "But Gerald is safe at Cambridge, thanks to your good offices."

So that was it. Prisk had been the second of the tutors employed to cram dear Gerald. Prisk and Marlow. And here, after Pluckrose's death, was the duke conducting a little veiled investigation. Not veiled from Marlow; there was a wariness about that young man that showed he suspected how the land lay. But—unless the man was an incomparable actor— veiled from the more aggressive and less apprehensive Prisk. . . . And now Prisk had raised his song and his glass together:

"O if my temples were distained with wine,
"And girt in garlands of wild ivy twine . . ."

Again he paused. "An epiphonematical passage," he said carefully.

For Hobhouse this looked like being too much. He opened his mouth as if to announce that it was not the Muses but a meteorite that he had come to seek. Appleby contrived unobtrusively to restrain him. The meteorite—or rather the absence of the meteorite—could wait. There was a matter of much more immediate interest going forward. The Duke of Nesfield had embarked on what Edwardian ladies would have called a smoking-room story.

Perhaps there was nothing so very odd about that. Sir Robert Walpole, a contemporary of the duke who built Nesfield Court, encouraged dirty conversation on the ground that it was the only sort of talk enjoyed by everybody. And at the moment the duke had rather an ill-assorted company to entertain. But with Hobhouse, at least, he was not being successful. That self-conscious representative of the higher constabulary, who had so recently been entertaining Appleby with certain of the more startling findings of his professional experience, was sitting frozen with horror. Other times, other manners. This was not at all the way the twentieth century expected its noblemen to behave.

But if Hobhouse contracted into an image of respectful disapproval Prisk expanded like a flower. It was soon evident that he carried not one but two invisible bags: a word-hoard and what might perhaps be called a love-hoard. And they had this in common: that their contents were curious, far-fetched and made smooth with handling. Nor did Prisk appear to be a mere passive collector of anecdotes of Cyprian experience. Much of what he had to say took the form of personal reminiscence. In fact, thought Appleby, a thoroughly dirty old man. It was a new light on Romance Philology.

The duke plied the whisky and listened attentively—so attentively that Appleby presently decided that Prisk was not the real object of interest at all. The duke scarcely glanced at Marlow—but it was on Marlow that some obscure experiment was being conducted nevertheless. How, then, did Marlow feel about it? He was not, like Hobhouse, shocked. He was angry. Or—to put it more adequately—Prisk's reminiscences pricked him to a cold fury which not all his wariness was able to suppress. And it was in the gauging of this that the duke was interested. Marlow, in fact, was to be goaded to the point of some outburst. That was the plan, and it was a plan which the duke had no intention of seeing upset by the arrival of a couple of policemen. And what was it about? Why was the duke thus exercising himself? Because these two men had been his guests—or employees. Because at the university which was one of his hobbies a scholar had—most shockingly—been murdered. Because of some piece of knowledge or train of speculation which had prompted him the day before to waylay the police and murmur, "I suppose it *is*—ah—Pluckrose?" Yes, because of that.

And now here was the young man Marlow—pale and gripping the arms of his chair. Why this fury? Young men, unless much inhibited by religious or other influences, are naturally given to Rabelaisian conversation among themselves. On the other hand they are commonly a good deal embarrassed and displeased upon encountering the same thing in markedly older men. An odd but incontestable fact of psychology, this. But did it account for the present situation? Appleby thought not. Marlow's reactions, stifled though they were, showed as being in excess of anything that could be covered by such an explanation. In fact there was only one reasonable hypothesis. . . . Appleby frowned. No, there were two hypotheses. Consider, for instance, the fact that the undergraduate Gerald would have to be present were the "reunion" to be complete. . . .

And there was the point that the Duke of Nesfield was far from pleased with the whole affair. Upon his face there was something drawn and strained which had been absent the day before. He was going to get at the truth but he was far from liking it. And perhaps he was going to get at the truth privately; had decided that his cryptic hint to the police was a mistake. Certainly he showed small disposition to acknowledge the professional existence of Hobhouse and Appleby here and now.

The duke disliked the affair. He disliked Prisk. One could discern this in the way he said "professor"; in the ever so slightly gingerly way he handed the man a glass. And, equally, it was possible to feel that Marlow he sympathised with. Which would fit in well enough. . . .

Only—thought Appleby looking at his untouched glass—there was so much to fit in. Sir David Evans's bust and Timmy Church's bigamy—how, for instance, could those be made to cohere with what was going obscurely forward now? And the meteorite: where did that have its place? Again, there was the lackadaisical Lasscock, whose frequent habit it was to sun himself in the Wool Court. And there was Miss Godkin of St. Cecilia's—that latter-day Lady Politick Would-be—murmuring mysteriously of the Foreign Office. There was all this and there was the as yet largely unexplored mechanics of the case. A not inconsiderable jigsaw— and one still perhaps without a focal point round which to build.

Appleby took a conventional sip at his whisky and looked at Marlow again. He was a young man who created a displeasing impression at first. One would probably write him down as flippant, hard, contemptuous, shallow—and inconsiderable. But perhaps all this was a disguise to hide strong and what he feared were unsophisticated and therefore disgraceful impulses. Actually, it might be, a markedly idealistic young man—and of course a tolerably able one. His wits were getting the better of his emotions now. Although evidently extremely allergic to Prisk in his present vein, he had caught at the essential fact of something artificial and contrived in the whole affair. And he was not going to be drawn. One could feel the tension slowly relaxing in him. Perhaps like Dr. Johnson on an altogether dissimilar occasion he had succeeded in removing his mind and thinking of Tom Thumb. If the duke had planned that Marlow should clarify the situation by jumping up and pelting Prisk with billiard balls his little piece of stage managing had failed.

In fact the party, thus obscurely at an impasse, was hanging fire. Prisk had passed suddenly from a state of bawdy volubility to one of moroseness and suspicion. Hobhouse was fidgeting. It might be as well to bring forward the matter of the meteorite at last. "This affair that was dropped on Pluckrose," said Appleby into the next silence; "it appears it came from Nesfield Court. That's why Hobhouse and I have ventured to

146

come out and see you." He looked innocently at the duke. "And perhaps that's why you took such a friendly interest in us yesterday, sir?"

The duke appeared to be studying a large and dreary Canaletto which hung above the fireplace; without taking his gaze from its green waters he slightly shook his head. "No," he said; "you are mistaken in that. I knew nothing of it until this evening. And I haven't heard properly about it yet; they just sent me across a message when your people rang up."

Hobhouse, with considerable hardihood, had produced a notebook. "Your grace," he said severely, "didn't know this thing had been stolen?"

The duke smiled charmingly. "I'm really afraid I didn't, inspector. It wasn't at all among my cherished possessions. Indeed, whether it can be called a possession of mine is a nice philosophical point. What do you say, professor? Can I be said to possess something the existence of which is unknown to me?"

Prisk shook his head. "In Nesfield Court," he said ponderously, "there must be much, duke, of which you are only unwittingly the impropriator."

"That's just it." The duke nodded as if something very safe had been said. "And it's difficult to keep one's hand on everything one *does* know about." He made a gesture, vague and apologetic, which seemed to comprehend the whole grotesque profusion of the building in which they sat. "However, I don't doubt that there was a meteorite, and that it was stolen. Martin"—he was addressing Marlow by his Christian name—"you used to mooch about the place a good deal; did you ever notice anything of the sort?"

Was there, Appleby wondered, an edge to this

question? Or was it merely the duke's habit of politely bringing everyone into the conversation in turn? Marlow was shaking his head. "No, sir. But then there are at least three separate museums about the place. And any number of collections and oddities and curiosities scattered here and there."

"That's very true." The duke was still apologetic. "Members of the family take it into their heads to form collections from time to time. My grandfather collected carriages; there are about eighty in the old orangery. And my uncle Hubert collected stage scenery; I believe it's still about somewhere. One hesitates to turn such things out. There's plenty of room, after all." He got to his feet. "Shall we go and find out? Mr. Collins may know, and I don't think it's too late to disturb him." The duke rang a bell. "Thomas," he said carefully to the answering footman, "will you give my compliments to Mr. Collins and ask him if I may bring in some friends?" He sat down again. "We'll give Thomas a good start." He looked at Appleby ironically and chuckled. "Say a hundred yards."

"Angelica Kauffmann," said the Duke of Nesfield. He took Hobhouse and Appleby each by an arm and drew them to a halt; then he cocked up his head until his commanding nose indicated the ceiling. "Woman must have been a sort of human fly. Not many places like this without some of her work. And she did the doors too. Come and look at this one. Wouldn't you call it rather a delicate arabesque?"

Prisk and Marlow had gone ahead; now, as a result of the duke's zeal as a cicerone, they were out of sight in some farther corridor. Nor did their host appear anxious to overtake them in the course of this pilgrimage to Mr. Collins; a few paces more and he had halted again before a portrait on the wall. "Lady Caroline Lamb," he said. "One of those portraits of her in page's costume. She must have been what they call a transvestist nowadays. My great-grandfather was rather struck on her at one time. After Byron, that was. What do you think about Byron?" The duke had turned amiably to Hobhouse. "Myself, I don't care for him at all."

"Do you care for Prisk?" Appleby dropped the question casually, while politely studying Lady Caroline's features.

The duke looked mildly surprised. "Dear me," he said; "what can I have done to prompt such a question?"

"Arranged matters so that he infuriates this young man Marlow, and then packed them off together down a lonely corridor. All this after having hinted more than a doubt as to whether Pluckrose was really the target designed for the meteorite. In fact, sir, it is quite clear that you are deliberately testing out the strength of Marlow's animosity. Does it extend to the positively murderous? And the experiment seems to me rather a risky one."

For some moments the duke said nothing; they moved on down the corridor and passed into a dimly lit saloon hung with pale blue silk. "Inspector," he said at length, "what is this that you have been putting into your colleague's head?"

Hobhouse, cautious and alarmed, made no reply. They had entered another corridor, white and cold, and were moving down an endless vista of bronzes set in alcoves on either side. "Yes," said the duke slowly. "I don't exactly expect murder and sudden death just ahead of us there; but in general you are right. If Martin Marlow is so unbalanced that he attempted to kill Prisk, then we might as well get at the truth. And it occurred to me that throwing them together again might bring the truth to the surface. Neither knew that I was asking the other this evening. But may I ask what you think it's all about?"

They had turned a corner and the sweep of a great staircase was before them; they began to climb. "Perhaps a girl," said Appleby. "These two were living here together for sometime. Perhaps Marlow had a girl—a pure girl or one whom he imagined to be so. And then perhaps Prisk, who clearly has a disreputable side to him—"

"It's not a bad theory." The duke reached the top of the staircase and quickened his pace. "Unfortunately it's not true."

"Unfortunately the truth concerns your grandson, Gerald, whom both these men were brought in to coach."

"Quite so." The monstrous house was flowing past them still in unending saloons and corridors. "Quite so. Gerald is a most attractive lad—and very much what one calls clean-living. Marlow became extremely attached to him—perhaps in an emotional, but certainly not in an unseemly way. Then this Mr. Prisk—whom I regret ever having retained—took it into his head to amuse himself by making what he called a 'man' of Gerald. He meant a sort of young Regency buck. He took Gerald up to town and introduced him to disreputable women. There would have been no great harm in that"—the duke's eye was momentarily on the shocked Hobhouse—"although it was certainly conduct extraordinarily unbecoming in a scholar

150

placed in a position of some confidence. But unfortunately Gerald is not at all that sort of boy. He reacted to these stupid but quite common experiences with a neurotic explosion: irrational feelings of guilt and so on. Not that *that* is anything very out of the way either. In my day there was always a bishop or two to whom parents would turn to set such matters right. Nowadays it's psychologists—and Gerald has one jawing away at him now. I don't myself attach very great importance to the whole affair. But the point is that this young Marlow was tremendously upset. He saw— and I suppose still sees—the lewd Prisk as having blighted Gerald's whole life. But it's his own life that is blighted, poor chap, if he killed Pluckrose. Perhaps he was just proposing to give Prisk a horrible fright, and the thing fell truer than he intended. Or perhaps there is nothing in my whole hypothesis—and I'm sure I hope not. After all, it would be astonishingly inefficient to manage to kill the wrong man." The duke halted and looked at Appleby hopefully. "Don't you think?"

"I rather do. But it happens that Pluckrose and Prisk shared a telephone. And if a telephone message was used to lure the victim, as it were, into position, then a mistake becomes more possible." Appleby frowned. "Does Prisk know that you know all this?"

"Certainly not. He has no idea that Gerald has confessed the whole thing to me. Otherwise I hardly suppose that he could sit with comfort at my table."

The Duke of Nesfield had perhaps somewhat the same constitution as his grandson. The leading of Gerald into evil courses shocked him far more than he cared to admit, and certainly he was very far indeed from forgiving the disreputable Prisk. . . . But now

surely even the recesses of Nesfield Court could not
much longer conceal Mr. Collins, and Appleby had
another set of questions to put. "About the meteorite,
sir. If it were here to be stolen presumably Marlow—
or for that matter Prisk—could have stolen it?"

"Presumably. But why anyone should want—"

"Quite so, sir. Why steal a meteorite? I'm coming
to see the crux of the whole matter as lying there. Is
there any conceivable reason why a man should steal
such a thing in order to drop it on—or near—another
man? We've had the suggestion that it was a matter
of symbolism, and there might be something in that.
It's a theory with two branches, so to speak. The meteorite might be attractive or relevant in virtue of its
general symbolism: the associations which such a thing
carries for every man. Or it might be attractive or
relevant in virtue of some *particular* symbolism: some
particular association which it had just for murderer
and victim and, perhaps, other specific people. But
now notice this. The meteorite was stolen; the meteorite was hurled down on Pluckrose. It doesn't at
all follow that the meteorite was stolen *with that end
in view*. So we must also ask: Is there any conceivable
reason why a man should steal a meteorite? Just that—
as a problem quite independent of the murder. For
instance, can such a thing contain precious metal?
Might it have a high degree of scientific interest?"

The duke smiled. "My dear sir, it's nice to hear one
question that one can answer. The meteorite could
have high scientific interest only for a *scientist*. And
such a person would have sufficient information to
know that I should be likely to relinquish the thing
at once for any reasonably accredited scientific purpose. A scientist wouldn't need to *steal* it. The idea

of a precious metal seems a more likely one. But somehow I feel that gold or platinum, say, doesn't happen in meteorites. We'll ask Collins to look it up. And here we are."

"May I ask one more question before we rejoin the others? It's still about the meteorite. Suppose that neither Marlow nor Prisk stole it. Would any of the other university people be possible—have the opportunity of noticing it, I mean, if it were about?"

"It seems to depend on just where about it lay. But a great many university people would have just as good a chance as Prisk or Marlow. You see, I give a party for them twice a year. And they wander all over the place."

"I see."

"In my mother's time they weren't let inside." The duke smiled his always faintly arrogant smile. "She had them in a book called 'Garden Parties Only' along with the city aldermen and the country doctors and the lower clergy. How remote those times seem!" The duke's hand was on the door before him; his voice was gently ironical. "Now I let them in. Twice a year. And what happens? They steal my meteorites." He opened the door. "Collins," he said amiably, "I've brought the police."

The room, Appleby reckoned in a vulgar comparison, was about the size of a small cinema. Everything showed cream and gold—including the greater part of the tens of thousands of books which clothed the walls. Ionic pillars supported a ceiling which was one swirling mythological battle-piece; Ionic pillars flanked a fireplace of green marble in which a great log was burning. And before this stood Mr. Collins, a rosy-faced old man wearing a brocaded smoking jacket and holding a churchwarden pipe. He had Prisk and Marlow comfortably placed on either side of him and was himself arranging a great silver bowl on a table. "Duke," he said when he had greeted Appleby and Hobhouse, "I think we have only to call for more lemons. Do you know how they came to give *Punch* its name? Because its first editor was Mark Lemon. I knew him well, Mr. Appleby; a fellow of infinite jest, of most excellent fancy. His friends knew him as Uncle Mark. Alas, my dear professor, *tempus ferax*"—Mr. Collins busied himself above his bowl—"*Tempus edax rerum*. Mr. Hobhouse, are you at your ease? Here is a lower and more comfortable chair. Morals and domestic furniture, they say, grow lower together. A suggestive thesis, Marlow my dear lad, for your learned pen. Pray draw up, gentlemen, draw up. Duke, it is nearly a week since you have assisted at these computations. Commonly I sit here of an evening now." Mr. Collins glanced round the vast room. "It is cosier in early spring. But had I known of your intended visit, I would have had fires lit in the library." His eye caught Hobhouse's surprised blink round the room and he chuckled. "Ah, Mr. Hobhouse, I often remind the duke of something said by the poet Coleridge when he was stopping in a deserted palace in Malta. He lived, he said, like a mouse in a cathedral. How admirable a phrase! And here at Nesfield we are all like mice in a cathedral—and waiting for the cat." Mr. Collins chuckled again and picked up a long-handled silver spoon. "Will it be a Cheshire cat? Well, the mob is distinguished by nothing if not by its grin. Will it be Dick Whittington's cat? I judge it will scarcely be amiably disposed towards the City of London. Will it be Puss in Boots? Ah, gentlemen, it may have boots but it certainly won't have breeches. The duke's cat is a sansculottic cat. And a sanguinary cat and a socialistic cat. But meantime the mice may play and the punch is ready. Professor, you will take a glass? *Nunc est bibendum*, Marlow, *nunc est bibendum*. And if *pede libero pulsande tellus* be ruled out by our advancing years, at least we may have a catch." And Mr. Collins, having served out the punch to his satisfaction, gave every indication of being about to break into song.

What used to be called Table Talk, thought Appleby. Perhaps the old gentleman wrote it all down afterwards and would one day publish it in a book. Table Talk by Dash Collins Esquire, Librarian to his Grace the Duke of Nesfield Court, K. G. ... And meantime it made another atmosphere somewhat inimical to brisk criminal investigation.

"Talking of cats," said the duke adroitly, "there is this one that has got out of the bag. The meteorite, Collins, the meteorite. Our friends here have discovered that it came from somewhere about the place and they have called to enquire. I don't remember ever having seen it myself."

"Probably you never have." Mr. Collins abandoned his singing posture and sat back comfortably by the fire. "Very probably you never have, duke. You bought it only a few months ago. And hard upon its arrival on this dim spot which men call Earth." Mr. Collins paused as if to savour the flavour of this quotation and of the punch together. "Hammond got you to buy it."

"Hammond?" said the duke, rather blankly—and then brightened. "Ah, yes, Hammond—of course.

Then Hammond is our man—and a very charming fellow too. Thomas, be so good as to give my compliments to Mr. Hammond—"

Mr. Collins shook his head. "You forget, duke. Hammond has left us. After he had catalogued the ceramics—"

"To be sure, the ceramics. Of course I remember that he came for that."

"He came to deal with the Pickering Collection."

"The Pickering Collection?" The duke nodded sagely and turned to Appleby. "Armour," he said. "Interesting stuff."

Mr. Collins shook his head indulgently once more. "Early scientific instruments," he corrected. "And when Hammond had done that, and most kindly lent Borrow a hand with the ceramics—"

"Ah, Borrow." The duke was confident. "The man with the beard and the mania for asparagus."

"Precisely. Well, Hammond, as I say, went back to the British Museum. You had only borrowed him, after all."

"A great pity. And have I only borrowed Borrow?"

Mr. Collins chuckled happily. "I fear not. But perhaps you could lend him somewhere. Otherwise we had better give instructions for more asparagus beds. And that reminds me of something I had intended to suggest to you about the peaches."

Appleby caught Hobhouse's eye and thought it wise to interrupt. "Perhaps you have heard, Mr. Collins, that one of the professors of the university has been killed. Somebody hurled this meteorite at him from a tower. So our investigation is really of some gravity and we are concerned to make the best speed we can."

"Dear me!" Mr. Collins took his pipe from his

mouth and looked comfortably concerned. "May I ask who the unfortunate man was?"

"His name was Pluckrose."

"You surprise me." Very deliberately, Mr. Collins got up and gave a poke at the great log on the fire. "I know little of Mr. Pluckrose—or indeed of any of the university people except our two friends here." And Mr. Collins bowed ceremoniously to Prisk and Marlow. "Nevertheless you could have named no name by which I should have been occasioned greater surprise. His grace"—and Mr. Collins, whom punch was inclining perhaps to old-world forms, bowed quite profoundly—"His grace is without the necessary information to be particularly startled. But hereby hangs a tale." He paused and looked doubtfully at the duke. "I suppose it isn't necessary to have a man of business present? I must confess to feeling that all this is unfamiliar and perhaps delicate ground."

For the first time the duke was mildly impatient. "Go ahead, man, go ahead. Lawyers won't help us."

"Then what I have to say is this." Mr. Collins puffed at his pipe. Was he, Appleby debated, looking rather apprehensively at Marlow? If so, it was only fleetingly, for now his glance was following a puff of smoke up to the great painted ceiling. "What I must say is this: I know who stole the meteorite. In fact I was present when the thing happened."

"Bless my soul!" The duke looked at his librarian in astonishment. "Why ever didn't you have it stopped?"

"Because the circumstances were such that I had to conclude that it was not, in fact, theft that was in question." Mr. Collins frowned—probably because he felt this sentence to be stylistically inelegant. "The

157

meteorite was removed under—how shall I put it?—under the most respectable auspices. This I had on Marlow's authority."

The duke swung round. "Martin, what is this? Have you known—"

"I don't know anything. I don't know what Collins is talking about." Marlow looked at once dogged and alarmed.

"I think that may be so. There is no reason why it may not be so, as the circumstances will make plain." Mr. Collins had turned earnestly to Appleby. "When Hammond first bought the meteorite for the duke it was stored somewhere about the house. Then it was sent away somewhere for scientific examination; it was weighed and photographed and no doubt analysed in various technical ways. Perhaps it proved to be without any special interest; I don't know. But when it was brought back Hammond had it put outside—under one of the little colonnades that flank the carriage drive by the lower of the east terraces. And there I happened to be strolling one morning when an open car drove up and there got out a figure that was vaguely familiar to me. I was quite unable to place the fellow, but I knew that I had met him on some social occasion. He walked up to the meteorite, examined it, and then called out to a gardener who was working near by. I could hear his words distinctly. 'My good man,' he said, 'be so good as to find help and lift this large stone into my car.' I think now that the gardener too must have seen this fellow among the guests here at one time or another. Certainly he did what he was told without misgiving. Of course an authoritative tone would go a long way with him—particularly when the object in question would appear to him as without any special value. Be that as it may, the meteorite was hoisted in the car, and away its new owner drove." Mr. Collins took a sip of punch, as if to recruit himself after this long narrative effort. "And now, I think, Marlow will know what I am talking about, and can take up the tale."

"I suppose I can." Marlow, it seemed to Appleby, was looking at once enlightened and perturbed. "But I didn't, as Collins seems to have supposed, realise that the car was carrying off the meteorite. I just didn't notice it. In fact I didn't know about the meteorite at all. I'd never heard of it—and I suppose I'd never walked that way since it was put there. All I noticed—and the point is, of course, that I happened to stroll up and join Collins just as the car was driving away—all I noticed was who the driver was. Collins asked me. 'Do you know who that is?' he said, and pointed down the drive. And I told him. And after that, I think, we just talked of something else."

Mr. Collins nodded. "Precisely so. Marlow told me who this fellow was, and the information must have dissipated any misgivings I may have had. The meteorite held no interest for me, and I doubt if I thought of it again from that moment till the time that enquiries began to percolate through this afternoon. Little did I suspect that the fellow was carrying off something which would be used to murder this unfortunate Pluckrose."

Appleby stirred in his chair. "And the fellow was—?"

Mr. Collins smiled happily—very much the verbal artist by whom a notable effect of climax has been achieved. "Why," he said, "none other than Pluckrose himself. That's the odd thing."

9

Pluckrose had stolen the meteorite. Pluckrose had bashed Sir David Evans's bust. These were both eccentric proceedings, or perhaps—reflected Appleby—a better word would be bizarre. And all sorts of questions presented themselves. Had Marlow, despite his protestations, been aware of the meteorite and seen it go? Had the incident somehow come to the knowledge of Prisk, who had also been at Nesfield Court at the time? But Pluckrose himself remained the chief enigma. Was his conduct—or what had come to light of it—susceptible of any rational explanation? Or had the Vice-Chancellor been right? A thing to remember about professors. They go mad.

But now Marlow had risen to take his leave—Marlow who must be suspected of having attempted to murder or terrorise Prisk in a sort of passion of indignation over young Gerald. It was a motive; it was a real motive if one granted a certain instability in the perpetrator. A lack of balance. Well, the meteorite itself had finally shown that.

Appleby frowned into the flare and flicker of Mr. Collins's comfortable fire. When the mind began to offer such little jokes it was about time to shut up shop for the night. But the duke had gone amiably out with Marlow—perhaps he was feeling contrite over the curious trap he had endeavoured to construct—and Mr. Collins was preparing to offer further entertainment to his guests. In place of the exhausted punch he was setting out whisky and soda. And then he looked up wistfully. "I wonder," he said, "if we might venture on something a little more interesting? I know that whisky is a good deal drunk nowadays, but I must confess that I continue to associate it with farmers' dinners nevertheless. And since Mr. Appleby has gained such information as we can give may we not allow ourselves a little license?" Mr. Collins had now produced a set of large and beautiful rummers. "*Antehac nefas depromere Caecubum*"—or his chuckle was at once bibulous and agreeable—"but I think we might bring it out *now*." And he produced a bottle of old brandy.

In Nesfield the trams had long since ceased to rattle; in the cinemas the silver screens were as blank as the mind after an unremembered dream. The subterraneous apartment in which the learned had held their deplorably named symposium the night before was given over to rats and spiders and in his private hotel Professor Hissey, sandwiched between retired ladies and commercial gentlemen, burnt midnight oil over *Annotatiunculae Criticae*. . . . Appleby cupped his rummer between his palms and glanced from the cautious Hobhouse to the still morose Prisk. In the course of the afternoon Pluckrose had been buried—and on

161

his beautiful white head Sir David Evans had worn a beautiful black silk hat. And now here was this cultivated old parasite dispensing liqueur brandy amid Horatian chirpings while the Duke of Nesfield spent an uncommonly long time bidding farewell to Martin Marlow. The numberless goings-on, thought Appleby sleepily, of human life. The disreputable goings-on of Professor Prisk, the man with the two invisible bags. . . .

Appleby sat up. Among academic folk that second bag must necessarily stay invisible. Very little in the way of disreputable goings-on is allowed. A good dollop of open scandal and out you go. But Pluckrose had been a busybody and malicious. Supposing he had found out something extremely uncomfortable about Prisk's private life? There was more of the likely stir of human passion in this, Appleby saw, than in the hypothesis of literary forgery or the like that he had entertained earlier. Suppose Pluckrose, for instance, had got hold of the shady business of Gerald, or of something a little shadier. Might not Prisk have thought him better out of the way? Again it was a motive, although wholly a speculative one this time. Had Prisk, then, had the opportunity of murdering Pluckrose? For that matter had Marlow, or Church, or Hissey, or Sir David Evans, or Miss Godkin? Or— again for that matter—his grace the Duke of Nesfield? All this must be obscure until tomorrow. To-day had been given to the *Dramatis Personae*; tomorrow must be given to Time and Place. Where had they all been when it happened? Where, for instance, had the somnolent Lasscock been—Lasscock who liked equally the seclusion of the Wool Court and of Miss Dearlove's orchard? Appleby became aware of Mr. Collins looking at him anxiously.

Mr. Collins looked anxiously at Appleby and then anxiously at the brandy-bottle. "I hope," he said, "that it isn't beginning to lose its life? Of course, it's a great mistake to suppose that even a great brandy will last for ever. But what we have here—"

This would never do. Appleby hastened to offer expostulatory and appreciative noises. Whereupon Mr. Collins, brightening, made as if to replenish the rummers. "My dear professor," he said to Prisk, "will you have"—and for a fraction of a second his voice hesitated—"another cigar?" He opened a silver box. "What a pity that you are not spending the night here! But there will be a clear moon for your drive back."

Which was a tactful way, thought Appleby, of suggesting that Prisk's share in the computations had gone as far as was wise. And certainly if the man had to drive himself back to Nesfield he had drunk enough. Enough and to no useful purpose, Appleby added to himself. For silence had descended upon Prisk; he was giving nothing away—not even a modicum of miscellaneous philological information. Only Mr. Collins continued to talk . . . to Table-Talk . . . a mouse squeaking in a cathedral . . . Samuel Taylor Coleridge Table-Talking: there was a nice cartoon by Max Beerbohm called that . . . *Zuleika Dobson* . . . Tavender . . . the point about Sir David Evans's bust . . . the proceedings of Mr. Hammond of the British Museum, a person of scientific mind. . . . All this was mere reverie—and yet surely in it were elements purposively striving towards fusion. Appleby tilted his rummer and the last drop of brandy evaporated under his nostrils; it was time for Hobhouse and himself to go. But here was the duke back again and it was Prisk who was going while Mr. Collins continued remorselessly to discourse—on port, on Japanese drama, on fox hunting, on conchology, on tobacco, on the painters of the Umbrian school. Appleby sat back again, resigned. But obscurely he knew that through the long corridors and lofty saloons of Nesfield Court, that across its broad terraces and down its long avenues, that from mile upon mile of the deserted, moonlit ribbon of road linking it to the city something urgently beckoned. *Now.*

The duke was in the room again. "I wish," he said, "that I could find it in my heart to be anxious about our friend the professor. Even Marlow is anxious."

"Marlow is anxious?" Appleby, as he echoed the words, got briskly to his feet. "Marlow took care to draw your attention to his belief that Prisk had drunk too much to be safe driving a car?"

"He did—and it's possibly true. I feel now that I ought to have done something about it." And the Duke of Nesfield shook his head—but not, it seemed to Appleby, with any very convincing appearance of dismay.

"Marlow went off first?"

"Yes—on a motor bicycle."

"And then there was quite a pause before you came back here and Prisk went off in his turn. Do you happen to know, sir, if his car was under anybody's eye?"

"Not, I should think, all the time. Of course a man brought it round for him and waited until he drove away. But Marlow had then been gone—or presumably gone—for some time. And that any one should have had an eye on Prisk's car in the interval is unlikely on the whole." The duke was about to pour himself out a rummer of Mr. Collins's brandy. But he broke off when he saw that Hobhouse had risen too. "You feel that you must be after them?" he said. "Well, I understand your point of view."

"I'm blessed if I understand *his* point of view." Hobhouse spoke impatiently as the Chief Constable's car swept round the first curve of the drive. "It seemed to me he quite liked that young man."

"Marlow? I think he does. But he doesn't like Prisk. He wouldn't be broken-hearted to see Prisk liquidated—which is immoral, no doubt. And he doesn't think the guilt of two murders greater than the guilt of one—a debatable point." Appleby was peering ahead in the bright moonlight. "And I think he puts the whole thing to himself this way. If Marlow killed Pluckrose in mistake for Prisk then Marlow is done for. Life holds nothing more for him—except perhaps the satisfaction of getting the right man before we catch and hang him. But, if this theory of Pluckrose's death is all wrong, Marlow didn't think to murder Prisk *then* and won't start doing so *now*, however much he may dislike the man. In a way the duke may be said to be out to clear Marlow. He presents Prisk at his most odious and then provides a nice empty corridor or a deserted drive. And if Marlow *doesn't* take advantage—"

"It's perfectly outrageous!" Hobhouse's indignation drove him to brusque interruption. "It's—it's positively feudal!"

"Feudal?"

"He thinks his own law better than the king's. He exposes this Prisk to a fearful risk for no better reason

165

than that he's a—a person of immoral habits."

Appleby chuckled—but his eye never left the road in front of them. "I admit there is something of the arbitrary baronial court about it. And would he expose Prisk to such a risk if the Gerald in the affair had been his agent's son, or the rector's son, or the gardener's son? Feed your egalitarian indignation on that Hobhouse. But keep your eyes open meantime."

They drove through the moon-blanched park. The ancient trees—single, in clumps, in groves—had gathered their shadows compactly round them; it was like moving amid a great archipelago in which the sea was motionless and silvered and silent. Once they drew up short as a small herd of fallow deer crossed the drive in single file, mysterious on some nocturnal quest; once, low to the right, they caught a glimpse of the great mansion, elaborate as a doll's house in some millionaire nursery. And then the car came to a halt before the park gates. From the lodge a man and woman came out together to open them. And Hobhouse called out through a lowered window. The man came up to the car.

"What has gone through lately—in the last hour, I mean?"

"The gentleman on the motor bicycle, sir. And then a car."

"Much interval between them?"

"No, sir. The car came up before we had the gates shut again."

"Did you notice anything particular about the way it was being driven?"

"No, sir." The man's tone was decisive, discreet.

Hobhouse sat back and the car gathered speed through the chase. "Marlow ought to have been further ahead than that," he said. "Suppose that after saying good-bye to the duke he—"

"Quite so." Appleby was tired and slightly impatient. "But there might be nothing in it at all. He might just have stopped for a bit to look at the park, at the deer, at the house. Tell the man to drive faster. He's got a clear road."

"What about more deer?"

"They can't stray across here. Look at the ditches on each side of us; there's a sunken fence."

Hobhouse gave the order. "Not a very nice place for a spill. But we'll be on the main road presently. There's the Abbey . . . steady!"

The car had braked hard; It swerved and stopped. Just ahead of them to the left a dark mass filled the ditch and rose in silhouette above it like a crouching monster with pricked ears, ready to spring. A horse would have shied at the threat—and the Chief Constable's chauffeur had reacted in something the same way. "Gawd!" he said. "That's a nasty one." It was a motor car with its back wheels high in the air.

They climbed out and ran forward. The car was an open run-about with the hood down, and it had gone helter-skelter into the ditch. Down the centre of this ran a wire fence on slender ferro-concrete posts. One of these posts had gone right through the floor boards, so that the car was like a beetle turned upside down and wantonly impaled. And clear in the moonlight a few yards off, giving rather the effect of an amputated antenna or wing, lay the prone body of a man. Appleby scrambled down and turned the body over. "Prisk, all right," he said.

Prisk, supine, stared wide-eyed at the moon.

"Dead," said Hobhouse.

Prisk's lips moved. "Selenitic," he whispered. "Selenologist. Selenotropic. Selenograph."

The Chief Constable's chauffeur took off his cap. "Gawd," he said. "A furriner. And calling for his mother, if you ask me."

Appleby, with a hand beneath Prisk's shirt front, shook his head. "Just a little lunar philology. And he's not much hurt." Hobhouse's glance went wonderingly from Prisk to the wrecked car. "A close shave," he said.

"Umph," said Appleby.

10

Professor Hissey picked up the coffee pot. "Appleby, my dear fellow," he said, "will you have a little more coffee?"

"Please." Appleby pushed his cup across the table. "And will you tell me about Pluckrose and the Vice-Chancellor's bust?"

"Well, well!" Hissey took up a fish knife and jabbed it vaguely at his bacon and egg. "You are developing quite a zest for the anecdotal side of our university life, I can see. And, talking of zest, may I pass you the Worcester sauce?"

"No, thank you," said Appleby, and bit into his toast and marmalade. "And I don't know that it's just idle curiosity. Anything you can tell might help."

Hissey nodded thoughtfully. "Prisk," he said, "has made no headway with it. In fact, its origin is quite obscure. Except, of course, that it has something to do with an orange."

"Dear me, no. I am speaking of the word zest. It

appears to have come from Portuguese through the French. The affair of the bust had nothing to do with an orange; it might rather be said to have something to do with grapes."

"Grapes," said Appleby. "I see."

"Sour grapes." Hissey chuckled innocently at this witticism. "You see, a little time ago Prisk was elected a Corresponding Member of the Prussian Academy. And Evans rather thought it was a distinction that ought to have come to himself. It was a most amazing business, and there is no doubt that Evans made something of an ass of himself. Pluckrose, who, I am sorry to say, always liked to make a little trouble, maintained that this rivalry or whatever it may be called was seriously disrupting university business. He was talking in this vein at Mrs. Tavender's party. I expostulated with him—when, as it chanced, we were standing beside Evans's bust. And then the thing happened. 'I tell you,' he said, 'that the man is green with envy.' And at that he took the bottle from his pocket and smashed it over the thing's head. And there, in a manner of speaking, was Evans—as green as you please." Hissey picked up a tea spoon and stirred carefully at the air in the vicinity of his cup. "I suppose," he added thoughtfully, "that Pluckrose might be described as a somewhat eccentric person."

"I suppose he might. Indeed, he's appeared to me in that role once or twice already. But this takes the biscuit."

"The biscuit?" Hissey looked methodically round the table. "Ah—I follow you. And the colloquialism does appear justified. It was a fantastic thing to do. Of course, there may have been more to the Prussian business than I am aware of. You might ask Prisk."

"At the moment, unfortunately, Prisk isn't available. He had an accident in his car last night and is laid up with shock. We'll call it an accident at the moment. Actually, it looks as if someone had monkeyed with the steering."

"Dear me! There has been much practical joking about the place of late, as you have no doubt heard. But I should hardly think that anyone——"

"Quite so. It was much more like attempted murder. And the possibility is that when Pluckrose was killed it was really Prisk who was the intended victim. This affair of the steering gear was a second shot. Tavender, who appears rather an acute person, envisaged something of the sort. If at first you don't succeed, shy, shy again. Only this time it wasn't a shy with a meteorite. It was a quick twist or two with a spanner."

Hissey sat back and looked thoughtfully at Appleby. He reached himself a piece of toast and buttered it with unusual precision. "Has it occurred to you," he asked mildly, "to canvas any other explanation?"

"Inevitably." Appleby smiled. "It's my business to do just that. There's the possibility that the two affairs are quite unrelated. Prisk appears to be a person of somewhat irregular life——"

"You don't say so?" Hissey suspended operations on the toast in order to register decent distress. "I had no idea of it. Or no *clear* idea." He fell again to comfortable mastication.

"And that sort of thing can raise up enemies. Or there might be this much connection between the two affairs. The spectacle of one professor being violently dealt with might have suggested the idea of dealing similarly with another."

"You don't think it might be a political conspiracy?" Hissey looked very acute. "There has been so much persecution of the learned all over the continent—" Hissey broke off and suddenly looked more acute still. "Or it might have been Prisk himself!"

"Ah."

"Suppose him to have murdered Pluckrose. It would be greatly to his advantage to establish the supposition that he had himself been in reality the intended victim upon that occasion. Interpreted so, the perpetration of a second shy, as you call it, would virtually clear him. But that is not all." Hissey was waving his knife quite dramatically in air. "We must not overlook the possibility of yet further subtlety. Suppose that the meteorite found its true quarry but that Prisk was *not* the perpetrator. It is then possible to suppose that this attempt upon Prisk is an effort at confusing the trail. We are intended to spot the possibility of a guilty Prisk ingeniously clearing himself in the fashion to which I have just alluded. We are intended to go off down that blind alley." Hissey paused, decently solemn. Then he beamed irresistibly, much as if the conversation had turned to the subject of *Annotatiunculae Criticae.* "I can see," he said, "that in the field of criminal investigation there are the potentialities of much intellectual delectation. One's wits can really be very fully employed. It is quite a new light to me."

Appleby chuckled. "Don't you ever read detective stories, sir?"

Hissey looked quite blank. "Detective stories?" he asked. "But yes, of course. A species of fiction which I seem to remember that Merryweather was fond of. Or was it Grant?"

"A species of fiction in which there would be some logical connection between Pluckrose's meteorite and the Vice-Chancellor's bust. A beautiful world." Appleby sighed. "A meteorite green with moss and a Vice-Chancellor green with envy—"

"Envy?"

It was Hobhouse's voice which had interrupted. He had hurried into the little dining room and now sat down between Appleby and Hissey. "Envy? You mean green with funk. I've just made an early call on Sir David. I thought he ought to know at once about this attempt on Prisk. So I told him. And what do you think happened? The man went green with funk."

Appleby sighed. "Something to remember about Vice-Chancellors," he said. "They go green with funk."

"The plot thickens." Hissey took another piece of toast. "Is somebody going to drop a meteorite on Evans? A gory business. One is reminded of Shakespeare's line."

"Shakespeare?" said Appleby.

Hissey nodded placidly. "Making the green, one red."

Going down the steps of the hotel, Hobhouse took a handkerchief from his pocket and mopped his forehead. "That was a really nasty joke—that one about Shakespeare. Pluckrose was one red, all right. You wouldn't believe a human body held so much mess. I wouldn't trust a man who can trot out a thing like that."

"My dear chap, we're not going to trust anybody. And I'm not sure *Macbeth* wasn't rather apposite. Macbeth, you know, got into a bloody business al-

173

though he wasn't altogether that sort of person—and then he just had to keep at it. This affair may have a pattern rather of that sort. Do you think Hissey might have murdered Pluckrose?"

"Might?" Hobhouse grunted impatiently. "That's just the sort of thing we're going to give to-day to finding out. Who was where and when. But if you mean in point of character, I should say yes. A lot of horrid things have been done by just such mild-mannered little men."

"No doubt. But I don't myself quite see Hissey murdering Pluckrose. In fact, I don't as yet see any of them doing such a thing—except perhaps Prisk."

"There are one or two people we haven't met yet. Somebody called Murn, for instance; who was Pluckrose's assistant. Murn is apparently a much older man. Disgruntled, perhaps. There might be something in that." Hobhouse did not sound particularly hopeful. "Somebody must have done it, after all. Unless Sir David was right, and Pluckrose launched himself off the tower, meteorite and all."

"And then proceeded to complicate matters by a ghostly interference with Prisk's car."

Hobhouse grunted. "You know, I can't help feeling we were on to something with that young man Church—the one the old fellow badgered about Galileo."

"We had certainly struck on something there. But I think it may be something substantially irrelevant. Dig about in a place like this and all sorts of odd things will turn up. The point is to bury the incidental ones again quick, before they begin to smell. But I don't know that Church's affairs will do that. And it's possible that we may have to exhume them a bit further.

174

I mean, they mayn't be out-and-out irrelevant. I can see how they might just come in on the fringes of the case."

"The case?" Hobhouse was ponderously sarcastic. "Would you be calling it that, now? I think I'd rather call it the mystery. The Pluckrose Mystery." Unlike Grant—or perhaps Merryweather—Hobhouse had no relish for romanticised versions of his craft. "And here we are. We'll go up the tower. You ought to have seen this hoist and store-room and what not long ago."

"No doubt. But, do you know, I think I'd like to have another look at the Wool Court first? A peaceful spot in which to order one's thoughts." Appleby stopped to light his pipe. "On the Mysterious Affair at Nesfield."

Once more they were walking the gloomy corridors of the university; once more a scurry of students and whisking gowns was about them. "Bit of a racket somewhere," said Hobhouse and opened the door which gave on the Wool Court. "Well, I'm blessed! Did you say peaceful?"

The fountain played soothingly—but amid a whirring and clanking uproar from the engineering shops opposite. And Appleby chuckled. "Light!" he said. "Light on Lasscock. This is his favourite haunt here, you know. And something about it has been worrying me. Too quiet for him by half after Miss Dearlove's orchard. But with these lathes and drills and things going it must be just about right for him. Homely, so to speak. I can understand his dropping in for a snooze. And if he's sufficiently convalescent perhaps he's here now. I'd like you to meet him."

"There's somebody under the tower." Hobhouse

had to raise his voice. "But it's what's-his-name—old Galileo."

Professor Crunkhorn was standing much where the deck-chairs had stood. Had he been reclining in one he would probably have achieved greater physical comfort. For his neck was craned backwards and his gaze was directed severely at the top of the tower. "Amateur detective on the job," said Appleby. "Magnifying glass in one pocket and false whiskers in another. And no doubt he's already left us several lengths behind. Now we engage him in a little learned talk." They advanced upon Crunkhorn, their footsteps inaudible amid the banging and clanking from over the way. "Good morning," said Appleby. "Have you still got Galileo in mind, sir?"

Crunkhorn, it might have been said, started like a guilty thing upon a fearful summons. But this was no doubt the result of being roused from some deep scientific abstraction. "Galileo?" he asked; "ah, yes—to be sure. And how, we may ask, would he have regarded this affair of Pluckrose? How, that is to say, in its scientific bearings? He would have been interested to know that the meteorite weighs between one and two hundredweight. And he would have pointed out that all bodies falling near the earth gather speed downwards at a rate approximately equivalent to thirty-two feet per second in one second if there is no matter to obstruct their progress. Even the statical mechanics of Archimedes—"

Hobhouse, not very attentive to this abracadabra, was looking up at the windows of the tower and scratching his jaw. "I suppose," he interrupted, "that if somebody managed to balance the thing on the sill of that projecting window and then levered it off it would fall quite plumb to earth?"

"It would, of course, fall in what, for practical purposes, may be called a straight line. Provided Pluckrose's chair had been correctly placed—and a preliminary experiment with some small missile would insure that being so—then as a method of murder the thing was foolproof." Crunkhorn frowned. "But it is all very puzzling, nevertheless."

Appleby glanced curiously at the mathematician. "Puzzling?" he said. "It's puzzling from several angles."

"No doubt. The figure of speech is a poor one, as a moment's reflection on the nature of angles will show you. But the sense of your observation I am not disposed to question. Altogether"—and Crunkhorn, apparently feeling that he had been a shade pedantic, made a sort of dive after more familiar language— "the death of Pluckrose is a rum go."

"And you still think it may have been the result of a joke that miscarried?"

"I do. And I ought to add that I was uneasy lest it might be my colleague Church who was involved. He shows at times a streak of brutal humour which I deprecate. But on consideration I am fairly sure that actual practical joking is not in his line. There is a young man called Pinnegar who would be more inclined to that sort of thing."

"Prisk's assistant?"

"Yes."

"On good terms with Prisk?"

"I think not."

"In fact, a likely suspect?"

Crunkhorn looked unexpectedly distressed. "It appears to be my fate, Mr. Appleby, to suggest suspicions. And that is foreign to my intention. I merely feel morally obliged to mention anything of a possibly significant kind."

Mathematics and humbug, thought Appleby, don't on the whole go together. The chances were that Crunkhorn's profession was honest enough. And there were several directions in which he might help. "I wonder, sir, if you can make any suggestion on one very odd point? The meteorite turns out to be the property of the Duke of Nesfield. He bought it some time ago on the advice of somebody in the British Museum—presumably on the supposition that it might be of some scientific interest. And it was, apparently, subjected to expert examination. We may have to follow up all that. But the point at the moment is this: the person who made off with the thing from Nesfield Court was Pluckrose himself. Can you think of any reason why he should do that?"

"Distinctly not." Crunkhorn was decided. "I don't believe that Pluckrose himself had any interests of that sort. He was a man curious in numerous fields of knowledge, but anything he was interested in we invariably heard about. He was an inveterate talker and controversialist."

"Might the meteorite have some merely monetary value—contain precious metals which would make it worth stealing?"

"Almost certainly not. Gold, platinum or silver have never been found in such things except in minute quantities. Moreover this meteorite—at which I took occasion to glance yesterday evening—appears to be of the common stony sort; it is unlikely to have a high metallic content; it would be a good deal heavier if it had. But the physicists will be able to tell you more than I can; as you know, they have charge of it now."

Appleby nodded. Hobhouse, who had been staring glumly at the fountain, turned to ask a question. "It wouldn't be valuable or important just because of its size?"

"Dear me, no!" Crunkhorn was amused. "There is a meteorite in Mexico which is estimated to weigh over fifty tons."

Hobhouse sighed. "Well," he said, "you couldn't drop *that* on a man."

"I suppose not. But if one did—" Crunkhorn paused and frowned. "It occurs to me that there is just one thing that would make a commonplace meteoric stone of immense interest: the presence in it of organised matter."

Appleby looked up. "Life?"

"Precisely. Needless to say, plenty of them have been cut up and examined for anything that might suggest the existence of organic matter beyond this planet. But nothing of the sort has ever been found."

"I see." Appleby's voice was suddenly oddly detached and absent. For suddenly he found himself groping with his obscurest intimations of the case; with nothing less than the truth as it was already striving to constitute itself deep in his mind. Once before he had known this sensation in the Pluckrose affair— when Tavender's gnomic utterance on the "associations" of meteorites had recurred to him as he lay in bed summing up the evidence two nights before. Now he glanced from Crunkhorn to Hobhouse. "How did we know it was a meteorite?" he asked.

Hobhouse looked momentarily blank. "How? Well, before you came we had the professor of physics, and a lecturer in geology, and a man from the city museum—"

"But of course it's a meteorite." Crunkhorn joined in impatiently. "One has only to look at it—"

"*You* have only to look at it."

"Traces of the characteristic crust—"

"No doubt, no doubt." Appleby was pacing restlessly up and down. He turned to Hobhouse. "But to *you*, and to *me*—it's just a big stone. . . ." He halted, almost comically rueful. "I'm not sure I know what I'm talking about," he said.

Crunkhorn raised his eyebrows. Hobhouse gave a grunt which sounded distinctly disapproving, and turned as if to leave the Wool Court. Then he stopped. "Somebody's coming," he said.

They all looked at the door by which they had emerged from the building. It had gently opened. For a moment nothing further happened. Then something large, floral and shapeless appeared. It was a cushion. And after it placidly toddled a stout and comfortable elderly man.

"Lasscock," Appleby said.

Pluckrose's chair was represented only by slivers which had been too small for policemen to bother picking up. The second chair that had stood beneath the tower someone had removed to the side of the court. And towards this second chair Lasscock, leisurely and unheeding, ambled now. He dumped his cushion in it, picked it up and moved placidly towards the three watchers. To the regular hum and clatter of the engineering shops had now been added the intermittent scream of some species of grinding machine and the dull thud and reverberation of what might have been a steam hammer. Perhaps because this made audible speech too strenuous an affair—perhaps because he saw no occasion for utterance—Lasscock said nothing. He merely bowed politely, set down his chair directly under the tower, patted the cushion into place, produced from his pocket a copy of *The Times*, and settled himself comfortably in the sun. The engineering shops pulsed and banged; it was just ten o'clock and a bell rang loudly; through the high windows of the long corridor flanking the court on this side came a clatter and shouting of students hurrying from lecture to lecture. It was all uncommonly like Miss Dearlove's orchard. And Lasscock closed his eyes. Then, as if mindful always of life's minor courtesies, he opened them again; gave a second—and as it were valedictory—bow; closed them once more; and settled the open newspaper peacefully over his face. Lasscock had all the appearance of being asleep.

"Well I'm blessed!" Hobhouse, not previously familiar with the habits of Nesfield's learned version of the Fat Boy, stared in astonishment. Then his gaze travelled storey by storey up the tower. "Of all the spots to choose for a quiet nap." His voice was positively anxious—much as if he expected a second celestial visitation to come thundering down from one of the windows above. "And it's not very decent, either."

Hobhouse had perforce to speak loudly if his indignation were to be communicated at all. And Lasscock, deceptively somnolent, apparently heard. For his voice came mildly from behind the broad expanses of *The Times*. "My dear sir," it said; "come, come. Don't doubt you're a sensitive feller and all that. But no good runnin' after morbid associations. Pluckrose's death very distressin' thing. Dangerous to let it lie on the mind. What the doctors nowadays call traumatic. Don't intend to act as if it were any concarn of mine. And cartenly not goin' to be driven to fresh woods and pastures new."

"Humph." Hobhouse looked at Lasscock—or rather at the empty villas and mansions of *The Times*'s back page—with strong disapproval. "And do you always sleep here?"

"Sleep?" Lasscock's voice sounded mildly surprised. "Commonly come here to think things out—when I happen to have a little leisure." With Lasscock *leisure* rhymed still with *seizure*—which somehow gave the word a particularly leisurable feel. "Not that I intend to think out Pluckrose. Business of that Lunnon feller—and yourself, from the sound of you."

"It certainly is." Hobhouse was extremely indignant. "And may I ask—"

"Mornin'."

"I beg your pardon?"

"Mornin' to you."

And *The Times* crackled faintly, as to a long indrawn breath.

They climbed the rather narrow staircase which, apart from the hoist, was the only means of communication between the store-rooms of the tower. Hobhouse breathed heavily, but not altogether from the effort involved. "Disgraceful!" he muttered. "Levity, I call it. An historian, did you say? If only he were a material witness and we could get him in the box we'd see that he got history." Hobhouse put something like venom into this obscure threat. "'Mornin',' indeed!"

Appleby laughed. "But he is a material witness. He

was there, you know, all the time."

Hobhouse came to an abrupt halt. "You don't say so!"

"But I do. I'll give ten to one that he toddled into the university as usual—and afterwards bolted back to Miss Dearlove's and had his half-term chill prematurely, just trusting that no one would remember seeing him about. The thing happened under his nose. Or rather, in front of his *Times*. The distinction is important, I'm afraid."

"You mean—"

"I mean that he woke up in his accustomed deck-chair and there was Pluckrose pashed and pounded beside him. A nasty shock. Disturbin'. You might even say odjus. But he isn't going to let it lie on his mind."

"Well!" Hobhouse almost exploded with anger. "It's utterly scandalous. He's made himself an accessory after—"

"I suppose he has. His attitude is certainly one of extreme quietism. But apart from his determination not to be bothered with the business he told me what must be more or less the truth. I can remember his words. 'Somebody dropped a horrid great rock on him from the tower. And I don't know anything more about it.' If Lasscock was asleep that will be really all he knows. He has simply suppressed the fact that he was present, that he saw that Pluckrose was undoubtedly and horribly dead, and that he made himself scarce. Avoiding anything traumatic, you know."

Hobhouse had turned round. "It's a criminal offence," he said. "Come along. We'll nip down to town and get a warrant and have him detained."

"My dear man, you've been trying—very rightly—

to drag me up these stairs for a couple of days. Don't let us have any more dukes in the case, for heaven's sake."

"Dukes?" Hobhouse paused, bewildered.

"First the noble Duke of Nesfield and now the noble Duke of York. Marching us up to the top of the tower and marching—"

Hobhouse had turned round once more—resignedly. "Ahr," he said. "Fond of a bit of literature, aren't you?"

"Literature?" Appleby, climbing again, slapped his thigh. "That reminds me that I'd quite forgotten *Zuleika Dobson*. But I don't know that she's going to be so important, after all. *Pickwick Papers* is much more in the picture."

"*Pickwick*?" Hobhouse was suddenly curious. "I know that book like the back of my hand, Mr. Appleby."

"Then you must remember the famous occasion"—and Appleby dropped his voice to a facetious whisper. "You see?" he concluded presently.

But Hobhouse shook his head. "I don't see that it makes sense," he said. "And, what's more, I'll tell you this. I sometimes think you're a bit off it." He climbed in silence and then paused again with a slow grin. "It's Lunnon," he said. "That's it. Lunnon feller." He laughed immoderately.

"Thirty-nine," said Appleby.

"Eh?"

"Thirty-nine steps."

"Ahr. Literature again."

"Or say twenty feet. So the storey we're concerned with must really be a very pretty height. Higher than

184

it looks, somehow, from down below." Appleby looked round him. "But we'll begin our inspection here."

They had climbed from the ground floor of the tower to the first storey. Here the windows were still flush with the walls and the place was no more than a big, squarish box, bleakly white-washed and containing a scattering of miscellaneous lumber: piles of pails and mops, two parts of an extension ladder, several enormous blackboards and a stack of framed, life-size photographs—presumably of university graduates whose insufficient distinction had earned them this oblivion.

"It looks bigger than the room below," Appleby said.

"So it is. It occupies the whole area of the tower. But, down below, part of that area is taken in for the dark room; and the hoist is recessed off too. Here, as you see, the hoist is just part of the floor. And plenty big enough for that meteorite."

"It would take two of them." Appleby walked over to the hoist and cautiously stood on it. Flush as it now was with the floor, it looked like no more than a sort of trap-door—except that the corners of it ran on metal pillars which stood parallel with the sides of the tower until they disappeared through a hole in the roof. "Rather like the sort of thing they have in railway stations, except that it isn't railed off at all. If the hoist were down at the bottom and you were up at the top you'd have to mind your step."

Hobhouse nodded. "Illegal probably. And there has been some sort of protection which I suspect the porters have knocked away. Easier to manipulate things. And, of course, at this level the thing is hardly used

185

at all—just when they want to stow away a bit of sizeable junk."

"But it's quite a complicated, electrically-controlled affair. You'd think it hardly worth keeping in order."

"It's used quite a lot between ground floor and basement. You see, as well as opening on the ground-floor store-room it opens on the dark-room too. And from there they use it to send things down to a basement room to be washed."

"I see." Appleby looked up through the square hole in the roof above him. "And the hoist goes right to the top?"

"Right to the low top storey under the roof. The works are in the pitch of the rafters. But the windows in the top storey are quite tiny. So the one immediately above this is the business storey as far as we're concerned."

"Then up we go. And why shouldn't we go up on the hoist? Just like a god at the end of a play."

Hobhouse looked puzzled, doubtless because plays of this sort were outside his experience. "Well, I could send you up, or you me. But if we both stood on the hoist I don't think we could reach the switch."

Appleby moved to the middle of the little platform. "Well," he said, "so long." He saw Hobhouse hesitate and then cautiously turn the switch. The hoist quivered beneath him and rose quite smoothly. It was an odd sensation. For a moment he was poised midway between the two storeys, and then the hoist came to rest as part of the flooring of the upper one. Appleby looked about him. The first impression was obvious. The place contained lethal objects galore. Here, close by the hoist, was the cast-iron sink. And there, by the wall, were the safe and the deed boxes, and on the other side were the squat ferroconcrete pillars which the engineers, learned in the Strength of Materials, used for bashing things. The cannon ball was not immediately visible, but no doubt it was concealed somewhere amid the general litter of the room. And Appleby turned to Hobhouse as he came puffing up the stairs. "Plenty of stuff left. What about a little experiment on your friend Lasscock down below?"

"Do you really think—?" Hobhouse looked sorely tempted, but presently shook his head. "It wouldn't do, Mr. Appleby; it wouldn't do. He could bring an action. Of course if we were making notes over there by the window we might drop a pencil on him, just by mistake."

"But he may have a weak heart, and the shock might be too much for him." Appleby crossed the room. "This is the window overlooking the court? It juts out, all right; these turrets are quite sizeable. And so are the windows themselves. And they open easily. And the sill is no more than nine inches from the floor." Appleby was now peering out and down. "Would it be possible to mistake one man for another down there? I suppose it would, particularly if one were a bit worked up. But Lasscock is pretty unmistakable. There he is. *Times* and all."

Hobhouse peered too. "Trusting chap. How is he to know it wasn't a maniac, who might just slip up and do it again? I say—you don't think it may have been Lasscock himself? He might get quite a kick out of sitting there afterwards."

"For what it's worth, I don't think it was Lasscock. When the thing happened he was sitting within a couple of yards of where he's sitting now." Appleby turned back into the store-room. "Measured, photographed, finger-printed and all?"

"Yes."

"What about that sink? It's been moved recently; there's a fresh scrape on the floor."

"That's right. We photographed it just in case it should be important. And the moving certainly wasn't done by our men. By the way, there were patches of damp here and there on the stairs and quite a pool in one place. I wonder if that might fit in with the theory of a joke gone wrong? Drop the meteorite near some one and then empty a bucket of water on his head."

"Humph. Dangerous and silly, but not necessarily impossible on that account. But why the meteorite? That's the crucial question."

Hobhouse sat down on the safe and raised the index-finger of his right hand; he seemed primed for some considerable logical effort. "Pluckrose stole the meteorite. What does one do with stolen goods? Hides them. He hid it here, and a pretty job he must have had getting it to the hoist. Somebody took the meteorite and pitched it down on Pluckrose—another pretty job."

"Getting it from a car to the hoist wouldn't be too bad, because the outer door down below is right on a side street. But getting it up even to this low window sill"—Appleby glanced round—"well, there are boards and iron bars and things, so I suppose it could just be done."

"But the question is, as you say, why use the meteorite? The safe looks a bit handier. I think the answer is this—and it pretty well excludes the theory of a joke. There was a murderer and he thought he was killing somebody else—Prisk, say. And he used something Pluckrose could be proved to have stolen and hidden here because he thought that would serve to incriminate Pluckrose."

Appleby was again standing on the hoist, staring upwards through the hole in the floor of the final storey. "Anything at all up there?" he asked irrelevantly.

"Absolutely nothing. And windows through which you couldn't drop a football. It happened here, all right. Look at the scratches on the window sill."

"Quite so. And your theory might be called colourable. You say that at ground-floor level one can get at the hoist from the dark-room?"

"Yes—as well as from the lowest store-room we began in."

"Then the dark-room must be the key to the whole thing."

"Well, well!"

"Set about killing a man and the first thing you think of is speed, and an alibi. And here, apparently, is a dark-room with a maze on one side and a hoist on another. A hoist on which I've just made a quick and comfortable trip from one level of this tower to another."

Hobhouse looked very solemn. "Do you know, I think I can just see what you're driving at. Go on."

"The thing is to get up here quickly, drop the meteorite and get down again—all with something like an alibi if it can be managed. Well, you go into the dark-room with someone else. Then you send that someone else off on an errand which will take, say, just three minutes. Then you slip into the hoist—"

"It's masterly." Hobhouse was more solemn still. "But there's just one snag. All you could slip into the hoist from the dark-room is a cat. Or say a spaniel.

You see, the hoist was designed simply for the store-rooms. Making it communicate with the dark-room was an afterthought. And they simply knocked out a hole big enough for their bottles and what-not. To get *yourself* from the dark-room and onto the hoist you'd have to go down a long corridor, into the street, back to the lower store-room and through the door by which we came in. Which shows"—Hobhouse was now almost demure—"that there's something to be said for taking a look round. Or even"—now he was simply reproachful—"for studying that bit of plan I drew. I think it shows the lay-out clearly enough." He paused. "Of course, I don't say that going off to see Miss Dearlove and all that wasn't necessary. But at the same time—" Again Hobhouse paused—this time abruptly, and upon a glance at Appleby's face. "Dash it all!" he said. "You knew all the time."

"My dear chap, your plan is so excellent that it is quite clear about the spaniel or cat. But it would be a nice theory wouldn't it, if it would work? And I apologise for pulling your leg."

"Umph. Well, the cat-hole's a pity. And the dark-room's neither here nor there."

Appleby shook his head. "I wouldn't say that." From his pocket he produced Hobhouse's plan. "We know a little about the people concerned; their temperaments and their relationships. Now we've got to get them taped. We've got to get the times fixed and every one of them pinned down on this." He waved the paper. "And meantime we'll go down to the ground floor again—for a look around." He stopped. "Talking of times, what's the time now?"

Hobhouse looked at his watch. "Just on eleven." As he spoke a bell clanged from somewhere below.

Appleby had crossed again to the window overlooking the court. The clatter from the engineering shops had stopped; the familiar turmoil of students released from their lecture rooms came faintly up. And Lasscock was stirring, raising himself, folding up *The Times*. He got to his feet, tucked his cushion under his arm and toddled away.

Appleby chuckled. "Really quite a methodical old boy. Been thinking things out, no doubt on the largest historical scale. And now he's off to give his pupils the benefit of the results. And, like Bernardo, he comes most carefully upon his hour."

"Ahr," said Hobhouse.

11

Mr. Athelstan Murn, who had reached the university within a comfortable couple of hours of luncheon, disentangled his purple muffler from his venerable beard and hung it, together with his hat and coat, on the door of his room. Turning away from this familiar operation his eye was caught and held by an equally familiar framed photograph which hung above an untidy bookcase. The photograph represented Mr. Murn's late chief, Professor Pluckrose, dressed in full academic costume and posed elegantly between a microscope and a row of test tubes. Mr. Murn stood for some seconds looking very placidly at the photograph; then, very placidly, he took it from its nail, walked across the room, and dropped it in the waste-paper basket. And then, as if this performance in itself represented a creditable morning's work, Mr. Murn lit his pipe and sat down in a comfortable easy chair by the window. From here Mr. Murn (who, after some fifty years of test tubes and microscopes, had come to find a mature satisfaction in the idle contemplation of the vagaries of human conduct) was able to study not only the environs of the university together with such persons as haunted there but also the whole panorama of smoky Nesfield which lay below. In such unpretentious observation Mr. Murn in a green old age had come to feel that the sum of human wisdom must consist. He liked looking at Nesfield and feeling reflective; he liked looking at miscellaneous passersby and feeling inquisitive; he particularly liked looking at girls who were both virgin and nubile and feeling—that they were mildly pleasant to look at.

To these harmless—and even philosophic—proclivities Mr. Murn was promising himself a larger measure of indulgence in the future. The Pest—for it was thus that Mr. Murn had long privately designated his principal—had been brought to judgment; and a great deal of unnecessary scientific activity could now be abandoned.

And yet Mr. Murn at the moment was not altogether free of his new world. He was troubled in his mind. He was troubled, for one thing, about the dark-room. He was troubled about the curious popularity that the dark-room had enjoyed just round about the hour of Pluckrose's death. . . .

Hissey had, of course, used it on and off for years; he was well known as a textual scholar and an epigrapher; in the course of a copious correspondence with other learned persons he was constantly in need of photographic reproductions of this inscription and that. It was a pity that Hissey so obstinately believed in his ability to do the work himself; it meant mess, spoilt paper, and sometimes broken plates. Still, Hissey's pottering around the photographic rooms was always explicable. Young Marlow, however, was a rarer visitor; occasionally he persuaded the laboratory assistant to make him rotographs or photostats but he seldom tried to do anything himself. There, nevertheless, he had been. And there, too, had been Marlow's usual companion, Pinnegar. In fact, a regular cloud of witnesses—but witnesses of what? And Mr. Athelstan Murn, forgetting his morning's labour of surveying Nesfield, turned his eye cautiously in the direction of his desk. Several times he did this, and on each occasion an observer might have remarked that his gaze was more troubled than before.

Mr. Murn stroked his beard—and paused as if he suddenly found the action disconcerting. Or even—the observer might have remarked—dangerous. . . . Mr. Murn rose and made his way to his desk; his hand went out to a lowermost drawer; he hesitated and returned to his chair. He looked doggedly out of the window. Two girls with short and blowy skirts were crossing the road to the university refectory, and Mr. Murn ought to have been pleasantly interested in four calves, in the glimpse of a thigh. Mr. Murn's gaze, however, though dutiful was abstracted; presently it was back once more on the drawer; and in a very few seconds Mr. Murn was again on his feet. But this time it was towards the waste-paper basket that he moved. He stooped, retrieved Professor Pluckrose and restored him to his nail. He stood back to observe the effect. Very evidently it displeased him greatly. Nevertheless Mr. Murn gave a resigned sigh and returned to his chair. He had scarcely had time to seat himself when there was a knock at the door. "Come in!" called Mr. Murn. He contrived to put a surprising amount of cheerfulness into the injunction.

This was because Mr. Murn instinctively felt that his awkward moment had come.

"A great loss," said Mr. Murn. "A great loss to science. And, of course, a personal loss, as I need hardly add." And Mr. Murn directed a glance of great pathos towards a photograph of the late Professor Pluckrose which hung above an untidy bookcase at the other end of the room.

"Quite so." Appleby looked decently solemn. "In fact, I understand that Mr. Pluckrose was a man who greatly endeared himself to all with whom he came in contact?"

"Just that." Murn's hand moved towards his beard, but suddenly checked itself. "The thing could not be better put; not even in an obituary notice." For an incautious moment the late professor's assistant looked disconcertingly merry. "It has been a terrible blow." And Murn, going hastily to another extreme, took a handkerchief from his pocket and brushed away a venerable and manly tear.

"We are finding it necessary to make a pretty exact check on the movements of everybody who was in this part of the building when the thing happened. My colleague, Inspector Hobhouse of the Borough Police, is at work on that now." Appleby paused impressively. "But as you, Mr. Murn, were closely associated with the dead man it has occurred to me that you may be able to tell us a little more than just that sort of thing."

"Certainly—anything that I can do, of course. And I rather understand from what you say that the affair is still a mystery?"

"Still very much of a mystery. We have made a little progress here and there, but the circumstances are still extremely obscure."

"Dear, dear! I am sorry to hear it." Murn settled himself a little more comfortably in his chair. "For instance, nobody saw it happen?"

"Not so far as our present information goes."

"Nobody, say, saw the assailant's features at the window of the tower?"

"I'm afraid not." Appleby looked curiously at Murn, who was himself looking with an expression of some anxiety in the direction of his desk. "I believe there is one witness who might possibly have been in a position to do so, but it seems likely that his attention was engaged elsewhere. In fact, he was thinking something out."

"Ah. I have come myself to feel that too much analysis is a mistake. I am inclined to recommend the superior uses of contemplation. I am disposed to conclude that the contemplative life produces the better nervous tone."

"No doubt, sir. But I don't know that it would altogether serve in my profession. And perhaps you could tell me something about Pluckrose's relations with his colleagues. Could they, for instance, be described as uniformly cordial?"

"Cordial?" Murn's mind appeared to be elsewhere and he answered incautiously. "The man was a pest."

"I beg your pardon?"

Murn blinked. "I was about to say that Pluckrose was a Pestalozzian. That is to say, as a teacher his methods followed the system of the celebrated Zürich reformer. But that is perhaps scarcely relevant."

"I should say not relevant at all. Though interesting, no doubt."

"As for Pluckrose's relations with his colleagues, it must be said that they were occasionally clouded. Dear fellow though he was, you will understand. He had a passion for the advancement of knowledge—often of other people's knowledge. And that, of course, led to trouble from time to time. For instance, he quite upset Hissey over some temple in Tartary."

"A temple in Tartary?"

"Yes—just the sort of thing that was none of Pluckrose's business, one might say. A German archaeologist—by name of Munchausen, if I remember alright—discovered in some unlikely place a temple with Roman inscriptions. They evoked a lot of discussion—some, I believe, are at Cambridge—and Pluckrose maintained that the whole thing was a fraud. Hissey is quite a friend of this Munchausen, and he was most upset. And there have been a good many frictions of that sort—and others even yet more trivial. You have no doubt heard of the affair of Prisk and the telephone."

"The telephone Prisk and Pluckrose had to share? Yes, we've heard of that one."

"And I fear it must be said that Pluckrose—dear fellow though he was—occasionally fomented quarrels. As well, I mean, as getting personally involved in them. For instance, there was some ill-feeling a little time ago between Prisk and our Vice-Chancellor, Sir David Evans. It was over a little matter of some distinction conferred by the Prussian Academy."

"We have a note of that too."

"Well, Pluckrose, I fear, did something to exacerbate it. Principally, no doubt, because he dislikes Evans. Indeed, I may say that between Pluckrose and Evans there was some rather serious trouble."

"Can you tell me what it was about?"

Murn looked quite uncomfortable. "It is really a most delicate matter. Or perhaps I ought to say a most indelicate matter. Among young men—yes. But when it comes to elderly men of not undistinguished position—"

Appleby stared. "Good Lord! You don't mean to say it was a woman?"

"I fear it was just that." Mr. Athelstan Murn glanced out of the window. "In fact, one might say it was a *girl*. I am myself strongly of the opinion that one ought not to get mixed up with them. Have a good look at them—yes. But when it comes positively to—"

"I see. Certainly a great deal of trouble would be avoided if you could persuade people to your point of view." Appleby paused. There had recurred to his memory the masterly insinuations of Miss Dearlove. "You really mean to tell me that Sir David Evans and Professor Pluckrose were at loggerheads over a girl?"

"Well, yes. Since you more or less asked me, you know." Murn looked quite reproachful. "Of course, it isn't very generally known. It just so happens—In fact, Miss Godkin could tell you more about it than I can. If you cared to approach her on such a topic. Though I suppose that sort of thing is just in your line."

"Miss Godkin!" Appleby was startled. "You don't mean to say that this girl was a *student*—a student in that lady's hostel, St. What's-its-name?"

"St. Cecilia's. But it is not, seemingly, quite as bad as that, I am glad to say. The young person has been living at St. Cecilia's, but she is not a student at the university. She is a German girl, temporarily under Miss Godkin's care." Murn paused. "And an absolute stunner."

"I beg your pardon?" Appleby was, if anything, more startled still.

"You should see her legs." Murn settled comfortably back in his chair. "And her—her bust."

"Dear me. An alluring girl, plainly." Suddenly Appleby chuckled. "*Zuleika Dobson!*" he exclaimed.

Murn shook his head. "I think not. I believe her name is Else Schmauch."

"No doubt. But Zuleika Dobson was a girl about whom a whole university went crazy. Would you say that something of the sort was the position here?"

"Fräulein Schmauch has certainly caused something of a sensation. Though I must say that her conversation—"

"So you know her?" Appleby looked sharply at Murn.

"As an acquaintance, my dear sir. Occasionally I dine with Miss Godkin in the hall at St. Cecilia's. There are—um—some interesting frescoes at which I am always glad to have a look. And I have met the young person in that way."

"May I ask if *you* have been at loggerheads with anybody over her?"

Mr. Murn, thus suddenly attacked, made an agitated grab at his beard—and promptly let it go, much as if it were a bunch of nettles. "My dear sir—"

"You have given me a number of facts, any or all of which may be valuable, which in effect suggest a number of possible motives for the crime which has occurred here." Appleby looked at Mr. Murn in the friendliest way. "I wonder if any of your colleagues,

199

equally obliging, could volunteer information on any little frictions in which you yourself have been involved?"

Appleby, thus rounding upon Murn, was doing no more than follow in a routine manner the unpleasant necessities of his calling. He had no reason to suppose that this elderly spectator of the human scene had any further secret to unfold. It was surprising, therefore, as well as gratifying that Murn should now throw his hands above his head in a gesture of despair. "I called him a viper!" he exclaimed. "Dear, delightful fellow that he was, I called him a horrible viper."

Very gravely, Appleby shook his head. "This is bad, Mr. Murn; this is bad, indeed."

"There had been a little misunderstanding over a piece of biochemical research in our department. I had been given to suppose that we were regarded as at work upon it jointly. And then Pluckrose—dear, impetuous fellow that he was—communicated the results to a scientific journal without making any mention of my name. Most unhappily, I was aggrieved. And I called him a viper."

Appleby produced a notebook. "And what is a viper? Something that one crushes, I should say."

Murn groaned. "And that was what I said. You have no doubt heard all about it. Several of my colleagues were present at the time. I told him that he was a viper whom it would give me great pleasure to crush beneath my heel." Murn groaned again. "How unfortunate it has all been! How it has spoilt the whole affair!"

"My dear sir, Pluckrose is dead. It is a beautiful fact." Murn was now looking at Appleby with a sort of open-eyed innocence that was extremely convincing. "I have dreamed of it for years. And now it is all spoilt by this terrible anxiety. By this fiendish plot to accomplish my ruin. You are *sure* nobody was seen at that turret window?"

"Naturally I can be sure of nothing of the sort. But so far no evidence of the kind has turned up."

With an agility surprising in so ancient a person, Murn sprang to his feet and moved towards his desk. "I will confide in you," he said—and opened a low-ermost drawer. "I have here an—an object which I discovered secreted in the dark-room shortly after Pluckrose's body had been found. Its significance I shall leave you to determine."

And Mr. Murn stooped, withdrew something from the drawer, laid it on top of the desk, and stepped back. Appleby advanced, stared—and then swung round much as if he suspected Mr. Murn of having performed a theatrical trick. Mr. Murn however was exactly as he had been before.

Again Appleby turned to the desk. What lay on it was a large, a white, a venerable beard.

Appleby picked up the beard and examined it minutely. "You say you found it?" he asked.

"In a cupboard in the dark-room. I'd hardly be likely to *buy* a beard, you know." And Murn managed to contrive a momentary appearance of mirth. "But it's extremely upsetting in the circumstances, you must agree."

"I think it's extremely interesting." Appleby had produced a magnifying glass and was giving an exhibition of the most orthodox criminal investigation. "There's dust on it—and if it's the same dust as is in the cupboard that will go a little way towards substantiating your story." He looked up. "And I may say that this is about our first clue—of a tangible sort such as one could thrust under the nose of a jury. This and a photograph of a scratched floor and a cast-iron sink. Would you mind coming along now and showing me just where you discovered it?" They moved towards the door. But before Pluckrose's photograph Appleby paused. "Did you see the body?" he asked abruptly.

Murn jumped. "The body? No. That is to say, I wasn't asked—"

"It didn't look like that any longer. Come along."

Murn made a distressed noise and followed Appleby from the room. They turned right and went down the corridor; through the high windows on their left light seeped in from the Wool Court. "By the way," said Appleby, "you know the fountain out there, Mr. Murn? It was full on when the body was discovered. Is that usual?"

"Decidedly not." Murn seemed to welcome this request for collaboration. "The fountain was designed for a much larger space, and was moved to the court when we built the new library. Turning it full on would make the devil of a mess."

"Which is more or less what happened. Can you think of any reason why?"

Murn considered. "I think I can. As you know, the engineering shops are opposite, and there are people working there most of the morning. I don't think the court can be observed from there, because of the arrangement of the windows. But it is possible—" He paused. "Perhaps we might step out and see."

They turned left down the next stretch of corridor, passed the problematical dark-room on their right, and went through the door which opened on the Wool Court.

Murn stroked his beard with something like renewed confidence. "Yes," he said, "it is rather as I thought. The engineers, you see, have one door giving on the court; it is over there by the corner opposite the tower. I believe it opens on what is called the forge room, which is very little used. But it is always possible that somebody might be about there. And if you wished to screen this opposite corner from observation you might do worse than simply turn the fountain full on. The valve is no doubt somewhere close by."

"You don't know just where?"

Murn started at the abruptness of the question. And then he smiled. "Mr. Appleby," he said, "I come from Norfolk. And I will answer you in the dialect of that county. You can't patch it on me. Beard or no beard, you can't patch it on me."

"It looks rather as if someone else is trying to patch it on you. And we might try a little experiment. You might stand down here and I might put on the beard and go up to the turret window. And you might decide how much I looked like you."

"I think you had better get someone else to decide." Confession and this little matter of investigating the fountain appeared to have soothed Murn's nerves; he glanced placidly up at the tower, placidly down at the spot where Pluckrose's chair had stood, and then led the way back into the corridor. They turned right and stopped before the second door. "I suppose, Mr. Appleby, that you know the lie of the land. This is called the photographic room, and the only entrance to the dark-room is off it to the right. And on the other side is Pluckrose's private laboratory—which is not, of course, the same thing as his private room. That is further up the corridor, just beyond the telephone he shared with Prisk. I don't expect there's anybody here."

They went in. The photographic room was long, narrow and lined with benches, sinks, shelves and cupboards. At the far end of the left-hand wall was a door leading to the private laboratory, and opposite this was a doorless aperture which was presumably the entrance to the maze. Murn was mistaken as to the room's being untenanted; at a small table sat Hobhouse taking down a statement from a white-coated laboratory assistant. This piece of business had apparently just concluded, for the man now rose and went out by the laboratory door. Hobhouse looked from Appleby to Murn—and from Murn to the false beard which Appleby still carried in his hand. "What you might call emergency equipment?" he asked.

Appleby nodded. "Emergency equipment for somebody, undoubtedly. This is Mr. Murn, and he is going to show us where he found the beard in the dark-room. How are things going?"

"Not badly, not badly at all. The information is coming together." Perhaps for the benefit of Murn, Hobhouse spoke in a peculiarly weighty and knowing manner. "I think I've got down the movements of most of the people concerned, and no doubt Mr. Murn will give an account of himself presently."

"Delighted," said Murn. "Anything that will assist in tracing Pluckrose's assailant. Poor, dear fellow that he was." And Murn looked solemnly from Hobhouse to Appleby and stroked his beard.

"Pinnegar is another gap so far." Hobhouse was

consulting his notes. "He's made off to London. Not, though, in anything that can be called an irregular way. He was due to do some work there, and he has leave, and he's left his address—a hotel near the British Museum. And, talking of the Museum, we put a call through to that Hammond, who made the duke buy the meteorite. The thing fell in a farm-yard in Lancashire a couple of months ago and just missed a yokel. So you might say that Pluckrose was its second shot. And then this Hammond made the duke pay the farmer something for it—though whether it was legally the man's property I don't know—and it was examined in various ways and found not to be of much interest to anybody. So it went back to Nesfield Court and lay about there until Pluckrose pinched it."

"Pluckrose pinched it? How extremely odd." Murn was clearly delighted with this piece of intelligence. "You know, that is what is so disappointing about science: everything follows in the dullest way from something else. Whereas when you get among folk you find a universe full of surprises. Not that I approve of becoming at all involved; the thing should be treated as a spectacle merely."

"We'll hope you're not involved in *this*." Hobhouse emphasised the repartee by pointing his pencil sternly at Murn. "Perhaps you will tell us what you were doing between ten-fifteen and eleven-thirty on Monday morning?"

Appleby interrupted. "Those are definitely the times?"

"Yes; I'm pretty sure of them now. Pluckrose lectured from nine to ten, and then saw a couple of students in his room. One of them had to run to get to another appointment at ten-fifteen. Nobody admits to having seen Pluckrose after that. And the other time is pretty well fixed too. A porter was going along the corridor here and thought he heard rather a loud swish of water. So he stuck his head through the door and there was the fountain full on. He went into the court and there was the body. He looked at his watch and it was just eleven-thirty."

Appleby nodded. "I've a note of all that."

"He went straight to the head porter, who rang for a doctor and the police. And as soon as he'd done that he looked at his clock and booked the thing. I've seen the entry: *Eleven thirty-four—accident in Wool Court.*"

"Businesslike. But seventy-five minutes is quite a long period to cover."

"That's so. But we shall probably narrow it down when we've made a certain gentleman talk."

Hobhouse said this with such a dark look at Murn that Appleby felt obliged to explain. "I may say that Hobhouse means Mr. Lasscock. There is some reason to suppose that Lasscock was there in the court, and was just waking up, perhaps, from his morning nap when the meteorite came down."

"God bless my soul!" Murn was really astonished. "But what has Lasscock to say about it?"

"Merely that he didn't come to the university at all on Monday. But we suspect that he is merely avoiding what he regards as involvement in something tiresome." Appleby looked ironically at Murn. "I mention all this—despite Inspector Hobhouse's obvious disapproval—because of what you say about involvement yourself. You seem to be somewhat of Lasscock's mind."

"I hope I should not keep clear of anything at the

expense of positive mendacity." Murn, who had recently built up so elaborate a picture of his fondness for his late colleague, wagged a virtuous beard. "And, as it happens, my answer to the original question is extremely simple. I was in the dark-room there on Monday morning from before ten o'clock until the news came to us of the accident. And I fancy that Atkinson, the lab man to whom you have just been talking, can substantiate that. It was his business to be here in the photographic room throughout the period concerned. And of course the only exit from the dark-room is by the maze and through this room."

"Except," said Appleby, "for a little opening to the hoist. And were you alone in the dark-room, Mr. Murn?"

"Dear me, no. There was a number of people there from time to time. And I rather fancy that Graves, the second lab man, was there continuously. Though often one doesn't much notice other people in the low violet light."

Hobhouse tapped his notes gloomily. "All that seems straight enough. Mr. Murn was in there all the time, all right—except that he went along to the refrigerator once or twice. And either in there, or in this room we're in now, were several of the others at one time or another. This Atkinson is pretty sure of himself on all that. Funny thing, really. These two rooms seem to have been quite a focus for the people concerned. Hissey, Marlow, Pinnegar, Tavender— though Tavender was after it was all over—pottering about for one reason or another. And Atkinson noticing all their comings and goings here, and Graves more or less aware of them in there"—and Hobhouse jerked his head towards the dark-room—"as if the whole thing was a kind of scientific apparatus for man-ufacturing alibis."

Appleby laughed. "Perhaps it was. Take Mr. Murn here. You say he slipped out now and then to the refrigerator—"

"For certain volatile fluids," said Murn placidly.

"No doubt. But if I go regularly to the refrigerator and it regularly takes two minutes, then to an Atkinson not positively attending to the matter six or even eight minutes will still register as two minutes. That's psy-chology."

Murn chuckled. "But not evidence. It wouldn't do to put under the nose of a jury, as you phrase it. Though I'm not sure it doesn't make me feel rather uncomfortable, all the same."

"There are all sorts of other possibilities." Appleby was crossing the room towards the maze. "This dark-room appears to be a sort of box. Always distrust boxes. You know the sort that is securely roped round each way, so that it appears impossible to open it? But one of the sides is really a sort of revolving door, with the rope as axis. And out the lovely lady crawls and—hey presto!—the box is empty." Appleby made a gesture in air. "And now, in we plunge. Mr. Murn, this is one of Hobhouse's big moments. He's per-suaded me to go places again. Instead of wasting time chatting with irrelevant persons like yourself."

"Have a care, Mr. Appleby. Right, left, right and left will take you in. But I advise you to feel your way."

Appleby had already taken one turn into the maze; he took another and found himself in pitch darkness. "And it was here that somebody hung up a skeleton?"

"Just half-way through." Murn's voice came from

close behind. "And painted with some sort of luminous paint. An extremely juvenile prank, such as one might read of in a school story. But I must say it gave me rather a turn."

"You came upon it first? What did you do?"

Murn laughed—and the noise bumped oddly about the little labyrinth they were threading. "I got Atkinson and Graves out of the way so that they wouldn't deprive Pluckrose of the benefit of the experience too. He gave a most heartening yelp when he walked into it."

"I suppose he was annoyed?"

"Extremely. And his reaction, as so often with him, was markedly eccentric. Most people believe that young Roger Pinnegar is responsible for the pranks that have been taking place. But Pluckrose insisted that the skeleton had been hung up here by the Vice-Chancellor."

Appleby came to a halt in the darkness. "By Sir David Evans! What an extraordinary notion."

"It is certainly not a fashion in which elderly philosophers are expected to behave. But it was Pluckrose's habit to maintain that Evans is slightly unbalanced."

"I understand that Sir David on his part believes something of the sort about professors in general." Appleby had now emerged into the dark-room. Nothing, however, was visible; the place seemed to be dark indeed. "Do you think that Pluckrose really—"

"I hardly think he could truly have supposed that Evans did it. But, of course, he may have connected it up in his mind with the somewhat delicate relationship existing between Evans and himself."

"In the matter of the fair Fräulein Schmauch? That's

another matter that really takes a little swallowing. Hullo—there's some light here after all." The outlines of the dark-room were beginning to emerge in a sort of low violet glow; it was an affair of sinks and benches, booths and cubby-holes, apparently so designed that a number of people could work independently at the same time. The place made a beautiful centre, Appleby thought, for the sinister game of hide and seek which it began to seem as if the Pluckrose business might have involved. "I suppose your eyesight accommodates quicker to it with practice; I'm only just beginning to see a thing."

"It's not really at all a bad light." Murn was now standing beside Appleby and Hobhouse was just emerging from the maze. "You can see most things, without much strain on the eyes. Now, over here is the cupboard I was speaking of. An empty cupboard—"

But Appleby had moved to the farther side of the room. "And this is the hatch that gives on the hoist?" He was peering at a small aperture in the wall, closed by a sort of sliding door or shutter. "It's most inconveniently small; I should say little more than a foot square."

Murn nodded. "I fancy they were afraid of light seeping in from the shaft. It's big enough for the few things we send downstairs from time to time. And there's the switch: a button for up and a button for down. But now, about this cupboard where I found the beard—"

"Talking of the beard," Hobhouse interrupted; "there you have one thing the hatch is big enough to take. You could send the beard down—or up."

*   *   *

Appleby had been moving towards the cupboard with Murn; now he turned back. "My dear man, what an astonishing perception. The beard goes up. And where does that lead us?"

"Presumably to the store-room again." Hobhouse, perching himself on a stool, raised his expository finger. "A fake Mr. Murn comes into the dark-room here. He sends the beard up the tower. He emerges, no longer a fake Mr. Murn. He goes up there himself and becomes a fake Mr. Murn again. He sends the beard down once more, returns to the dark-room, again not a fake Mr. Murn. He retrieves the beard and leaves the dark-room—"

"Again as a fake Mr. Murn." Appleby turned to the venerable figure of the late Pluckrose's assistant. "And now you know, sir, how the police mind works."

"I must admit it is a beguiling theory." Murn had grasped his own beard, rather as if apprehensive that it too might be whisked magically into the hoist. "Only I'm not sure that the procedure which Inspector Hobhouse suggests isn't needlessly elaborate. Surely the person whose mysterious activities he is sketching could simply put the beard in his pocket and take it to the tower that way."

Hobhouse shook his head. "It's a big beard; a fine beard, if one may venture to say so. And it would crush it badly to stuff it in a pocket; Spoil the effect of the subsequent disguise. If there was really some plot to display somebody like Mr. Murn as pitching down the meteorite from that window I do think there may be something in my idea. I wouldn't say that I see the thing quite clearly"—Hobhouse's voice was appropriately modest—"but I fancy that something might be worked out."

"I don't think you are allowing yourself a big enough cast." Appleby, who had laid the false beard down on a bench, took it up again and peered at it seriously in the dim light. "I rather sustain Mr. Murn's objection about the pocketable nature of the thing: I doubt if it would be much the worse ten minutes later. But if you suppose *two* people engaged in some plot to impersonate Mr. Murn—"

"Dear me!" Murn amiably chuckled. "I can scarcely envisage myself as enjoying such popularity."

"If you imagine two people with a beard between them, then this little entrance to the hoist might be uncommonly useful."

"But wouldn't two people provide themselves with two beards?" Hobhouse was extremely serious. "If you had a job of murder on hand, a little extra expense—"

Appleby threw the beard down on the bench again. "The whole thing takes on the air of a theatrical farce. People disguised as each other bob ceaselessly in and out of the wings. Let's hope it's a tolerably well-constructed show."

"I doubt it." Hobhouse shook his head gloomily. "Too much material, if you ask me. The Vice-Chancellor's bust, and the young man you say is a bigamist, and this beard business, and Prisk and his car, and grudges about the duke's grandson or the Prussian Academy or Zuleika What's-her-name—well, it will take some pulling together."

"No doubt. But Mr. Murn wants to show us his cupboard."

Murn nodded. "An empty cupboard, to which I happened to go on Monday afternoon. And there was the beard—and nothing else."

"Exactly," said Appleby. "No question of too much material in this case."

"I opened it and put in my hand, intending to make sure of a space on which I could store some plates." And Mr. Murn opened the cupboard door and suited his action to his words. "What was my surprise—"

Mr. Murn's voice faded; in the dim violet light he stood transfixed. And then, very slowly, his hand emerged again. It clutched not one but two large, white, venerable beards.

12

Hobhouse, with a bundle of false beards under his arm, closed the door of the photographic room behind him. "I rather fancy that dark-room," he said. "You know where you are with it. Rather a pity Pluckrose wasn't killed in there, if you ask me."

Appleby shook his head. "It's a box," he repeated. "Always avoid murders in boxes. Unless the lid is off, mark you."

"And would you say the lid is off here?"

"Decidedly. The setting isn't of what you might call the insulated type. The victim isn't shut up in a box with just so many people, one or more of whom must be responsible for the crime. Pluckrose may have been killed by any one in Nesfield; he may have been killed by the Man in the Moon."

"Quite a likely suspect, if you come to think of it." And Hobhouse smiled, much pleased with this bold stroke of fantasy.

"So we have simply to take the likeliest people as

the objects of our first enquiries. And if that is no go then the less and less likely. Until we are checking up on the Bishop of Nesfield and the Lord Mayor of Nesfield—"

"And the Duke of Nesfield. And then we retire on our pensions and hand our notebooks to our successors. Meanwhile—"

"Meanwhile we are talking of boxes. And on our way to inspect a small specimen just down this corridor. Between Prisk's room and Pluckrose's. And here it is. I wonder if it's a regular thing to have two men share a telephone in this way?"

Hobhouse nodded. "Apparently it is. There are quite a number of these little boxes about the place. And all locked, so that the instruments can't be used by just anybody passing along a corridor."

"What sort of locks?"

"Quite rubbishing. And one key is likely to fit a good many boxes."

Appleby tried the door of the little box on the wall. "Locked now. And what about the switch-board operator?"

"She knows where any call comes from. At the time and so long as she remembers, that is. Naturally no record is kept of calls within the house system." Hobhouse fished out a notebook and thumbed it over. "On Monday morning the girl remembers just two calls on this machine. She's hazy as to the times, but she knows they were both before the fuss of Pluckrose's death. The first was a call to this machine; somebody ringing through for Prisk. She doesn't remember where the call came from, and she doesn't remember recognising the voice."

"Somebody ringing through for Prisk? That means

she would give two rings, and then pause, and then two rings again until there was an answer, or until it was evident no one was going to reply?"

"Just that."

"Does the girl remember Prisk answering?"

"She remembers that somebody answered, but she doesn't remember if it was he."

"And whether the call was answered quickly or not?"

"She doesn't remember that either."

Appleby tapped thoughtfully at the little locked box. "Well, the possibility of error is clear. Pluckrose, say, is here at the open box, and about to make a call. The thing rings—the first of two rings for Prisk. But Pluckrose picks up the receiver impatiently or absent-mindedly, and if the message is brief and clear may suppose it to have been for himself."

"Quite so. And there's a point in favour of that idea which we didn't know of when we considered it before. The second call in which this instrument was involved was a call *by* Pluckrose, so it may have been the one he was about to make when the bell rang. And it was to the Vice-Chancellor." Hobhouse paused and it was clear that he had something remarkable to communicate. "Only the Vice-Chancellor denies it. Well, aren't you surprised?"

"I don't know that I am." Appleby looked soberly at his colleague. "You know, Sir David Evans is in this thing. Whatever we may think of the scandalous story of him, Pluckrose and a woman—or girl—"

"Is there a difference?"

"There is to Murn's mind. Anyway, I say Evans is in the affair. Hence his extraordinary performance

216

when we interviewed him. And hence, no doubt, his subsequent funk."

"The funk followed on his hearing of the attempt on Prisk—if it was that. When I saw him again about this telephone business he was just short with me. Rather like Lasscock. Mornin' to you."

"Lasscock's turn is coming. A full and free confession from that eldest son of Morpheus is badly overdue. But about this call: the girl is quite sure?"

"She's in a bit of a stew now that Evans denies the thing. But quite clear all the same. There was a call to Evans through this machine—"

"He takes his own calls direct?"

"Not normally. But on Monday his secretary was away ill and nobody had been put in her place. So the call—if there was a call—went straight through to him. Somebody asked for the Vice-Chancellor from this instrument and was put through. Evans said 'Sir David Evans' and this somebody said 'Pluckrose here.' And then the girl plugged out."

"She's sure it was Pluckrose?"

"No, she's not. It's an interesting thing. She's sure of Evans. But she's not sure about the voice at the other end. It's worth noting that, I think, when you consider that the voice said 'Pluckrose here.' Even if she hadn't recognised his voice at the time you'd expect her, when recollecting, to think she had. That's psychology, as you might say. But I'd prefer a few finger-prints myself. And I'm having a man along to look for them on the telephone presently."

"And then?"

"Well, of course we can't go about like story-book sleuths demanding impressions from all and sundry; it would pretty well cost us our jobs. But perhaps, at this stage, we can pick up a few from people's personal property on the quiet. Now, Pluckrose's and Prisk's apart, whose prints would you like to hear of inside this box?"

Appleby considered. "Marlow's," he said. "Marlow's or Pinnegar's."

"And now we come to times and places." Hobhouse, who seemed quite contented to turn the corridor into a police bureau, leant against the telephone box and again thumbed his notebook.

"And distances. For instance, if Evans got a telephone call from here asking him to come over to Pluckrose's room, just how would he do it?"

"He would have to come right round the building." Hobhouse considered. "No. He could cut through the engineering department and across the court through the door of what's called the forge room. And then through the door in the corridor here."

Appleby nodded. "It looks as if a time factor may be important, so that we have to look out for all that. You say that you've got most of the people pretty well taped?"

"Not too badly." Hobhouse produced a loose sheet of paper. "I've got them between ten-fifteen and eleven-thirty. And if we find that Lasscock can time the thing more or less to the minute we'll be not too badly off. Though, mind you, I've no information on the movements of the Man in the Moon."

"We can consult a nautical almanac." Appleby took the paper from Hobhouse. "It simply covers the people who seem to have been most in the picture?"

"Just that. Pluckrose first. And then the rest in alphabetical order. And even if the criminal is an unknown X we shall be working towards him by eliminating these."

Appleby took the list and studied it.

Pluckrose, Henry Albert. Lectured from nine to ten; manner normal. Saw students in room till ten-fifteen; manner normal. Subsequent movements unknown.

Church, Timothy. Tutoring in his room till ten fifty-five. Alone in room till eleven-ten. Tutoring again till eleven fifty-five.

Crunkhorn, Richard Meredith. Spent entire morning undisturbed in own room. No confirmation available.

Evans, Sir David. Arrived at university shortly before ten. Secretary absent. Visited by professor of philosophy at ten-five; interview over ten-twenty. Claims to have remained in his own room until shortly before eleven. Then decided, as is customary with him, to go over to refectory for cup of coffee. On his way strolled about for some minutes enjoying mild sunshine. Owing to warmth of day returned to own room to change coat. Then went direct to refectory, where observed about eleven-fifteen. Stroll authenticated by porter, who glimpsed Sir David returning to main building; vague however as to time. Remained in refectory until joined by Hissey (see below).

Hissey, Stanley Rutgersius. Consulting with librarian till ten-twenty (confirmed). Returned to hotel for book (no confirmation yet). Remembered book not at hotel but university. Returned to university. Remembered some prints left in dark-room. Went into photographic room. Asked Atkinson the time, as he had an appointment at eleven-ten. Atkinson said time ten-fifty. Went into dark-room. Found Graves developing some of his plates. Remained helping till eleven twenty-five. Then remembered appointment and was about to leave when news came of Pluckrose's death. Took news to Sir David Evans in refectory; then returned to own room.

Lasscock, Theodore Almeric de la Tour. Claims not to have been at university at all. Failed to meet first class of the day at eleven, or to send note of his absence. If he arrived about ten, went straight to Wool Court and decamped about eleven just possible that he might come and go unobserved. But witnesses to his presence likely to be found (bus conductor, stray students, any-one passing through court).

Marlow, Martin Christopher. In dark-room from ten-fifteen till news of accident arrived. Confirmed by Atkinson.

Murn, Athelstan. As Marlow, but made several short trips to refrigerator.

Pinnegar, Roger. Left for London before this part of investigation undertaken. Looked into photographic room and dark-room about ten-fifteen. Noticed by two students in street outside tower just as one student was asking other the time. Time was ten thirty-five. Student believes watch reliable. Pinnegar probably making his way to refectory, as there reading papers and drinking coffee about ten-forty. Remained there and seen talking politely to Sir David Evans (see above) about eleven twenty-five.

Prisk, Peter Patterson. Nervous prostration following car accident before this part of investigation undertaken (physical injuries nil, but doctor vouches for genuineness of subsequent collapse). Seen to arrive at university about ten. Had no academic engagements during morning. Believed to have been continuously in his room and no record of being seen elsewhere except just before eleven, when he enquired for his assistant, Pinnegar, in photographic room and dark-room.

Tavender, Hubert Wylie. Spent early part of morning in town, negotiating with a picture dealer on behalf of his wife. Arrived at university about eleven and went first to refectory for cup of coffee (story confirmed). Crossed side-street to main building about eleven-fifteen and records noticing door of store-room at bottom of tower as standing open. Went direct to classroom and met students at eleven-twenty (five minutes late). Conducted seminar class till twelve forty-five. Has no further information (*Hobhouse*: you are sure there is nothing else you can tell me, sir? *Tavender*: Nothing—or nothing that would be believed by any judge or jury in the land; and that must be the same thing from your point of view. *Hobhouse*: This is a very serious matter, Mr. Tavender. You are sure you have nothing to add? *Tavender:* Nothing, I do solemnly swear. *Hobhouse*: I am not asking you to swear, sir. I am not even taking a formal statement yet. *Tavender*: Nevertheless I swear it—by the beard of the prophet, my dear man).

Appleby handed Hobhouse back the paper. "I call that a very pretty document. And with a nice kick in the tail."

"That about the beard?" Hobhouse shook his head. "It might be a coincidence, I suppose. But, if you ask me, that Tavender is a mischievous sort of chap. And what would he mean by that stuff about a judge and jury?"

"Presumably that he possesses information of so fantastic a character that no credence would be given to it were he to divulge it."

Hobhouse frowned. "Such as?"

"Well, it might be a circumstance fantastic in itself; or it might be a circumstance fantastic chiefly in virtue of the character of a person or persons involved in it. For instance, if one saw Pinnegar stuffing that cupboard with spare beards that would be fantastic in the first category. But if one saw Crunkhorn or Evans doing the same thing that would be fantastic in the second. And, by the way, though Tavender may be an extremely irresponsible person he is certainly by no means a fool. And when he has a little joke there will probably be some salt of wit hidden in it somewhere." Appleby looked at his watch. "And now I'm going to arrange a little luncheon party."

Hobhouse put his notebook in his pocket with some alacrity. "Well, I must say I could do with a nice steak. And it will go down on your expenses, not mine."

"But you're not being asked. I said arranging, not giving. And, as it's uncommonly short notice, I think to save time—" And Appleby, producing an instrument from his pocket, applied himself to the door of the telephone box. "Not much of a lock, as you say." The door had swung open; he picked up a directory, referred to it, and lifted the receiver. "Central, please."

Half an hour later Appleby climbed to the top of a bus, walked forward to the front seat and sat down beside Timothy Church. "Hullo," he said. "Going this way?"

Church, who was sunk in some gloomy reverie, gave a perceptible start. "Astonishing!" he said with irony. "It's really astonishing how you people work things out. And I own up. I'm going this way."

"Nothing like a little confession. It disburdens the heart."

"I'd rather prefer to disburden the bus. You'd find the trams very comfortable. Or wouldn't Scotland Yard run to a taxi? Some people get sick on top of a bus." Church paused darkly after these witticisms. "How's your nasty murder?" he asked.

"So so. The outworks of the mystery are beginning to yield. On the other hand fresh complications continue to sprout. Beards, for instance."

"Beards?"

"There's a cupboard in the dark-room which grows beards. Inside, that is to say. False beards just like Murn's. Three have turned up so far. Now, what would you make of that?" And Appleby looked enquiringly at Crunkhorn's assistant.

"I'm not required to make anything of so silly a story—praise God." Church was pulling fiercely at a large pipe. "And if you ask me, this squashed Pluckrose business is an absolute blight. . . . You're sure the bus doesn't make you feel a bit queasy?"

"Quite sure, thank you. I continue to look forward to my luncheon."

"Your luncheon?" Church, momentarily suspicious, glanced quickly at Appleby. "Where's your local friend?"

"Hobhouse is investigating other aspects of the case."

"Blast the case. You can't reconstitute Pluckrose. Best let the thing alone."

"Which is the opinion of that curious fellow, Tavender. A most irresponsible man."

"He's nothing of the sort." Church spoke with sudden intellectual impatience. "If Tavender says let the thing alone you'll find he has a sober reason for it."

Appleby looked curiously at the young man beside him. "What sober reason could there possibly be, Church, for ignoring a very grave crime?"

"None, really—I suppose." Church responded quickly to Appleby's appeal. "But, realistically considered, there's a great deal of rot in retributive justice. And Tavender may know something which suggests that the truth would occasion more scandal than it is worth. A university is an important place, after all. And the public is so dam' dumb."

"A university is much too important a place to be let become a happy hunting ground for licensed murderers. And, by the way, what you attribute to Tavender I was myself rather inclined to attribute to Evans at one time."

"Oh, him." Church put much into the monosyllables.

"A desire to hush the thing up. Incidentally, if Tavender feels like that he has acted most illogically more than once. For he's gone out of his way to present me with several valuable hints."

"Sporting instinct, I suppose." Church was sud-

224

denly gloomy again. "Blast the whole thing. It's like it is sometimes with the Method of Least Squares. I can't get it out of my head."

"I see. And when you have problems enough of your own—"

"Exactly." Church pulled himself up, suddenly startled. "What do you mean?"

"Mrs. Church being a bit troublesome, I suppose." Appleby spoke quite casually. "Particularly with Miss Cavenett about."

Church jumped to his feet. "Sorry," he said. "But this is where I get off."

Appleby got up too. "Is it? Same with me, oddly enough." He followed Church down the steps. "The Mrs. Churches, I ought to have said."

They got off the bus and walked down a side street in silence together. Only half way down Appleby spoke. "I say, Church," he asked curiously, "did you ever sleep with any of them?"

Church made no reply and they walked on in silence still. An indiscreet question. But human nature, reflected Appleby, is so extremely curious a thing. And one has the instinct to investigate where one can.

In the gardens of St. Cecilia's Hall young ladies, equipped with secateurs and suitable gloves, gathered flowers. On the terrace other young ladies walked with Miss Godkin's dogs. Under trees young ladies sketched. And through open windows and across the lawn floated the strains of violins and harps, pianos and cellos, discoursed by young ladies for whom, by the doom of Miss Godkin, musical accomplishments had been decreed. One could see at once that

225

throughout the Hall refined cheerfulness and cultivated gaiety reigned. Indeed these qualities, together
with punctuality, needle-work, dips into *Country Life*
and *The Queen*, unpainted fingernails, intelligent conversation, politeness to servants and the use of Received Standard English, were required by Miss
Godkin from eight-fifteen in the morning to ten
o'clock at night. Young ladies who so far wished to
become girls again as to read film mags, make bets
on horses, discuss boys, discuss girls, toast bloaters
before gas fires, consume grocer's port, fan dance,
croon, pinch, weep, become deliciously sick on chocolate peppermint creams, tell each other about their
homes and their neighbours, their mothers' troubles
with hire-purchase and their fathers' triumphs with
dogs: such recalcitrant elements could indulge their
back-slidings only in the nocturnal seclusion of the
spare, but dainty and maiden-like, cubicles with
which Miss Godkin provided them. By day life at St.
Cecilia's was elegant and controlled; it combined,
Miss Godkin was accustomed to say, the variousness
and verve of a noble household of the Renaissance
with the dignity and repose of an English country seat.
And some of the girls had to stay three whole years.

Miss Godkin herself was a prominent figure upon
the scene as Appleby and Church walked up the drive.
Standing under a cedar on the lawn she was giving
instructions to two gardeners of decorously mature
years. She was attended by two young ladies who were
learning how to give instructions to gardeners. As
their allotted path in life was that of primary school-
teaching in an industrial town it was perhaps far from
certain that they would ever bring this particular
branch of knowledge into play. But—as Miss Godkin

was fond of saying—one can never tell nowadays; and for this reason two of her charges were thus chosen daily to enjoy the more intimate experiences of superior living. They fed at Miss Godkin's table and there was Georgian silver and coffee out of Crown Derby Cups. The silver was not so bad; it would take a most unluckily savage bite to make any permanent impression on it. But from first stir to last sip the Crown Derby was sheer agony throughout.

"Dear Mr. Appleby, how good of you to come!" Miss Godkin advanced in what might be called a garden-party way—to which was added however a faint touch of conspiratorial and business-like feeling. "Mr. Church, we are glad to see you." Miss Godkin turned to Crunkhorn's assistant with a nice glide from cordiality to gracious condescension. "And now here are Miss Bearup and Miss Fisher." And Miss Godkin proceeded to introduce Miss Bearup and Miss Fisher to Appleby, and Church to Miss Bearup and Miss Fisher. From which Appleby concluded that the curious bee about the Foreign Office must be buzzing in Miss Godkin's head still. Indeed he could hardly otherwise have contrived to arrange with the somewhat mystified lady a luncheon-party on his own terms.

"And now where, I wonder, is dear Else? Mr. Church, she is quite a friend of yours, I believe. But she will turn up presently, I don't doubt. The bell will ring at any moment, and she is a most punctual girl." Miss Godkin paused on this and smiled meaningfully at her two charges. "But here is another of our guests." And Miss Godkin again advanced over the greensward. "Miss Cavenett?" she said enquiringly. "How do you do?"

Mr. Church's Miss Cavenett had marked the particularity—not altogether festive—of the occasion by arriving in a taxi; and now she suffered introductions in an ominous quiet. Mr. Church was understood to mumble something to the effect of having met before. Miss Cavenett, having received from Appleby over the telephone the vague impression that she was being invited into the heart of her fiancé's harem, treated Miss Fisher and Miss Bearup to a species of rapid refrigeration of which the icy breath might have been felt half across St. Cecilia's spreading lawns. And this was hard on Miss Fisher and Miss Bearup. They were expected to be lady-like; whereas Miss Cavenett had all the horrid liberty and resources of a gentlewoman. Under the most genial circumstances they would have had some little difficulty with their hands and feet; Miss Cavenett was unconscious of the even more anxious business of turning the head upon the neck— and it was most probable that she had never as much as heard of Received Standard English. As they all walked towards the house Appleby, although he ought no doubt to have attached himself to Miss Godkin, contrived to get these unfortunate young people one on each side of him. "I think," he said, "that you have an awfully jolly place here."

Miss Bearup turned her head cautiously until she might just conceivably have glimpsed the tip of Appleby's nose. "It is very pleasant," she said. "It is so spacious and restful."

To this Appleby made no reply—and, oddly enough, Miss Bearup appeared to be encouraged by his silence. "In fact," she added in something like a half-whisper, "it's sometimes a bit *quiet*. If you know what I mean."

"I think I do." Out of the corner of his eye Appleby could see Miss Godkin doing her best with Joan Cavenett, and Timothy Church glowering along by himself. "I should imagine it's all right for a time."

"That's just it," said Miss Bearup, and both she and Miss Fisher looked with sudden admiration at a stranger of such philosophic penetration. "And there are things one learns, I must say. Amelettes and amateur theatricals and what to do to the stalks of flowers. I expect it all helps later on. And how to speak distinctly. Not that I think people didn't hear me pretty clearly before."

"And the Facts of Life," said Miss Fisher incautiously.

Miss Bearup laughed—engagingly, Appleby thought. "Miss Godkin gives little talks on that. And sometimes there's a fact or two thrown in that might be really useful, if you ask me. But the rest requires a pretty strong stomach, as you might say." Miss Bearup now looked full at Appleby—and her stride lengthened on the grass. "You know," she said, "sometimes it's just god-awful being a woman."

"I say"—Miss Fisher too now was an ally—"why did that girl look at us that way when we were introduced? Is she something too frightfully grand?"

"Not as far as I know. I believe she mistook you for other people."

"How very odd!" Miss Fisher glanced cautiously over her shoulder. "You know, odd things do happen at St. Cecilia's from time to time. Particularly since these foreigners have taken to drifting through."

"The German girls?" Appleby dropped the question casually. "How do you find you like them?"

Miss Fisher looked at Miss Bearup, as if this were

a complex matter requiring the superior gifts of her friend. And Miss Bearup scowled with a frankness that would have occasioned Miss Godkin acute distress. "You get the facts of life from them, all right," she said. "Facts of death and hell let loose. And they're nice kids, only a bit jumpy because of what they've been mixed up with. Not that we see a great deal of them, because they're not really at the Hall. Miss Godkin just picks them up somehow."

"Parlour boarders," said Miss Fisher.

Miss Bearup remained serious. "I wouldn't like to be made to feel about my own country like some of those people are. You know, all that will have to be stopped, if you ask me. Don't you think?"

"Hitler's Germany?" Appleby nodded. "Yes."

Miss Fisher frowned. "It will mean our men being killed, and the children bombed, and people like ourselves going and making things in factories?"

"Yes," said Appleby. "It will mean all that."

"Well, it must just be stopped, all the same." Miss Bearup kicked a divot out of the lawn with a vicious skill which might have frozen Miss Godkin's blood. "Hullo, there she is."

"The latest one," said Miss Fisher. "A bit different from the others. In fact, an absolute . . . well, you'll see for yourself."

Appleby was already seeing for himself. He had no need of any one to tell him that the girl in the black frock, who now stood waiting for the party by a french window, was Fräulein Schmauch. Nor did he need to be told that she was, too, Zuleika Dobson. The Germans are not strong in the production of fatal women but occasionally they produce a masterpiece. And Fräulein Schmauch was that. She was tall and perfectly proportioned; her features were regular, her skin was ivory and her eyes and hair were black. But these and other charms were quite obviously only so many *points d'appui* upon which the total and uncommunicable effect of Fräulein Schmauch was based. Meet her, and clearly you had to make up your mind at once. Either you must let your thoughts dwell carefully on other things or resign yourself to the rapid and uncontrollable growth of sheer amatory obsession. And, likely enough, Fräulein Schmauch would pay no attention to you. But whether this neglect was that of the replete tiger or of the unspotted and milk-white hind it would not be easy to say. For of Fräulein Schmauch's superlatively compelling attributes a large inscrutability was not the least.

Of all this—and doubtless more—Miss Cavenett was rapidly aware. And if the awareness had the effect of returning Miss Fisher and Miss Bearup to a welcome obscurity in her regard it was far from contributing to the ease of the ensuing luncheon. This took place upon a dais from which Miss Godkin could survey the body of her charges, who sat at narrow tables and restrainedly conversed across a barrier of tastefully ordered flowers. Miss Godkin, while keeping an eagle's eye upon the larger scene, directed the conversation of the immediate party into artistic channels. Miss Fisher and Miss Bearup were required to show knowledge of Mr. Pasmore and Mr. Duncan Grant; Fräulein Schmauch was consulted on Ernst and Klee. Fräulein Schmauch had little to say; as her voice when she did speak had a low, husky quality which played alarmingly upon the spine this was perhaps all to the good. Timothy Church, who might have been expected to eat in glowering or embarrassed silence, was unpredictably gay, his spirits being perhaps raised by a sense of some imminent resolution of his fate. But, all in all, it was an uncomfortable meal, and general relief was produced when Miss Godkin rose and pronounced grace. "And now, my dear Else"— and Miss Godkin cast her conspiratorial glance at Appleby—"I want you to take Miss Cavenett and Mr. Church and show them the new herb garden; it is really doing remarkably well. And you, my dear girls,"—and she turned to Miss Bearup and Miss Fisher—"have work to do, I know." This was evidently a well-understood formula of dismissal; Miss Godkin's two victims of the day withdrew after correct farewells; and presently Appleby and his hostess were in the garden again alone, with Fräulein Schmauch and her charges disappearing round a clipped yew hedge.

"Well," said Appleby, following them with his eye, "I think perhaps they may work it out."

"Work it out? Really, Mr. Appleby, you must understand that all this has puzzled me a great deal. I think I may say that commonly there is not much at St. Cecilia's that I don't know about. Not that the girls are not allowed their proper privacy and reserve, of course."

"Of course," said Appleby politely.

"But ever since Sir David arranged that these German girls should come to me from time to time—"

"It was Sir David who arranged that?"

"I am quite sure that it was really the dear duke."

"A much more likely man to organise the thing, I should say."

"To *organise* the thing? Dear me, I am quite puzzled again. But I gathered that Sir David was merely carrying out the duke's wishes, and that there was a considerable *inwardness* to the whole affair." Miss Godkin looked cautiously round the empty lawn, as if fearful of being overheard. "Had it been Sir David alone I should scarcely have agreed. Particularly since—"

"Particularly since Fräulein Schmauch has arrived and exercised such a fatal power over elderly men."

"Precisely so; you appear to know all about it." And Miss Godkin looked at Appleby in surprise. "It has been extremely embarrassing—particularly as I have sometimes feared that the thing could not but be remarked by the girls. Perhaps you know that Sir David Evans himself—"

"And Pluckrose and Professor Prisk?"

"And these as well. Dinners and theatres. In a place like Nesfield one just can't behave in that way. I have been particularly apprehensive in regard to Mr. Prisk, whose reputation is the reverse of good. Mr. Lasscock, who is a close friend of mine, has recently discovered the most incontrovertible evidence of that. It has been most worrying."

"I am sure it has. And now with murder added—"

Miss Godkin gave what could only be called a yelp of dismay. "Mr. Appleby, you can't mean to suggest that there is any connection between that horrible affair and *St. Cecilia's!*"

"There has been this rivalry, as I suppose it may be termed, over your latest German protégée. And it is possible—well, to construct a tenable theory connecting either Evans or Prisk with the crime. Not that there aren't other factors too. There are plenty of motives lying around, though I don't know that any

233

of them is quite as strong as I would wish. And, for what it is worth, I am inclined to guess that Fräulein Schmauch's place is merely on the outskirts of the affair. . . . I wonder how those three are getting on."

"Else and Mr. Church and this Miss Cavenett? Will you please explain what you mean by saying that they have to work something out? Do both the young women want to marry him?"

"Dear me, no." Appleby halted and looked mildly at Miss Godkin. "One of them is married to him already."

"Mr. Appleby! Have you had me arrange this luncheon to further some horrible collusive divorce?" Miss Godkin was aghast. "Following upon a disgraceful clandestine marriage?"

Appleby shook his head. "I don't know that anything of the sort will be necessary. For although Church is married to Fräulein Schmauch—"

"Oh dear, oh dear!"

"—I doubt whether the marriage is legally valid. You see, he has been married before."

"Married before!"

"Quite often. In fact to *all* those German girls—or at any rate to a good many of them. And now he wants Miss Cavenett."

Miss Godkin, with a complete failure of the principles of deportment, grabbed wildly at a garden chair. "Mr. Appleby," she gasped as she sank down, "am I mad?"

"I am quite sure you are not. But a fair part of the world is—and the disease is particularly bad round about the centre of Europe."

"This is wholly bewildering. I quite fail to follow you. I cannot see what possible connection there may be between the state of Europe and this Church's monstrous career of bigamy."

"Bigamy? Well, I'd hardly call it that. Knight-errantry sounds better by a long way."

"Knight-errantry! Are we to understand that Mr. Church tours dragons' caves and tyrants' dungeons picking up *wives*?"

Appleby sat down. "Yes," he said soberly. "He does. Or he tours Himmler's Germany, which is much the same thing. And I believe that other young men have been in on it too, and that it is something which the Duke of Nesfield has found a good deal of satisfaction in financing and organising. Suppose, Miss Godkin, that you're the daughter of a Jewish professor in Berlin. Or suppose you're a Munich girl who has worked for the Social Democrats or for anybody those gentry don't like. What's your best chance? To marry an Englishman or an American quick and get away while the going is good."

"But surely—"

"And it's happened quite a lot. Plenty of men have made formal marriages with German women just to get them away. And so far the Nazis haven't come down on it. But this of Church I suspect to be an ingenious and organised affair, given a romantic, Scarlet Pimpernel top-dressing by a nicely calculating brain at the top. So far, Church has refused to divulge the truth even to his fiancée. . . . By the way, who is Fräulein Schmauch?"

"I'm afraid I really haven't any idea." Miss Godkin looked particularly distressed as she made this appalling social confession. "Though I was assured by Sir David that she was a girl of good family. And clearly she is well-bred—"

"In fact, clearly not Fräulein Schmauch. In other words the scheme—which has been using this beautiful place of yours as a sort of clearing house, if the term may be used—has a little more to it than simple knight-errantry, after all. There must be plenty of important people in Germany who might act more freely one day if the daughters, say, were out of the possible clutches of the Gestapo."

"Mr. Appleby, this is most astounding! I had, of course, some idea that these girls were more or less in the position of refugees who wished to live quietly here for a while. But I had no idea of the adventurous and—and matrimonial circumstances in which they came to me. Though I felt, you know, that some *diplomatic* element might be involved. The Foreign Office—"

"Quite so." Appleby sheered hastily off this delusory topic. "What is important at the moment is that we should keep quiet about the whole thing. Which is why I particularly hope that it will prove wholly unconnected with Pluckrose's murder. And now I am afraid I must be getting back to the university."

"But, Mr. Appleby, whatever am I to do with those three young people? They may be having a most fearful row at this moment."

"Miss Godkin, I am quite sure that you are very capable of dealing with *any* three young people. And probably—now that we have forced an issue—they have got it settled by this time. I rather expect that Church and Miss Cavenett will announce their engagement straight away."

Miss Godkin, though visibly gratified by Appleby's assertion of her competence, looked extremely perplexed. "But I don't see how they can do that. If he has been married several times already—"

"The records will be in various consulates about Germany—and it wouldn't be at all surprising if they were all unaccountably mislaid. Moreover there has probably been a whole jungle of false passports and the like through which a court would just refuse to cut its way. To which we may add the great improbability of any of the girls concerned making any claim that a real marriage occurred. On the whole I think Miss Cavenett will see that the right thing to do is to go straight ahead."

And Appleby took his leave. Out of the corner of his eye as he went down the drive he saw Mr. Church, Fräulein Schmauch and Miss Cavenett returning from the herb garden; he saw too Miss Godkin rise from her chair and stand for a moment as one who ranges some necessary battalion of small talk about her. Perhaps her guests would stay to tea and there would be more discussion of Paul Klee and Max Ernst, of Mr. Pasmore and Mr. Duncan Grant. And Appleby chuckled. So much, surely, for *Zuleika Dobson*. And now if he could confine himself to the central aspect of the case, to what might be called its Pickwickian core. . . . But before he reached the bottom of the drive Appleby was frowning thoughtfully again. He was not, after all, entirely sure that he had wholly disengaged the thing from that tiresomely magnetic German girl. What, for instance, was the wholly fantastic information that Tavender possessed? Appleby had a disturbing feeling that it might point back to St. Cecilia's. And to St. Cecilia's, somehow, he had no wish himself to return.

13

It is further evidence of the compelling personality of the young woman who called herself Else Schmauch that Inspector Hobhouse, as he munched sandwiches gratuitously provided by the university refectory, had her pretty constantly in mind. Never having met the girl, he was not in a position to meditate her charms; and it was therefore necessarily as a mere unknown force that he regarded her. But, even so, his reflections must be taken as a weighty tribute to her allure. Hobhouse put a good deal of trust in allure; it was his experience that it was generally to be found in one corner or another of any sanguinary case; and in the Pluckrose affair Fräulein Schmauch appeared to be the only person capable of providing it.

Pluckrose had been murdered; to Hobhouse this at least appeared certain. And then there had been an attempt to murder Prisk; from this conclusion one could only escape by the difficult hypothesis that Prisk had ingeniously staged the affair of the motor car himself. And then Sir David Evans, knowing about Pluckrose and hearing about Prisk, had gone into a blue—or green—funk. Now Pluckrose, Prisk and Sir David had, it seemed, been as three elderly moths fluttering round the ineluctable lamp that was Fräulein Schmauch—and from all this might not a tolerably clear picture be built?

Suppose that this unknown girl had already an established lover; suppose him to be a man passionately jealous and homicidally inclined. Might he not have killed Pluckrose, attempted to kill Prisk—and even now be preparing a similar short way with that third amatory nuisance, Sir David Evans? And might not an awareness—or a sense—of this well account for Evans's panic? That these men should pursue an amour until even the most unbalanced lover felt that they must be so dealt with was sensational and fantastic in the extreme. But Prisk, at least, was definitely a person of loose principles—and then had not the fellow Tavender hinted at knowledge so extravagant that it just wouldn't be believed?

Having got so far Hobhouse stopped short—stopped short because, on his present information, he had come up against a brick wall. He had no present means whatever of providing the German lady with her necessary lover. At Nesfield University just nobody of the right sort appeared to be about. The place might hold its natural complement of quiet sensualists, effective and ineffective, practising and theoretical; but the homicidally passionate proprietor of a fatally attractive female Teuton was just not there. In the experienced judgment of Hobhouse only Marlow had a touch of any such temper. And Marlow, as far as was known, belonged to another context; his only known grudge was against Prisk alone; and that had nothing to do with a girl, Teutonic or otherwise. An attempt to take this theory further must, in fact, await the return of Appleby. Of the young man Church, about whom Appleby had given those mysterious intimations of bigamy, Hobhouse would have liked to have hopes. As far as the Pluckrose affair went Church appeared to be without an alibi for the fatal fifteen minutes round about eleven o'clock.

Eleven o'clock. . . . Hobhouse, his brow suddenly darkening, swallowed down his last crust—for refectory sandwiches have crust all round—and rose to his feet. For before him of a sudden was the vision of the unspeakable Theodore Almeric de la Tour Lasscock, of whom there was such good reason to believe that he had witnessed a quite grotesquely bloody murder and straightway picked up himself and his cushion and toddled off in quest of undisturbed peace of mind. Hobhouse sharpened a couple of pencils—when really hot on a trail he often snapped one off at the point—and went in search of this extreme exponent of non-cooperation.

In Lasscock's room he found two girl students sitting on the absent scholar's table comparing snapshots. They were waiting, they explained, for Mr. Lasscock, who was known to be with the Vice-Chancellor and due presently to return. Hobhouse might have waited too; instead—and on no very clear premises, except that his impatience was great—he formed the design of confronting Lasscock with his turpitude in the presence of Sir David Evans. Having decided on this more or less dramatic procedure he proceeded to march without ceremony into the Vice-Chancellor's room.

The sunlight was on Sir David Evans. But Lasscock, by pushing his own chair round the desk until it was side by side with Sir David's, had ensured that the sunlight should be on him too. And whereas Sir David was under the necessity of posing in the sunlight Lasscock had only to bask. Lasscock basked and Sir David weightily talked—presumably on some aspect of the administration of historical studies in the university. Sir David talked and Lasscock sat with his hands finger-tip to finger-tip in front of him: an attitude which contrived to suggest some degree of judicial attention, and thus to discount what might otherwise have been a disconcerting impression of obliviousness in Lasscock's features. For Lasscock's eyes were closed; his mouth might have been detected as slightly open; his breathing was regular and easy. One could almost believe him asleep. But every now and then his fingers would part; hang suspended, as it were, upon Sir David's words; and then close in affirmation, or at least in cognisance, of whatever had been said.

It was upon this scholarly and deliberative scene that Hobhouse burst. Lasscock and Sir David Evans, sitting side by side, looked at him with astonishment and mild reprobation, much as two first-class passengers of controlled behaviour but decided views might regard a person who flung himself down on an opposite seat while flourishing a green ticket. "Inspector Hobhouse," said Sir David sternly, "you preak in upon important business, look you. Perhaps something urgent has occurred?"

Hobhouse produced the first of his pencils and pointed it. He pointed it at the countenance of Lasscock which, rosy against the Vice-Chancellor's rows of sunlit calf and morocco, showed like a peach lazily ripening against an ancient wall. "I have important business too, sir. I have come to tax Mr. Lasscock—"

"Bless me! Feller has changed his job." Lasscock shook his head in mild astonishment. "Policeman, when I last saw him. Goin' round with the Lunnon man. And now he's hopped into the Inland Revenue. Like some of the Lepidoptera, my dear Evans. A pest as a caterpillar and then a pest as a butterfly later on." Lasscock opened his eyes quite wide upon Hobhouse. "But it's no good, sir; no dashed good at all. Nothin' to be taxed on. Brother sold the last acre years ago. Not a penny left in the Funds. Supportin' myself like a little school teacher. Sweat of my brow." And Lasscock produced a beautiful canary-coloured handkerchief and gave his forehead a sort of symbolical dab.

"I have come," said Hobhouse, breathing hard, "to *charge* Mr. Lasscock—"

Sir David rose to his feet. "Inspector Hobhouse, do I understand that you hold a warrant to arrest—"

"No, sir; nothing of the kind." Hobhouse, thus unhappily taken up, floundered momentarily and the accusing pencil wavered. "I have come to—to represent to Mr. Lasscock the seriousness of his having withheld important information from the police. He claims not to have been at the university on Monday. And now, acting on information received"—Hobhouse boldly advanced this useful if mendacious formula—"we have reason to believe that statement to be inaccurate; deliberately misleading, I am afraid it is necessary to say. In fact I am inclined to suspect that Mr. Lasscock saw the whole thing."

"Saw the whole thing!" Sir David sat down again—quite abruptly.

"Mr. Lasscock was sitting in the Wool Court when the meteorite came down and killed Pluckrose. Mr. Lasscock, I say, was there as he commonly is at that hour, sitting in a deck chair. And, for all I know, he may have been staring straight up at the tower." Hobhouse paused. "The statement that he was elsewhere is a very serious matter indeed."

"Statement?" said Lasscock. "What djew mean by statement, officer? Lunnon man got it in his notebooks, signed and properly witnessed?"

Hobhouse struggled with his extreme indignation. "You distinctly stated to Detective-Inspector Appleby of Scotland Yard—"

Lasscock shook his head indulgently and turned to the Vice-Chancellor. "Feller isn't talkin' about a statement at all. Talkin' about a private conversation with this Appleby 'tother mornin'. Gentlemanlike chap but seems to get things confused. Drowsy mornin' in Miss Dearlove's orchard—excusable perhaps. But inclined to take a severe view of this Hobhouse, 'pon my soul."

"Do you mean"—Hobhouse rapped his pencil on Sir David Evans's desk, and the point promptly snapped—"Do you mean flatly to deny that you said—"

Momentarily disengaging his finger-tips from their contact with each, Lasscock pointed to a desk calendar. "Notice the date?" he asked. "Monday quite a long time back now, ain't it? What's the Chief Constable goin' to say when he larns that you haven't yet taken formal statements from people you believe to be concerned? 'Course I was sittin' in the court. And down the thing fell."

"Very well!" Hobhouse contrived to control himself sufficiently to fish his second pencil unbroken from his pocket. "And now will you have the goodness to tell me—"

"Stop!" Sir David Evans, who had been listening to all this in evident perturbation, jumped up, strode across the room and flung up a window. "My dear Lasscock," he said as he turned round again, "you must haf a care. It iss not to be porne, look you, that we should be intimidated in this way. You must carefully consider eferything you should say. We had petter haf advise, we had petter haf your solicitors, pefore anything more iss said."

"Attorneys?" Lasscock very definitely shook his head. " A pack of six-and-eightpenny rascals and odjus jargon-mongers. I think I can look after myself—obleeged to you, all the same. And it was like this. Of course I was sittin' in the court; reclinin', you might say—"

The Vice-Chancellor fiddled at random with papers on his desk. "Lasscock," he said, "I peg you to stop and reflect." He turned to Hobhouse. "I consider it my duty to protect Mr. Lasscock's interests in efery way. He iss a most valued and respected colleague of mine, look you. I will not see a friend—a close personal friend—do anything rash, I say. There must pe no more of this now, inspector. If you wish—"

"My dear Evans, you are too dam' solicitous." Lasscock was now looking at Sir David with a good deal of covert curiosity. "But the officer may as well have the story now as later. There I was, reclinin' in the court and workin' one or two things out. It may well be I was lookin' up at the tower—"

"Lasscock, I peg you to reflect—"

"—only, you know, my eyes were closed, likely enough, and perhaps I had put the *Times* over my face as well. I find I work things out best that way. Well, at eleven o'clock the bell went—and a nasty great clankin' thing it is, that always wak—stops me from workin' things out at once. And I started up, I dare say. And there was Pluckrose, sittin' opposite. And then down this hijjus great thing came." Lasscock, for one who had to guard against unpleasant incidents lying on the mind, related this catastrophic circumstance with remarkable composure. "Nasty mess it made, too. I was a bit splattered, if you don't mind my mentioning it."

The Vice-Chancellor had turned pale beneath the white halo of his hair. "You mean to say," he almost whispered, "that you *saw* Pluckrose killed?"

"Just that. Distressin', of course. But then it was Pluckrose, you know—which made it not quite so bad."

Hobhouse's pencil, which had been racing, snapped. "And you mean to say," he almost shouted, "that you just cleared out?"

"Of course I went over to have a look." Lasscock fished in a pocket and placidly handed Hobhouse a fountain pen. "There could be no doubt that the feller was dead; indeed spectacular is the only term you could apply to the result the nasty thing had achieved. Well, I picked up my cushion—I commonly take a cushion out there—and came into the main buildin'— intendin', you know, to mention the affair to the porter."

"Mention—!"

"It seemed the proper thing to do at once. I don't think gals go much into the court, but one wouldn't like one to stumble on just that. Though it's surprisin' what gals can stomach: know Miss Godkin?"

Hobhouse made a strangled noise. "And *did* you see the porter?"

"As a matter of fact I didn't. I looked at my watch as I was goin' down the corridor and saw that my next lecture was a bit overdue. So I felt I'd better leave Pluckrose for the time—the dead to bury their dead, you know—and get on with the business of the livin'. If Nesfield students can be described as livin', that is to say."

"And *did* you lecture?"

"Well now, I didn't. I went back to my room for my gown and then a dam' queer thing happened. I began to feel dam' queer. After all, I suppose an affair like this Pluckrose business doesn't happen every day."

"It certainly does not." Hobhouse spoke with fervent emphasis. "So you felt queer. And then?"

"All I could do for a bit was just to sit down and recover. And by the time that was over it was too late for the lecture; all the students would have gone. So I went along the corridor again and peeped out at the court. And there they all were, fussin' round the body. The thing, you might say, had been taken out of my hands. So I got my hat and coat and went home to my lodgins."

"And it doesn't occur to you—"

"I'm glad that you've got round to me eventually." Lasscock tapped his fingers together precisely. "It's comfortin' to be able to feel that the police are thorough, even if a bit slow. Gives one a sense of security. And although I didn't see anythin' and can add nothin' to your case, it's obviously the right thing that you should come to me in a routine way. But mind you have a clearer notion of what I say than that engagin' but incompetent feller in the orchard."

"Mr. Lasscock"—this time Hobhouse tried speaking more in sorrow than in anger—"do you realise that you are our only witness that the crime happened just on eleven o'clock?"

"Is that so?" Lasscock looked only mildly interested. "And might that be of importance to your investigations? The possibility hadn't occurred to me. But then I am quite unschooled in that sort of thing."

During the latter part of Lasscock's narration Sir David Evans had been sitting at his desk with his beautiful head sunk meditatively in his hands; now he looked up and fixed the historian with an extremely penetrating glance. "And you mean to say," he asked, "that you saw *nothing* except what you have described?"

"Nothin' at all. How could I, my dear Evans? I was in—in a considerable abstraction until the moment the thing fell."

"Nothing in the nature of an—an appearance at one of the windows of the tower?"

"Certainly not." Lasscock shook his head comfortably. "As a witness I can be of no use whatever. The only other thing I noticed was that someone had turned the fountain full on. It was drenchin' the path across the court. But clearly that has nothin' to do with the case."

Without any warning whatever Sir David Evans rose and pointed a minatory finger at the astonished Lasscock. "It is tisgraceful, look you! You haf impeted the police in the execution of their tuty! Hear you, Mr. Lasscock, I am tispleased; I am more than tis-

247

pleased—I am intignant!" The Vice-Chancellor's thickening Cambrian accent suggested that this statement was indeed true; he closed his finger so that what he held in front of him was a clenched fist, and this he proceeded to brandish in an extremely temperamental way. "You haf prefaricated, sir; you haf shamelessly prefaricated!"

Lasscock's eyes opened wider than Hobhouse had ever seen them and slowly he sat bolt upright. "Sir David," he said with much dignity, "I don't at all understand what you're gettin' at."

"It iss pad, Mr. Lasscock. It iss more than pad; it iss suspicious." The sibilants fairly hissed from Nesfield's Vice-Chancellor; he might have been a railway engine blowing off superfluous steam. "It must be infestigated, sir; the police will infestigate, sir; you shall account for yourself, look you, Mr. Lasscock."

"Well, I'm blessed." Lasscock too got to his feet—not exactly briskly but yet with a good deal of decision. "And what about the attorneys now? It might be a good idea to call one of the tedjus fellows in on your own account. And ask him about slander and defamation of character and that sort o' thing. Close personal friend indeed—pshaw!"

"It shall be reported on, Mr. Lasscock; it 'shall be tiscussed. The Chancellor shall know of it, sir. It iss not conduct pecoming a scholar."

Lasscock, who had been holding his canary-coloured handkerchief in his hand, returned it very deliberately to his pocket and turned as if to leave the room in silent indignation. Sir David, who now seemed to find it necessary to stand on his toes, followed with every appearance of positive physical menace. "And hark you, Mr. Lasscock, it iss not conduct pecoming a chentleman——"

With his hand on the door-knob Lasscock turned round. "You silly old goat," he said. "You fuzzy headed, muddle minded, muddy thoughted leek-eater." Lasscock spoke still in the most dignified way. "You ode bawlin', chapel crawlin' upstart. Afternoon to you." And Lasscock turned to Hobhouse. "Common thing, " he said. "Often obsarved. Noted by Tennyson. The schoolboy heat, the blind hysterics of the Celt. Afternoon to you, too."

And Mr. Lasscock was gone.

There was no particular reason why, at this juncture, Hobhouse should judge it useful or desirable to put Professor Hissey next on his list. Perhaps he simply remembered him as a notably mild-mannered man, whose bearing and conduct were likely to afford a pleasing contrast to the deplorable scene which had just concluded. Be this as it may, Hobhouse found himself making his way to the celebrated epigrapher's room. It was empty and—it occurred to him—surprisingly tidy. The pictures—photographs, for the most part, of inscriptions in what Hobhouse sagely took to be Greek—were straight on their nails, and a great many files were ranged in an orderly way on the shelves. There were moreover such evidences of well-regulated bachelor comfort as a tea-pot, kettle and spirit stove behind a screen. And there was a tin of mixed biscuits into which Hobhouse, unaccustomed to sustaining himself on a sandwich throughout the day, was tempted to dip. He contrived however to resist this unprofessional impulse and went on to seek Hissey at his hotel. There he found the scholar in what was apparently his private sitting-room, peacefully arranging multicoloured slips of pasteboard in a card index.

Hissey beamed upon his visitor. "My dear sir," he said, "come in; come in and tell me how you are progressing in this deplorable affair." He turned to the maid who had shown Hobhouse up. "And, Martha, should there be muffins, I don't at all see why we shouldn't have rather an early tea. See what can be done, there's a good girl." He beamed again upon Hobhouse, who was much impressed by this intuitive understanding of the carnal needs. "If you will take the chair by the window, Inspector, I believe you will find it reasonably comfortable. And please forgive me if I go on with my job. It is almost purely mechanical and will not preoccupy me in the least. At the moment, as it happens, I have a good deal on hand."

Hobhouse sat down. "I think, sir," he said affably, "that I might say much the same thing myself."

"Is that so? Is that really so?" And Hissey looked up rather vaguely at his visitor. "I suppose a thing of that sort does at times take not a little working out. From one or two things that Merryweather has told me during the last few days I can well imagine that it may be so."

"Um," said Hobhouse, slightly mystified. He was wondering if there would be a muffin each, and whether there would be anything else as well.

"I hope that he is coming too? Grant, I ought to say. Or rather Appleby. I am extremely interested that Appleby should have taken up so novel a career." And Hissey worked with a good deal of concentration at his coloured cards, so that Hobhouse was inclined to doubt the quality of his interest in anything else whatever. "What a pleasant day it has been." Hissey

250

craned his neck slightly in order to look out of the window, rather as one who would corroborate a random guess. "One really longs to go out and stroll in the sun. But I am under some pressure of work at the moment, tiresomely enough." And at this Hissey got to his feet and fell to rummaging among piles of papers on a large table; there was, Hobhouse noted, a good deal of disorder in this more intimate retreat. "Now, what can have become of that Roman villa at Gub-Gub? I always mix it up with Dab-Dab, I am sorry to say." He shook his head, perplexed. "Is it not Shakespeare who speaks of Memory, the warder of the brain? Marlow would tell us at once. I find myself that it is a most capricious faculty. The important things one tends only too often to forget. Whereas entirely secondary and irrelevant matters can assume quite a haunting power over the mind. . . . Dear me! Here is our tea already. Martha, you are a most commendably festinate girl." And Professor Hissey, already reaching for the tea-pot, chuckled happily at this piece of learned badinage. "Sugar, Inspector? And cream"—he peered into a jug—"or milk, as I fear I ought to say?"

After Sir David Evans it was extremely soothing. Hobhouse ate a whole muffin in silence—and this seemed to suit Mr. Hissey very well. Mr. Hissey coped with his tea with one hand and his card index with the other; Hobhouse, marking the smooth precision with which he worked, and guessing that the process had been going on uninterruptedly for hours, felt that he was at last gaining a convincing breath of that higher and rarefied air which academic persons are supposed wontedly to breathe. But presently Hissey paused. "And how," he asked, "is our poor friend

Prisk? Automobiles have always appeared to me to be somewhat dangerous contrivances, as so many of our recent innovations are. I was extremely sorry that he had so bad a spill."

Hobhouse reported on Prisk's health—at some length, because he was a little puzzled as to how to proceed. His business, he now felt, was once more to go round the people concerned, taking a tug at an alibi here and a jab at a motive there. But he had chosen Hissey in rather an idle spirit and the hospitality of his reception made his position delicate. There were three muffins, all told, and plum cake and a plate of chocolate biscuits. Hobhouse, therefore, went slow. "I believe, sir," he said presently, "that it was you who took the news of Mr. Pluckrose's death to Sir David Evans?"

"Indeed?" For a moment Hissey received Hobhouse's question rather as if it were a piece of stray intelligence to be civilly received. And then he nodded. "To be sure I did. I was up in the dark-room, you see, when they brought the news. And I had an obscure feeling that everyone ought to do some thing. That was why I volunteered to break the news to Evans. Perhaps I don't use quite the correct expression; perhaps I ought to say *give* the news"—and Hissey looked quite anxiously at Hobhouse for his opinion—"though I have no doubt, of course, that Evans was very upset. He *looked* upset"—and Hissey frowned momentarily, as if there was something disturbing in this recollection; "very upset indeed." For perhaps a couple of minutes Hissey worked silently at his cards. "There was something odd about Evans's appearance," he said.

Hobhouse was startled—not so much by the words

as by the almost undoubted fact that Hissey had spoken them to himself, without any thought of communication to his visitor. Hobhouse, from over his tea cup, looked covertly at his host. Yes, Hissey was frowning thoughtfully—much as he frowned at his little cards. Only at the moment, and for almost the first time since Hobhouse had entered the room, his hands were empty. The man's concentration and abstraction were alike complete.

And Hobhouse too was thoughtful. What had this normally absent—and, upon the occasion in question, surely agitated—scholar remarked about Evans on encountering him some thirty minutes after Pluckrose's death? Or had it been something about the way in which he received the news? For instance, had the Vice-Chancellor failed to register adequate shock or surprise? But it was something slightly different from this that was suggested by Hissey's words. Evans's appearance had been odd. . . . And suddenly a grotesque vision presented itself to Hobhouse's ordinarily unimaginative mind. He saw Sir David Evans sitting drinking coffee in the university refectory in his wonted way—but with his beautiful white hair matched by a beautiful and Murn-like white beard. And Mr. Hissey, that abstracted man, was aware that about the Vice-Chancellor's appearance there was something a little out of the way. . . .

But this was absurd. Hobhouse accepted a chocolate biscuit and tried something else. "According to the statements we have collected there were several people with you in the dark-room when the thing occurred."

"The thing?" Hissey was at his cards again; for a moment he looked up to glance over the tea table.

"Ah, yes. Now, what day would that be?"

"Monday."

"And this is—?"

"Thursday."

"To be sure." Hissey smiled apologetically. "One rather loses count of the days, you know, when one doesn't go to bed."

"Doesn't go to bed!" Hobhouse was astonished. "Don't you go to bed, sir?"

"Dear me, yes. I fear I am really becoming quite careless in my speech. I meant during the last few nights merely. It is my habit when real pressure of work comes along. I ought to add that your visit is really a most pleasant relief. May I offer you another cup of tea? I think you were saying something about the dark-room?"

"I was saying that there were several people there with you at eleven o'clock on Monday, when Pluckrose was killed."

"Eleven o'clock? Do you know, I have the impression that it was a good deal later than that? By the time I got to Evans—"

"Quite so, sir. But some time had elapsed before anybody found the body. Or rather should I say, before anybody admitted finding the body. But that Pluckrose was killed just on eleven o'clock is now certain. We have the evidence of Mr. Lasscock, who actually saw it happen."

Hissey, who was again at his table searching for papers, turned round abruptly. "Lasscock! *Lasscock saw it happen!* My dear sir, however can that be? Surely we should have heard—"

"Mr. Lasscock had reasons of his own—somewhat peculiar reasons of his own—for—well, for withholding this information for a time."

"God bless my soul!" Hissey walked slowly to the tea-table and mechanically poured himself out another cup of tea. "I think I may fairly say that you astound me. And you say that he can actually fix the hour?"

"More or less to the minute."

Hissey picked up a piece of plum cake. "I should imagine that such a discovery must constitute a decidedly favourable turn in the investigation. . . . Ah, there is Dab-Dab at last." And Hissey, his mind clearly half on his cards again, made a dive back to the piles of documents. "Though I should suppose that a course so extraordinary as that of withholding information on so grave a matter would rather shake Lasscock's credit in your regard."

"Well, sir, in a way it might." Hobhouse smiled tolerantly; his feelings for the somnolent historian had become much more kindly since his spirited denunciation of Sir David Evans. "But we find in our work that people can act in very odd ways and yet be straight enough witnesses when it comes to the point." And Hobhouse nodded sagely; replete with muffin and chocolate biscuit, he was inclined to philosophic generalisation. "Yes, sir. Queer things happen in our profession."

Professor Hissey smiled. "That," he said, "is just what Bob Sawyer's friend says in *Pickwick*."

"*Pickwick*?" Hobhouse was brought momentarily to a stand. "Do you know, that reminds me of an odd thing Mr. Appleby said? He said that *Pickwick Papers* was mixed up with this case. That it had to do with one of Mr. Pickwick's immortal discoveries—something like that."

"How very odd." Hissey, who had been moving his

slice of plum cake approximately in the direction of his mouth, was so struck by this circumstance that he paused, looked at the cake in one hand and a pink card in the other, as if in some uncertainty as to which it would be reasonable to file. "How very odd, indeed. But then so is what you tell me of Lasscock. And I still cannot help feeling that he is not altogether to be relied upon. In so *minor* a matter of chronology, that is to say." And Hissey chuckled his innocent chuckle. "I believe it might be demonstrated that the surer you are of your reigns and dynasties and centuries and so on, the more inaccurate are you likely to be on what falls out between breakfast and luncheon. So I hope"—and now Hissey looked quite serious—"that you won't hang anyone just on Lasscock's word."

"It's the judge and jury who will do that, sir." Hobhouse was serious too. "But at least I don't think there will be any mistakes in the particular you mention. And I'm not saying that Mr. Lasscock can point to the guilty person; all he can do is to point, in a manner of speaking, to the innocent ones. Anyone we can fix round about eleven o'clock—"

"I see." Hissey had produced another file of cards and was still working tirelessly at his index. "To one unaccustomed to that sort of thing it is all very well—well, queer, in your own phrase."

"There's plenty that's queer enough for a police museum in this case." Hobhouse took the last chocolate biscuit. "The beards, for instance."

For the second time in this curious interview Hissey was plainly startled. He looked at Hobhouse with what was, for him, an unusual expression—an expression of sudden and decided caution. "Did I understand you to say beards?"

"Beards. No doubt you know Professor Pluckrose's assistant, Mr. Murn, and the fine white beard he has? Well, Mr. Murn himself found an exactly similar beard—a false one, of course—in a cupboard in the dark-room. He found it not long after the crime."

Hissey was silent.

"And then—and this is the extraordinary point— Mr. Murn was showing us the empty cupboard again where he had found the thing. And there in the cupboard again were two more beards of just the same sort."

There was silence in Mr. Hissey's room, but its owner was no longer absorbed in his learned labours. He was staring at the window, with a sort of mild attention suggesting that he rather expected some one to drop in that way.

"I don't suppose, now, that anything would occur to you about that?" Hobhouse asked the question at random. "I mean, there isn't anybody or anything with whom it might strike you that the beards could be connected?"

"I should connect false beards with the stage. Or, better perhaps, with amateur theatricals. In fact they might well belong to the university dramatic society; it has, I believe, a very considerable collection of properties—if that be the word. Marlow is in charge of all that. He is a very considerable actor, I have been told, and has worked for the society with great enthusiasm."

Hobhouse considered this colourless but possibly pregnant statement carefully. "Then, sir, you would be inclined to associate Marlow with the beards?"

"No."

Hissey's reply was as decided as it was brief. And

as monosyllabic utterance was contrary to his habit and probably to his code of manners Hobhouse looked at him in surprise. "Well, perhaps it is a tenuous connection, sir. The beards may have nothing to do with this dramatic society."

"I am almost certain that they have." Hissey paused, and Hobhouse suspected that he was in the throes of some obscure ethical problem. "I may say, in fact, that I am assured that these beards come from the society's collection." Hissey appeared to be gaining time. "I can see," he said carefully, "that any testimony relating definitely and unambiguously to a crime it is one's duty to advance; in fact to come forward with whether taxed or not. But in the case of some dubious and perhaps scarcely even collateral circumstances, when one might well be involving an innocent person in grave suspicion—" Hissey broke off and walked over to the window. "May I say," he presently continued apologetically, "that there is matter here on which I would like to consult Appleby? He is an old pupil of mine, as you know, and I should have a good deal of confidence in his judgment on any point touching the moral sciences."

"Quite so, sir." Hobhouse, though faintly nettled, was a model of diplomacy. "And now I think I had better be getting along. I'm sure I've kept you from this big job of yours too long already."

"Not at all, not at all." And once more Hissey amiably beamed. "And I am so pleased that there were muffins. I may say that there are crumpets every second day, and I have always regarded them as a distinctly inferior dish. It is pleasant, however, to feel that soon there will be cucumber sandwiches. I am *ver egelidos refert tepores*, as the poet says."

"Just so, sir. And good afternoon."

"One moment." Hissey raised a detaining hand. "I am afraid I have behaved very foolishly. A craven scruple, as Shakespeare has it, of thinking too precisely on the event. After all, the fellow was plainly in so merry a mood about it that it would be absurd to impute any sinister intention."

"I'm afraid I don't—" Hobhouse was completely mystified.

"Tavender. I may as well tell you at once. The reason that I am so certain of those beards having come from the dramatic society's store is that I saw Tavender walking away with them. With two beards. And—let me see—on Tuesday afternoon. He was chuckling heartily. And he would have been rubbing his hands together—you know the way he has—only, of course, he was clutching a beard in each."

14

"I've called a meeting," Appleby said.

"A meeting?" Hobhouse was perplexed. "Whatever is that?"

"A meeting of all the people concerned. Don't you always call a meeting?"

"I never heard of such a thing!" And Hobhouse looked at his colleague aghast.

"This affair has gone on long enough. And it's holding up something really rather intricate which I happen to have on in town." Appleby's expression was quite solemn. "So I think we'd better clear it up."

Hobhouse thumbed his notebooks with a gesture of something like desperation. "But the whole case is at sixes and sevens. Think of this business of Tavender and the beards. He's practically a new element and fits in just nowhere. Think of the weird behavior of Evans. Think of Pluckrose, killed with his own stolen meteorite. Think of Prisk's car. Think of that bust. Think of the appalling clutter of possible motives: the

260

Prussian Academy and the boy Gerald and little mis-understandings over biochemical research and your German girl—"

"There is certainly plenty of material."

Hobhouse groaned. "And the alibis, Mr. Appleby! Think of the whole complex situation round about eleven o'clock—I ask you, have we got it analysed out? And if you bring all those people together—"

"They'll talk."

"Oh dear, oh dear!" Miss Godkin herself could not have expressed more complete dismay. "But that's just what we've had already—floods of it. And nothing whatever has emerged. Bless me, Mr. Appleby, we don't even know whom the meteorite was intended to kill."

"Never mind. Somebody does—and perhaps they'll tell."

"And perhaps you'll offer the meeting a little reading from *Pickwick Papers*?" Hobhouse's irony was gargantuan.

"I certainly might. Chapter XI, it would be." Appleby looked at his watch. "And now I think we'd better get along. We can't have Pinnegar and we can't have Prisk, but the others will all be there."

Hobhouse thrust his notebooks in his pocket with a gesture suggesting that he had small intention of taking them out again. "Very well. But you ought to have Prisk, I should say. He must be involved some-how or there wouldn't have been that business with his car. But Pinnegar seems to have no particular place in the picture. He's merely—" Hobhouse broke off. "There you are!" he said. "If you will hurry along like this things just will get overlooked. If there isn't some-thing about Pinnegar there is about his friend Marlow.

261

I got the message only half an hour ago. They got what are pretty certainly Marlow's finger-prints from his room and they correspond with impressions found inside that little telephone box."

"And so they ought." Appleby nodded equably. "Marlow made a bogus call, all right. And as for Pinnegar, it's likely enough that he is in—well, say up to but just short of his neck. And wouldn't you say that we've seen less of him than of any of the others?"

"I suppose that's so."

Appleby smiled. "Well, that's always suspicious in an affair like this."

Large and square and high and gloomy, the tank-like board-room sucked in the dusk. Shadows were gathering like a fine web in the corners and soon the blanket of the dark would be drawn round the cowering nymphs and goddesses, ending their day-long shamefast strivings. Wandering in their fragile prison of trellises and vines the hermaphroditic figures of Burne-Jones had taken on a greener pallor. Round the walls the departed worthies swam uncertainly in their daguerreotype and photogravure and oil; and round the table the present scholars of the university sat almost as uncertainly as they. After all, it was an occasion decidedly out of the common run of things. They looked with some anxiety at Appleby, who had sat down at the head of the table with a little sheaf of notes.

"Sir David and gentlemen," Appleby said, "I have asked you to come together in this way in the belief that you may be able—and willing—to assist in the conclusion of the rather difficult investigation I have had to undertake. In the past few days I have made,

I believe, considerable headway. Nevertheless it is necessary to say that the case"—he paused and looked deliberately round the table—"that the case against Professor Prisk is by no means complete."

There was an instant subdued hubbub in the board-room; it was cut by Tavender's voice—sharp, almost alarmed. "Prisk is not here. Will you be so good as to tell us at once whether he is under arrest?"

"Mr. Prisk is, as most people know, at present in a nursing home in the city—following what had the appearance of being an accident to his car. Like other people possibly concerned, he is under the observation of the police."

"Most unsatisfactory." Tavender appeared to have taken upon himself a spokesmanship which would more naturally have been Sir David Evans's. Sir David was merely looking apprehensive and shaken; Tavender looked—and sounded—formidable. "This is most unsatisfactory," he repeated, "and, I judge, extremely irregular."

"Pluckrose was killed at eleven o'clock on Monday morning by a heavy stone—a meteorite—cast from a window of the tower." Appleby had ignored the interruption. "The meteorite was, as it happens, his own property. Or that is a polite way of putting it. The dead man had apparently conceived himself as entitled to remove it from the grounds of Nesfield Court for some purpose of his own. Why he should have done so surreptitiously I am not prepared very satisfactorily to explain; for it seems very probable that the duke would have given it to him for the asking. But the Vice-Chancellor has an ingenious theory, based on somewhat abstruse psychological premises, that a large stone of this kind might hold a morbid

263

fascination for Pluckrose; and if this is so it might explain his impulse to make off with it secretly. Be that as it may, Pluckrose stored his booty in a little used store-room; and from that store-room it was, ironically enough, pitched down on him with fatal results."

"This is mere unsubstantiated statement." Tavender was speaking again. "Is there any evidence whatever that Pluckrose stole the meteorite? For steal is apparently the right word."

"He stole it all right." Marlow, from near the foot of the table, spoke nervously and abruptly. "Mr. Collins, the duke's librarian, and I saw between us what leaves no doubt about that."

"Very well, he stole it. Pluckrose, after all, was a very eccentric man." And Tavender tapped the table in front of him. "But murder and an odd act of kleptomania are very different things. Nobody is going to be troubled about Pluckrose making off with a chunk of rock. Accusing Prisk of killing Pluckrose, however, is a much more grave affair. We should hear the evidence at once."

Appleby nodded. "That is very true. And I don't say that there is very conclusive evidence yet. But there is enough, in my opinion, to justify the present method of attempting to sift the situation further. Let me tell you something which happened on Wednesday afternoon. I met Prisk coming away from Mrs. Tavender's and had some conversation with him about the case. I pointed out that we did not as yet at all clearly know against *whom* the attempt with the meteorite had been made. But the peculiar matter of the shared telephone made it not altogether unlikely that it was he himself who had been the intended victim.

I pointed out to him—took care to point out—two consequences of this possibility. The first he might regard as comforting—and it was this: if the attempt had really been against him, then he hadn't made it; he would be cleared of attempting to murder Pluckrose. The second was more disturbing: if the murderer had tried to kill Prisk and had failed, then he might very well try again. I left these two ideas with Prisk—and you will see pretty clearly that they constituted a sort of trap. He might be tempted, that is to say, into *staging* an attempt on his own life by way of confusing the trail. And that very night the thing happened; we came upon Prisk, more or less uninjured, in the middle of a very pretty car smash. A bold man could certainly have contrived the thing himself. But I imagine that the nervous strain involved would be considerably greater than that produced by a genuine accident; and this will account for Prisk's present collapse."

There was a murmur round the long table and again Tavender broke impatiently in. "All this is extremely oblique and questionable. And we have heard nothing that goes to the heart of the matter. Why should Prisk want to kill Pluckrose—not, presumably, because he was irritated about a telephone?"

"Almost certainly not." Appleby paused. "Perhaps Sir David Evans might be able to suggest a motive?"

Sir David, who appeared to be much more concerned with watching Tavender than Appleby, looked abruptly up the table and raised a threatening hand in air. It seemed likely that this whole suggestion was to be denounced as disgraceful and displeasing. But instead Sir David lowered his hand and shook his handsome head. "No," he said quietly; " I haf no suggestion, Mr. Appleby."

"No private circumstance in the relations between Pluckrose and Prisk about which you yourself might be in a position to be specially well informed?"

There was silence in the board-room as the wraith or spectre of Fräulein Schmauch was thus paraded down the table. Sir David put an uneasy finger between his neck and starched collar—and was then apparently enabled to shake his head again in a measured way. "No," he said shortly.

"Quite so. We can expect no other reply." Appleby paused and made some show of consulting his notes. "We don't need to find any reason why Prisk should want to murder Pluckrose. For it was not in fact Pluckrose whom he intended to murder. It was Mr. Lasscock."

Tavender, who had walked down a corridor chuckling and with a beard in each hand, was certainly looking both serious and perturbed now. Indeed, most of those present were. Only Lasscock himself, perhaps, remained wholly placid; and his was the first voice to be articulately heard. "'Stonishin' thing," he said. "This Lunnon feller smart chap. Gets to the bottom of it. Sense of security. No faith in that local man. Remarkable about Prisk; often thought I saw somethin' nasty in his eye. Hijjus close shave, come to think of it. Fell out well in the end, though. Rid of Pluckrose. Prisk too now, by the look of it."

Appleby rapped on the table, like a chairman calling a meeting to order. "Let me point at once to a very significant factor in a case of this sort: any *known habit* on the part of one of the persons concerned. Mr.

266

Lasscock may be described as eminently a person of regular habits. For instance, he contracts a chill quite regularly half-way through the academic term."

There was a guffaw from Timothy Church and a laugh—oddly high and nervous—from Martin Marlow. But Lasscock himself nodded his head solemnly. "Parfectly true," he said. "Never struck me before. Always happens round about that time. Find the best cure is regular tots of rum. Most sovereign stuff."

"And in fine weather he makes what is apparently an almost daily visit to the Wool Court. He goes there with a cushion round about ten, settles it and a deck chair on a particular spot, thinks out various historical problems till just after the stroke of eleven and then goes about his work. Well, Sir David and gentlemen, where is that particular spot? I can tell you myself, because I have seen Mr. Lasscock pick up a chair and carry it there. It is the identical spot on which Pluckrose's chair rested when Pluckrose was killed. And it always would be that spot. Only if somebody else chanced to be occupying that spot already would Mr. Lasscock be obliged to pitch his chair a little to one side or another. You will see where this leads. A murderer up in the tower could reckon on Mr. Lasscock's being exactly below. And if another man happened, by chance and for once in a way, to occupy that spot on a certain fatal day—well, it was Mr. Lasscock's good fortune and that other man's bad luck."

"And the motive?" Tavender asked the question without taking his eyes off Sir David Evans. "We found no motive for Prisk's attempting to kill Pluckrose. Why should he attempt to kill Lasscock? Did he disapprove of his half-term chills?"

"Prisk tried to kill Lasscock because Lasscock knew

too much about his private life. I had this information from Miss Godkin, the Warden of St. Cecilia's, only this morning. Prisk is a person of scandalous habits, as the Duke of Nesfield could testify and as many people are more or less aware. But Mr. Lasscock, if Miss Godkin is to be believed, has happened upon the most incontrovertible evidence on the point—and may have been disposed, for moral or other reasons, to make the matter public. And that would be the end of Prisk as the holder of a university chair. The motive of the attempted crime, in fact, is abundantly clear."

"All this is most disturbing." From a shadowy corner far down the table Professor Crunkhorn's voice came, level and severe. "Whatever positive force there may be in Mr. Appleby's contention, it seems difficult at present to bring forward any negative considerations. But there is one matter which has been in the forefront of my own mind—and I think Mr. Appleby himself served to put it there. It is the matter of the meteorite. Pluckrose stole it; which is strange enough. But why should Prisk design to use it to kill Lasscock?"

"The answer is that he didn't. Prisk, having realised that the spot on which Lasscock was accustomed to sit gave him the sort of opportunity he wanted, went up to the store-room on Monday morning with no definite missile in mind. If there was something suitable he would use it. If not, he would simply reconnoitre, and accomplish his design another day. The meteorite was not in his mind in advance, and probably he knew nothing about it. Actually there were all sorts of suitable objects lying about. For instance, there was a heavy cast-iron sink and I think at first he proposed to use that; the sink has plainly been scraped along the floor. Then, spotting the meteorite, he chose that—probably as being heavier and bigger. We have most of us wasted a good deal of ingenuity in canvassing the possible symbolisms and significances of the meteorite. It must have had some significance for Pluckrose—he wouldn't have stolen it otherwise—but afterwards it simply becomes a heavy object lying about. It has no other associations whatever. And Prisk's proceedings were extremely simple and straightforward. He didn't trouble about any sort of alibi. But he did, by the way, take one step to lessen the risk of being seen at any awkward moment. In the engineering department there is one door opening on the Wool Court, and from here it would be possible to see the store-room window in the tower—the window from which Prisk had to operate. How could he avoid the chance of being seen? The answer, as it happened, was quite simple. He had only to slip into the court a little earlier and turn the fountain full on. The result was a considerable mess, but it certainly precluded any awkward observations being made by a stray engineer."

"It's not true!"

In what was now full dusk in the board-room Marlow's voice rang out as if involuntarily. And in the same instant lights snapped on above the table. Appleby, standing by the switch, turned slowly round. "No," he said quietly. "It's not true. But we'll have the truth now—Mr. Marlow."

Marlow had risen to his feet. But now, with the eyes of the whole room upon him, he sat down again, trembling violently. "Pinnegar and I planned—"

Appleby raised his hand. "I'm sorry to have to talk so much," he said. "And I'm sorry to have put up a story just to startle Mr. Marlow into an avowal. But I'm afraid I have to do a little more talking still."

"Inspector Hobhouse and I went carefully into everybody's movements, as you may well imagine." Appleby was back at the table, consulting his notes. "We tabulated them and considered them as the basis of possible alibis. And here is what we have for Mr. Marlow: *In dark-room from ten-fifteen till news of accident arrived. Confirmed by Atkinson.* No other alibi is as good except Mr. Murn's. And even Mr. Murn's turns out on scrutiny to be inferior—for although he too was in the dark-room he made, as he was accustomed to do, a good many trips through the photographic room to the cold-storage room and back. Marlow, then, had the clearest alibi of all. He also had a false beard exactly like Mr. Murn's."

If there had been sensation before there was something like furore now. Even Hissey, who hitherto had sat through the meeting in a sort of mild impatience doubtless occasioned by the thought of his card indexes, looked extremely concerned. Crunkhorn was engaged in some sort of altercation with Church; Tavender was speaking in low, urgent tones to Sir David Evans; Lasscock had risen, walked round the table and sat down beside Marlow, who sat trembling still, and with his head in his hands. Murn, on the other side, stroked his beard and looked extremely uncomfortable, as if he would gladly have exchanged this particular human spectacle for a well-equipped bench of retorts and test-tubes.

"And Marlow, as Professor Hissey has told us, is quite an accomplished actor." Appleby continued to talk in matter-of-fact tones. "When I have mentioned

270

these two facts I have taken you to the heart of the matter. Or as near to it as I need at present do. For it is not my intention at the moment to discuss Marlow's motive for attempting to murder Prisk—"

Marlow raised his head. "Prisk!" he said.

"—for attempting to murder Prisk. That motive has nothing to do with anything at the university; it concerns an incident of a very distressing kind which belongs to an altogether different place; and I shall leave it to your Chancellor to convey it to you at a proper time." Appleby paused and glanced round an auditory which was now very impressed indeed. "It is sufficient to say that Prisk was the intended victim; that the plan miscarried for reasons which I can, I believe, analyse; and that Marlow then made another attempt of which you have heard something: the attempt on Prisk's car.

"Let me remind you of the character of the darkroom; it is a dimly-lit place in which several people can work simultaneously without being more than intermittently aware of one another's presence. But all goings and comings are observed—mechanically and inattentively perhaps—by the assistant Atkinson, who works in the photographic room which affords the only means of egress. Very well; Marlow goes into the darkroom at ten-fifteen. Then at the appropriate moment he slips into the maze, dons the beard, adopts Mr. Murn's gait and slips out to a telephone. He calls Prisk and Prisk answers—at the instrument he shares with Pluckrose. But Marlow is agitated and there is some betrayal in his voice. Now, Prisk is wary about this telephone; he is apprehensive, too, of the practical jokes which have been taking place. And so he does an odd and malicious thing. Pluckrose is passing;

he says, 'One moment,' and hands the receiver to his colleague with a word that the call is for him. Marlow, unaware of this, simply makes an appointment on some pretext in the Wool Court—where Mr. Lasscock is already slumbering and a chair is already set—and rings off. Then he hurries out and turns on the fountain, for the identical reason I have already given. Next he goes up to the store-room. He seizes first the iron sink—probably already selected as his weapon—and then changes his mind and gets up the meteorite. He looks down and clearly distinguishes Mr. Lasscock, *Times* and all. The other figure, then, is his man. He releases the meteorite, hurries down and back through the photographic room, removes the beard in the maze, and is back at work in the dark-room within perhaps eight minutes all told. And all that Atkinson is aware of is one of Mr. Murn's customary goings and comings, which he will scarcely mark as being longer than usual. And that is the whole story of a tolerably ingeniously planned crime."

There was silence in the board-room. And then Tavender spoke, very quietly. "It isn't the whole story. And it isn't the right story, either."

"It has been far from my intention to assist in any hounding of Pluckrose's murderer." Tavender looked cooly round the table. "The thing is so incredible that no jury would believe the truth; at the same time the scandal which a trial would occasion would do the university the gravest injury. No good end would be served, therefore, by an attempt to secure a conviction. In other words it is a bad business all round and the only comfort I can discern lies in the undoubted fact that Pluckrose was an unpleasant fellow.

"It was my intention, then, to let the matter alone. I must confess, even, to having thought it expedient a little to complicate the trail; that was in the matter of the redundant beards. One beard suggests a one-man show; it occurred to me that an *embarras de choix* in this particular might suggest a conspiracy; and hence the cupboard which positively grew the things." Tavender chuckled. "The action, being intended to mislead the police, was no doubt criminal. But the motive was altruistic; I wanted the Pluckrose affair buried in hopeless muddle and a futile scandal avoided. And towards that consummation we should be fairly launched at this moment, had not the fatal ingenuity of Mr. Appleby worked out this extraordinarily ingenious case against Marlow. Of course I can't see Marlow hanged. He had nothing whatever to do with the business."

Tavender paused. Appleby, quite still at the head of the table, kept his eyes on his papers; he might have been a chemist patiently awaiting the step-by-step unfolding of an experiment.

"Marlow had nothing to do with the business?" Crunkhorn was speaking, slowly and carefully. "But, when Marlow was prompted to rebut the supposed case against Prisk, I understood him to admit that he and Pinnegar had planned—"

"That was something quite different!" Marlow, now sitting back in his chair, looked rather wildly round the room. "The fountain . . . Pinnegar and I had planned a joke . . . a joke against—" And then Marlow threw up his head in despair. "Oh, lord," he said, "what a ghastly mess! If you just let me collect my wits for a minute I'll explain—"

Tavender waved an impatient hand. "Marlow can

explain what he pleases later. And it isn't my business to explain anything, thank goodness. I've only to tell you what I saw. It was the beard. And the beard wasn't on Marlow. It was on Evans."

There was hubbub again. Marlow was shaking his head in some obscure negation, as if more wildered than ever. Church was leaning across the table and endeavouring to shake hands with him, apparently by way of celebrating the fact that the whirlwind had passed on to engulf the older generation. Lasscock was looking at the Vice-Chancellor in open-mouthed astonishment and speculating, no doubt, on what might be considered conduct unbecoming a scholar. The others questioned, exclaimed or called loudly for silence. And at length Tavender once more made himself heard.

"The beard was on Evans—which means, you might say, that the boot is on the other foot." Tavender paused to laugh complacently over this indifferent jest—and perhaps to heighten by suspense the effect that was to follow. "The beard was on Evans and Evans was coming out of the tower. The time was between eleven-ten and eleven-fifteen. Somehow I don't think that Marlow will hang."

"It is all lies; it is all hallucinations!" Sir David, who had been quite silent for some time, sprang to his feet and gesticulated wildly. "There was jokes, look you; there was impertinences!"

"And another thing: it was clearly Evans who had turned on the fountain. He had got himself pretty well soaked in the process. It added to the fantastic appearance of the whole affair." And Tavender leant back, grimly enjoying himself. "Just what happened was this. I had been in town during the early part of the morning and when I got up here I went straight to the refectory and had a cup of coffee. When I came away and was crossing the side street I noticed that the door of the store-room at the bottom of the tower was open. And then I noticed Evans coming out. He was more or less his own proper self except, as I say, that he was soaking wet. He came out without seeing me—but he did apparently see a couple of students who were opposite the Great Hall and who might spot him at any moment. It was then that he did this fantastic thing. He dodged back into cover and a moment later came hurriedly out, fantastically disguised as Murn. And then he slipped along the other side of the road, as quickly as he could while preserving something of Murn's manner. It wasn't the sort of thing one sees every day."

There was a silence of stupefaction in the board-room. Appleby looked up and glanced round. "You will see," he said, "that by means of a little shock tactics we have arrived at what is at least a modicum of fresh and surprising information. Sir David, do you admit that certain circumstances took you to the top of the tower on Monday morning, that when you were alone there you looked down and saw what had happened in the court, and that you then got away as quickly as you could, using a certain false beard in the process?"

"It iss true. There was impertinences." Evans nodded his dignified head with every appearance of restored equanimity. "And Pluckrose was tead and it was tifficult. Reticence appeared to pe the prudent policy."

"Mr. Marlow, do you admit that Mr. Pinnegar and

yourself planned and perpetrated a joke against the Vice-Chancellor?"

"Yes."

"And Mr. Tavender, did you find a false beard and stow it away in the dark-room; and later, believing that the whole matter had better rest in obscurity, did you add to the confusion with more beards?"

"Just that. And perhaps the confusion could have got on very well without me. I doubt whether many people here feel the affair to be exactly pellucid yet."

Appleby nodded gravely. "The matter is complex and there is a good deal that is still obscure. Several important matters have not yet been mentioned: for instance, a temple in Tartary, and a ladder, and the Strength of Materials." He paused and for a second his eye seemed to catch that of someone far down the table. "I think that some of you may want a little time to reflect, or for consultation with each other or with myself. I would suggest that we disperse now and meet again after dinner. Say in two hours' time."

The proposal seemed to meet with general favour and the company filed from the room. In the long corridor bleak, bare lights burnt sparely. Appleby, his notes under his arm, said a word to Hobhouse and disappeared. Outside it was quite dark.

Darkness was absolute in the board-room. It was as if the nymphs were departed, leaving no addresses, and as if the bewhiskered worthies had faded, seeking a more kindly limbo. A rat crept softly among the university calendars and a night wind blowing down the chimney faintly rustled the invisible silk of the Duke of Nesfield's gold and scarlet gown. Frozen amid their loaded vines the creatures of Burne-Jones awaited recreating light and from far away in the city the sound of horns and motors echoed up the hill. The second hour moved to its close.

Appleby was the first back; the lights snapped on and he came in rather wearily; an observer might have remarked that he was as pale as Aphrodite and her smock. He sat down at the table, put his notes in front of him, took one glance round the empty and silent room, and began to read sombrely at the first page.

Wednesday Morning

Arrived yesterday afternoon and got the general hang of the case.

Why should a man murder in this way, using a meteorite which only the uneducated could suppose to be an instrument of death by misadventure? Because either (1) the meteorite was the handiest thing or (2) it was the only thing or (3) there was attached to it a symbolism satisfactory to the perpetrator and possibly significant to some third party or (4) this particular meteorite had associations calculated to mislead or (5) a meteorite generically regarded has associations calculated to mislead. The last possibility is the most subtle and Tavender at the symposium last night seemed to have it in mind (a). A combination of the above factors is also a possibility.

The body has been quite remarkably crushed.

Jokes. As these have been current the crime may be (1) a joke gone wrong in some such way as Crunkhorn suggests or (2) deliberately or fortuitously intertwined with a joke or jokes itself innocently intended. Tavender again has seen something of this; he suggested correlating the crime with the matter of the skeleton in the maze and with the facetious possibilities of the Prisk-Pluckrose telephone.

There has been the odd circumstance of the porter's tortoise and its engendering my Aeschylus theory. In fact I find myself canvassing all the curious associations of the death-from-the-air complex (a). Even so remote an association as that of Damocles.

The Duke of Nesfield has reason to apprehend that somebody else was actually the intended victim. Here there may be a situation which (1) bears out the duke or (2) has been deliberately exploited by the murderer to confuse the trail or (3) introduces such a confusion by chance or (4) is capable of exploitation later to get people rattled and talking: the old technique!

Consider the shared telephone. This might be used in contriving (1) a murder or (2) a joke. And it might introduce a factor of error or miscarriage into either of these. I feel that here is rather a chancy element to embody or exploit in a planned crime.

A planned crime?

Sir David Evans is concerned to befog the affair. Just the role for a metaphysician. I doubt if he tried to kill anybody. He would have it remembered that professors go mad. It is doubtful if the cold light of statistics would bear this out but certainly dons are often highly-strung and pervertedly ingenious folk—see any learned journal.

Why turn on the fountain?

The dark-room. If one of those ingenious persons were planning a crime it might well occur to him to exploit this. *Or if he were improvising measures to escape the consequences of a crime?* The lie of the place is so like the main theatre of a crime story!

Old Hissey, the eminent epigrapher, turns out to be professor of classics here now; he is going to put out a book. Along with Evans he is the only person to convey an impression of disingenuousness so far. Marlow and Pinnegar? Well, Pinnegar perhaps a bit scared.

Back to notes marked (*a*) above. I have a dim, rather startling notion. I say dim, though—mistakenly or no—its first dawning was like a flood of light. I've been had by floods of light before now.

Wednesday Evening

Miss Dearlove of the moated grange, the dirty mind. Evans and Pluckrose were both after one girl. Why not? But one imagines in rather an ineffective way: chocolates, dinners, theatres, flowers. Common enough. But then such a situation hardly gives scope for homicidal passion. Here conceivably is a more or less extraneous, but complicating, factor. It opens the whole tiresome business of private lives. Nosey-parker Pluckrose may have known too much about, say, Prisk.

Lasscock, the man who knows something *but not much*.

Marlow was a tutor at Nesfield Court. The duke's supposition that some other victim was designed connects, then, with Marlow.

Church's girl, Church's bigamy, Miss Godkin and the Foreign Office. The inwardness of all this is pretty clear and it appears as a side issue. But it may conceivably connect with the Evans-Pluckrose-girl complex *(b)*.

Sir David Evans's bust. The heart of the mystery lies here. So it is a pity I find it baffling!

Tavender recommends a reading of *Zuleika Dobson*, the story of a girl who proved fatally attractive in an academic society. The hint here tends to bear out *(b)* above.

If Prisk killed Pluckrose Prisk may fake an attack upon himself, thus suggesting Prisk as the intended victim in the first place. *But so may some one else*. That is to say, if there is a discoverable motive for *X's* killing Pluckrose it will suit *X* now to contrive the impression that Prisk and not Pluckrose was originally aimed at *(c)*.

Wednesday Night

At Nesfield Court we have had a revelation of the sort of man Prisk is in the story of Marlow's friend, the lad Gerald. Here is a true homicide-motive for the first time. But it is a motive for Marlow's murdering *Prisk*. And, telephone and all, I distrust the notion of the wrong man's having been killed.

And we have discovered that Pluckrose stole the meteorite.

Why should a man steal a meteorite?

Well, what is unique about a meteorite?

Pluckrose stole the meteorite; Pluckrose bashed the bust.

BILL STUMPS HIS MARK.

Thursday Noon

Why did Pluckrose bash the bust green? An explanation comes from Hissey (green with envy).

Hissey triumphantly finds possibility *(c)* above. Making the green, one red. Hissey's little joke. Lasscock would wake at eleven.

Crunkhorn on fifty-ton meteorite.

The sink was moved and this suggests that there was no previous plan to use the meteorite—although, if I am right about Bill Stumps, its use was something like poetic justice *(d)*. The sink was picked up to use; and then the meteorite was seen, and used instead. See *(a)* above and *(d)*. We are dealing with a masterpiece of improvisation.

The false beard. False beards are used for *jokes*. Bogus telephone calls are used for *jokes*. It is a great *joke* to turn on a fountain on some one. Consider Evans's quickest route to Pluckrose. Here then is a fortuitously synchronising joke. And there was damp on the tower stairs: the joke and the tragedy at a sort of hide-and-seek, forming a syndrome. This, worked out, will explain all the facts. Pinnegar has decamped—but as one might from a scrape, rather than from a crime.

Extra beards. These represent simply a malicious spoke in our wheel. Thrust in by Tavender, I should say. (And I shall never know how much Tavender knew; he is a natural born detective, I am inclined to believe.)

Thursday Afternoon

The affair of Timothy Church's bigamy has cleared itself up on the expected lines. The grotesque Evans-Pluckrose-Prisk embroilment with the magnetic German lady explains Evans's concern to conceal the joke played on him; there he was in the tower with his lewd rival Pluckrose dead below!

Can the joke be got clearer? I think it can. By a little after ten Lasscock is comfortably asleep in the court. He may wake up for the fun, or he may not; it is not very material to the jokers. Somewhere about ten-twenty Marlow rings up Evans on the Prisk-Pluckrose telephone, represents himself as Pluckrose and asks Evans to come over urgently. Evans therefore takes the short route through the Wool Court. Pinnegar meanwhile has disguised himself as Murn (overcoat, hat and muffler as well as the beard probably); he dodges out before the astounded Evans, turns on the fountain and drenches him. Evans, his Celtic spirit roused, pursues the elderly-seeming jester. Pinnegar bolts round to the tower and up the staircase to the top floor. Evans still follows and Pinnegar gives him the slip by coming down the hoist—having abandoned the beard. Evans is completely winded and more or less collapses; and meanwhile the murderer is at work on the floor below. So that when Evans recovers and looks out of the window there is Pluckrose dead beneath him. He hurries downstairs, taking Pinnegar's abandoned beard with him—and thus leaves no trace of the affair except puddles on the stairs. At the doorway he is fearful of being seen, so on a sudden impulse he claps on the beard until he is well down the street. Then, perhaps, he attempts to stuff it in a drain—whence it is retrieved by the interested

Tavender and later secreted in the dark-room cupboard: the first of Tavender's little jokes. Evans hurries to his room (glimpsed by the porter); changes his jacket (warm day, he said, and something odd about his subsequent appearance, Hissey told Hobhouse); and goes to the refectory as usual. Note as a pleasant coda to all this unhappily timed buffoonery that he is there presently engaged in polite conversation by a beardless Pinnegar.

This gets a great deal out of the way, at least to my own satisfaction. I hope to get corroboration by staging a general show-down this evening.

And now it is all plain sailing:

The Munchausen inscriptions are at Cambridge
The bust was new—and it turned green.

And:

The meteorite was on record as only recently arrived on earth.

And:

The noise of a steam hammer; the Strength of Materials
The forge room is little used
The prime association of meteorite is *from above*
The extension ladder
The hoist will go up to the top storey
The hoist can be operated from the dark-room
The weight of the evidence.

15

John Appleby put his notes in his pocket; he brought out a letter and laid it on the table in front of him. Crunkhorn came into the room followed by Hobhouse and Marlow, and at short intervals the others arrived. Appleby looked at nobody and said nothing, seemingly lost in some sombre reverie of his own. Hobhouse, counting the people as they came in, eventually leant forward and whispered to him. And then Appleby spoke.

"I have here a letter addressed to the Chancellor of the university by Professor Hissey. I have spoken to the duke on the telephone and he has given me permission to read it to you."

And Appleby picked up the letter from the table, opened it and read—slowly and in a clear, unemphatic voice.

MY LORD DUKE,

I am informed by Mr. Appleby of the metropolitan police that the lamentable events which have lately taken place within the university have been to you a matter of personal concern. It is for this reason—and because your Vice-Chancellor, by an irresponsible frolic unhappily implicated in the affair, may wish for the moment to stand aside—that I venture to address this letter to Your Grace. I shall be as little tedious as may be. Of what I have to say the greater part must necessarily be explanatory. Nevertheless the essence of my purpose is apologetic. I am sorry that I punched Pluckrose on the jaw. The fact that he thereupon fell under the steam hammer; that in falling back I pressed against the valve-lever; and that as a necessary consequence Pluckrose was instantly killed: these are points upon which remorse would be inappropriate, as they were concomitants fortuitous and undersigned. But I am sorry that I punched the man on the jaw.

I am sorry that I involved Prisk in the risk of a serious motor accident. Legally and morally, this act was attempted murder. I would not have done it had I not had a great deal of work on hand. Night after night I sat up trying to get through with this, but I was early aware that Appleby was progressing too rapidly for me. It became clear that something must be done. Otherwise *Annotatiunculae Criticae* would never be completed, for I believe that there are few opportunities for

285

scholarly disquisition afforded to occupants of a condemned cell. The particular clouding of the issue which I attempted was possibly but indifferently conceived—but I was tempted into feeling that if it could be made apparent that Prisk had always been the predestined victim I should be in a considerably stronger position. It was an uncomfortable night, with its long lurking round Nesfield Court.

And now I must be something more systematic. But first let me repeat that this letter is motivated by ethical concern. I am anxious—I have from the first been anxious—that all the facts of the matter should be known and that justice should ultimately take its course. I have no wish to avoid the consequences of the unhappy deeds which have been forced upon me. This being so, you may ask—with a recourse to that Latinity which is but one evidence of Your Grace's distinguished abilities:

Quid est, Catulle? quid moraris emori?

And the answer is, of course, that I have not wanted to hurry up and die; I have had, I reiterate, too much work on hand. It would be no exaggeration to say that, from the first moment of my realising that Pluckrose was dead, I have been entirely engaged in arranging what might be described as a series of delaying actions. At first my expectations were modest; I sought for no more than a few days in which I could order my papers and prepare one or two learned trifles—significant only to myself—for the press. Later I saw that I might take somewhat larger scope, and at least get out my projected book. But that this was not to be and that the twitch of the tether—or should I say halter?—was imminent I realised upon learning from Inspector Hobhouse, an amiable if unwary officer, that the perspicacious Appleby had penetrated to what may be called the Pickwickian or Stumpsian aspect of the case.

And now let me tell you about Pluckrose. He was an interfering fellow, if ever there was one—and in a peculiarly laborious way. He would get up enough of another man's subject to enable him to take more or less effective ground in his badgering activities. He did this with my own subject, which—perhaps it is necessary to mention—is that branch of classical archaeology known as epigraphy, or the science of deciphering inscriptions cut in stone. Of recent years we have had to deal with one or two odd cases of fraud or forgery in this department of knowledge; and, hearing of this, Pluckrose took an extraordinary notion into his head. He declared—no less—that the inscriptions on the celebrated Tartary obelisks recovered by my honoured teacher and close friend Professor Munchausen of Riga were an out-and-out fake! This nonsense was tiresome enough, but there was worse to follow. Pluckrose, in addition to being a busybody, was a chemist. And he declared his intention of undertaking a chemical experiment which should prove the truth of his assertion.

Although extremely annoyed by this grotesque and offensive talk, I was not actually alarmed until the startling incident at Mrs. Tavender's party. It was here that Pluckrose explained to me the nature of the test he proposed. More or less freshly cut stone, he declared, could be made to respond to chemical action in a manner altogether different from stone the surfaces of which had been exposed to the air for many centuries. It was his intention to go up to Cambridge and empty a vial of fluid on the inscriptions. If these had indeed— as he asserted—been cut within the last two or three years the surfaces thus recently exposed would react by turning green. And to make good this assertion Pluckrose perpetrated his astounding and offensive attack upon Sir David Evans's recently chiselled bust. It will certainly occur to you—as it certainly occurred to Appleby—that this was very imperfect evidence of Pluckrose's being able, or disposed, to carry out his threat. A colourless liquid which will act as a green dye when exposed to air is likely enough, but a similar fluid which will distinguish between old and fresh cut stone is altogether less probable. Had this struck me at the time, how different might the issue of the whole affair have been! *Sed haec prius fuere.*

I expostulated with Pluckrose more than once, endeavouring to urge the disrepute into which his futile and disgusting experiment would bring both Nesfield and academic people in general. I expostulated with him on that fatal Monday morning in the Wool Court, having previously made an appointment for the purpose. This was at ten-thirty, and the place was suitable as being commonly quiet and secluded—with only Lasscock, perhaps, asleep under the tower. But on this morning the Wool Court was somewhat uncomfortable; the fountain had been turned full on and—owing to the direction of the wind—only Lasscock's corner was entirely dry. I had, of course, no idea of what this matter of the fountain meant—or that at that very moment Evans was pursuing the disguised Pinnegar to the topmost storey of the tower. I drew Pluckrose into the forge room, a little-used place in which the engineers have their drop hammer and one or two other pieces of heavy apparatus. He was very offensive. It was there that I punched him on the jaw.

The hammer had pulverised the man; it was extremely awkward. In a sense the thing was pure accident, for I had certainly not the remotest conscious intention of killing him. But I had knocked him under this terrible machine and by an inadvertent movement I had released the mechanism. What Freud has called the psychopathology of errors was plainly involved; that obscure mechanism of the mind which makes the unconsciously suicidal man cut his chin while shaving!

Here then was Pluckrose dead—a prosecuting barrister would doubtless say neatly and ingeniously despatched—and through the instrumentality (shall we put it?) of one with whom he could very probably be proved to have been involved in a dispute. I do not think that I have ever been in a more awkward situation—in "so tight a place," to use the popular expression.

For the very tolerable ingenuity of the dispositions that I proceeded to make I am disposed to claim little applause. I acted as a man in a dream, and yet with the most efficient calculation and despatch. It seems likely that the same powerful and hidden forces which I must admit as having been a factor in Pluckrose's death were continuing to operate—and with a similar automatism.

The leading principle was obvious. It was half-past ten and Pluckrose had just been killed. I must give to the fatality the appearance of having taken place at some other hour—an hour at which, demonstrably, I could not be involved. I have gathered from Appleby, that this is called constructing an *alibi*; the Latin is indifferent but the meaning clear.

There was a tarpaulin which must have been used to shroud some mechanism of the engineers'; and in this I bundled the body. I carried it across the Wool Court—no mean feat—and set it in a deck chair directly under the turret window and hard by Lasscock. A newspaper, which I had in my pocket I placed over the crushed torso, so that glimpsed only for a moment Pluckrose would not appear too obviously dead to a sleepy man. For I knew that Lasscock would be awakened by the eleven o'clock bell and all my plan turned on that. I took back the tarpaulin. There was a mess in the forge room. I had to risk that for a time.

I went round the building and up the tower. This must have been only minutes after Pinnegar came down; and during everything that followed Evans was resting, or lying exhausted, in the top storey. By how much would the terrors of the affair have been increased had I known of this extraordinary circumstance!

There was an extension ladder in the store-room immediately above ground level; I took the two parts of it up separately and assembled it; it stretched from the window-sill to the hoist.

I got hold of the iron sink—and then I saw the meteorite.

It was plainly that. But only something like clairvoyance can explain all that I immediately knew about it. For I knew at once that Pluckrose himself had hidden it here, and in furtherance of a plan of the most extreme ingenuity and malice. Mr. Pickwick, when at Cobham, discovered an inscription which he rashly declared to be of extreme antiquity—but a little analysis showed that it read BILL STUMPS HIS MARK. Pluckrose has possessed himself of a meteorite well-authenticated as having only recently arrived on earth. He proposed to remove all but the inobvious traces of the thing's being indeed a meteoric stone; to do this and then to fake an inscription which I might later be induced to accept as genuine ancient work. And then Pluckrose would spring his mine: the Greeks or Romans or whoever it might be had, then, contrived to carve an inscription on a body thousands of millions of miles away in interstellar space!

So you can see why I took the meteorite and not the sink; you can see, perhaps, two reasons. "'Tis the sport to have the engineer hoist with his own petard"—and I was certainly in a position to do that. But it also occurred to me how inevitably a meteorite sets one thinking in terms of impact from above; and this I had to enforce by any subtle power of suggestion I could command.

So I got hold of the meteorite—*rudis indigestaque moles*—and heaved and levered it on the ladder. It was a terrific weight, and yet not, I suppose, capable of doing at all the damage that the drop hammer had done. In fact the weight of the meteorite might have been awkward evidence. And I suppose Crunkhorn to have had something of the sort in mind when, according to Appleby, he said something about a fifty-ton meteorite.

And now mark the situation. One end of the ladder lay on the window-sill and the meteorite lay on the ladder. The other end of the ladder lay on, and was tethered to, the hoist—the hoist raised some eighteen inches above floor level. *And the hoist could be controlled from the dark-room.*

You will see that there is little more explaining to do. I hurried to the dark-room, taking care that Atkinson should note the time: ten-fifty. And then, just on the ringing of the eleven o'clock bell, I sent the hoist a few feet *up*, and so tipped the meteorite out and down. It was a curiously godlike sensation: *eripuit caelo fulmen*. But there followed a period of some strain. I had to wait in the dark-room until the news was brought to us. I had to trust that, in the general consternation, no one would think to go up to the tower until I could slip up myself and dismantle the ladder. I had to trust, too, that I should then be able to get round to a still-deserted forge room and clean up the hammer. The fact that Lasscock simply made off without giving any alarm considerably increased at least the second of these risks—and the stress of the situation generally. And later, of course, it appeared for a time as if his continued silence might upset my "*alibi*" altogether. All these matters, however, fell out well enough in the end.

But I had reckoned without Appleby—and it is curious that I should have had a tendency to confuse him with Merryweather and Grant, persons, it must be recorded, of but mediocre mind. It is pleasant to reflect that the concentration and efficiency with which he has brought his natural talent to bear upon the case may be due in some measure at least to his pursuance as an undergraduate of the grand old fortifying classical curriculum. I did not see a great deal of him in those days, but I recall that he brought me essays from time to time and it is possible that I did a little to assist him in the business of straight thinking.

And now, with apologies for claiming your indulgence thus long,

    I am,

    My Lord Duke,

    Your Grace's obliged and humble servant,

    S. RUTGERSIUS HISSEY

His Grace the Duke of Nesfield, K.G.,
Nesfield Court,
England